Realizing the Distinctive University

MARK WILLIAM ROCHE

Realizing the
Distinctive University

Vision and Values, Strategy and Culture

University of Notre Dame Press

Notre Dame, Indiana

University of Notre Dame Press
Notre Dame, Indiana 46556
www.undpress.nd.edu
All Rights Reserved

Copyright © 2017 by University of Notre Dame

Published in the United States of America

Library of Congress Cataloging-in-Publication Data

Names: Roche, Mark William.
Title: Realizing the distinctive university : vision and values, strategy and culture /
Mark William Roche.
Description: Notre Dame, Indiana : University of Notre Dame Press, 2017.
Identifiers: LCCN 2016049588 (print) | LCCN 2016052199 (ebook) |
ISBN 9780268101466 (hardback) | ISBN 0268101469 (hardcover) |
ISBN 9780268101473 (paper) | ISBN 9780268101480 (pdf) |
ISBN 9780268101497 (epub)
Subjects: LCSH: Universities and colleges—United States—Administration. |
Education, Higher—United States. | Education, Humanistic—United States. |
BISAC: EDUCATION / Leadership. | EDUCATION /
Decision-Making & Problem Solving.
Classification: LCC LB2341.R57   2017 (print) | LCC LB2341 (ebook) |
DDC 378.73—dc23
LC record available at https://lccn.loc.gov/201604958

∞ *This paper meets the requirements of ANSI/NISO Z39.48-1992
(Permanence of Paper).*

Contents

Acknowledgments

I want to thank those who in diverse ways helped me grasp the value of academic community or offered persuasive commentaries on early drafts.

As an administrator I was blessed with superb mentors, to whom I remain grateful even today. As chairperson at Ohio State, I reported to, and learned greatly from, Deans G. Michael Riley, David Frantz, and Kermit Hall. As dean at Notre Dame, I worked closely with, and developed under the guidance of, two excellent provosts, Nathan Hatch and Tom Burish.

Every higher administrator has a support staff that includes associates. As chairperson I benefited from working with associate deans, and as dean I learned from the associate provosts. Such support persons were especially important to me early in my tenures as chairperson and dean. I would like to thank in particular Chris Zacher at Ohio State and John Affleck-Graves and Reverend Timothy R. Scully, C.S.C., at Notre Dame.

As dean one works with an array of donors, who make a tremendous difference. In my case, many of those donors served on the Arts and Letters Advisory Council. They and others became a great source of inspiration and support, for which I will always be grateful. A few of their stories are embedded in these pages.

In the course of my eleven years as dean, I appointed and worked with a dozen associate deans and more than fifty department chairpersons. I learned from them in immeasurable ways and I owe all of them considerable gratitude. Many of them will see their work mirrored in these pages. I would like to name the two associate deans who helped me in unusual ways, particularly during my partial leaves: Chris Fox, who was my first appointment as associate dean, had bold aspirations for the university and the spirit of an entrepreneur; Greg Sterling, who became in my final years my second-in-command, provided a peerless level of support and counsel; his work ethic knew no limits. I would like here as well to thank my successor, John McGreevy, whose work I allude to in these pages and whose effectiveness as dean has been matched only by his modesty and generosity.

Helpful was the feedback of many colleagues. Several focused their specialist lenses on various sections: Brandon Roach on regulatory burden, Jean Gorman on development, and Joe Russo on financial aid. Ted Fox offered helpful comments on the introduction. Kathy Cunneen, Ann Donahue, Bill Donahue, Carsten Dutt, Jim Heft, Bruce Kimball, Jim Nolan, and an anonymous reviewer made valuable suggestions on the entire manuscript. Dolores Vargas kindly checked the works cited section against the narrative.

It would be difficult to express in words the gratitude I owe my wife, Barbara, not only for her patience as I worked in administration for seventeen years, but also for her continued graciousness as I continued thereafter to invest in teaching and writing. Because of her extraordinary intelligence and the range of her capacities, I also learned tremendously from her.

I benefited importantly from the counsel of the administrative colleagues and staff persons with whom I worked, at both Ohio State and Notre Dame. I also learned greatly from my faculty colleagues. In recognition of their work and our common enterprise, I dedicate this book to my colleagues in the College of Arts and Letters at the University of Notre Dame, including not only those who worked with me during my tenure as dean but also those who are now advancing the college in ways I could never have imagined.

Introduction, or How I Almost Managed to Become Someone Else

From 1997 to 2008, I served as dean of the College of Arts and Letters at the University of Notre Dame. One day my staff ushered me into our conference room for one of the brief birthday celebrations they occasionally arranged. I was a bit late. They had waited for me before beginning to sing, and I joined in with full voice, but I quietly paused after a while and whispered to one of my colleagues, "Whose birthday is it?"

"Yours," she said.

With twenty-one departments and more than five hundred faculty members in the college, my identity as dean was overwhelmingly collective, and forgetful immersion in its day-to-day responsibilities had become a way of life.

But I didn't adjust to the identity of dean immediately. A week or so after I had started, I set up a meeting with our computer technician, Dave Klawiter. "Let's meet at eight o'clock tomorrow in Harry's office," I said. "Harry" was Harry Attridge, who was my predecessor and had since moved to Yale. Dave responded, "Maybe you should start calling it *your* office."

When someone would ask where I worked and what I did, for years I simply said that I taught at Notre Dame. Somewhere along the way I made the transition to, "I'm dean of Arts and Letters." I became the role I was playing.

I served for eleven years, six more than I originally intended. But I had learned that it takes time to make substantive changes, so I stayed longer than I had planned.

In eleven years I made many mistakes. And yet I learned many lessons as well. Experience is fed in part by reflection on mistakes. I hope in this book to help others avoid pitfalls by offering a kind of surrogate narrative experience. But the book is not only about mistakes: It is about intellectual principles in administration and strategies for moving from vision to implementation. It offers an analysis of best practices, with particular stress on the value of distinctive mission. More than twenty-five years ago, Henry Rosovsky, at the time dean of Arts and Sciences at Harvard, published a splendid book called *The University: An Owner's Manual.* One might think of this book, as one of the readers for the press suggested, as *The Distinctive University: An Operator's Manual.*

I once heard a president say he had no power. He meant that he could not take any action without strong support from below. What he said is not quite true. Certainly, there are areas where an administrator must and should defer to the faculty. At Ohio State the chairperson never overturned the department after a good and substantive discussion, but he or she had the right to argue persuasively for a given position. A dean tends to defer to the faculty in certain areas as well. The only time I ever even contemplated overturning our legislative body, the College Council, on a curricular matter was when our classics department proposed a classical studies major, in addition to its majors in Greek and Latin, that would require no knowledge of Greek or Latin whatsoever. That seemed bizarre to me and a minority of faculty colleagues, both in the department and the college. The College Council vote was mixed but positive, and I chose to honor the vote. It turned out that the major, which already existed at several peer universities, was a success and led indirectly to higher enrollments, even in Greek and Latin; the classical studies majors *wanted* to know Greek and Latin. The majority was right, and I was wrong, though wise enough to defer.

Even though I love small discussion classes, I am also a fan of superb lectures, which model high standards of thought and elocution, inspire students, and encourage them to work through the material analytically, synthesize ideas, and develop questions as they listen. A few colleges and universities have lecture classes that everyone says you must take. At Williams College, the Introduction to Art History served this prominent role; as recently as 1988, 58 percent of the graduating class, representing majors across the full spectrum of the arts and sciences, had taken the year-long lecture course (Toomajian). When I became dean, I proposed that we elevate our best lecturers by creating the temporary designation Notre Dame Master Lecturer for those faculty members who were excellent scholars, had very high student evaluations, regularly taught courses with more than a hundred students, and did not inflate grades. My colleagues were aghast that I would introduce such a concept to a community that prizes small classes; they gave the idea a resounding no, and I had to retreat.

Still, there are unambiguous areas where an administrator has considerable power or means to elicit motivation; these lie above all in vision, personnel, and budget.

First, academic leaders can inspire and motivate faculty toward a vision that is widely shared. The most powerful and enduring tool of any administrator is vision, and the ideal strategy for motivating faculty members to further the university's goals is to collaborate with them to craft an appealing vision. When we act because we identify with a vision, we are intrinsically motivated. A vision must be collectively formed, but there is no question that the role played by academic leaders is central.

The second realm involves personnel, that is, hiring faculty, making tenure decisions, and appointing academic leaders: the first case requires considering candidates put forward by the departments, and the latter two cases require consulting with faculty members. Although these decisions, which determine the personnel who will carry out a vision, are made in consultation with faculty, administrators tend to have the final say.

Finally, budget expresses vision through priorities and differential allocations. The apportionment of resources is normally not an issue of faculty governance. Departments may request a faculty position from the dean, but they do not vote on whether they will receive it. The faculty has a right to be consulted and informed, but it does not have authority over budgetary decisions. And it is through the budget that incentives are most fully realized and, indeed, that negative consequences can be felt—for example, when only minimal resources are allocated to weaker departments. In this book, I tell the story of how I worked with vision, personnel, and budget without holding back tales of my own missteps.

For a university to flourish, it needs to embrace a distinctive vision and instantiate or embody that vision in specific practices. I use my own experience at Notre Dame as a lens through which to tell of the challenges as well as of the best and worst practices in realizing the idea of a distinctive university. Though many of my examples come from Notre Dame, which can be viewed as unusually distinctive, my goal is to use this university simply as an exemplar. Decades ago Burton Clark identified a set of distinctive institutions, focusing on small liberal arts colleges: Antioch, with its work-study program and community participation; Reed, with its combination of intellectual vigor and nonconformity; and Swarthmore, with its signature honors program. Religious colleges, single-sex colleges, and historically black colleges are further obvious examples of distinctive institutions that inspire allegiance, dedication, and affection. George Dennis O'Brien ended his postpresidential memoir with a plea for more distinctive and mission-driven universities, ones with a "specific character" and, drawing on the language of Burton Clark, an "institutional saga" (217). More recently, Jonathan Cole has lamented the "lack of differentiation among our leading universities" and called for "a more intense search for individual identity" (*Toward* 274, cf. 61).

One can criticize many universities for looking too similar to one another and employing as their markers vague and indistinguishable rhetoric, which often amounts to fostering excellent research and educating future leaders. I have heard more than one high school senior announce after a tour of multiple college campuses, "They're all the same!" Despite the trend toward similarity in self-presentation, all colleges and universities are at some level distinctive, though along a spectrum, with some more interchangeable and others more distinct. In fact, most American colleges and universities do see themselves as distinctive; more than half of the nation's private colleges and universities, for example, are religious. Although one can learn from other universities and their practices, each college or university benefits by making general practices its own, by being different. In this light, processing stories about other distinctive colleges and universities can be helpful. Clark's book sought to help us understand distinction through case studies. More recently, George Keller has written a case study about Elon University, and Bill Bowen has offered general insights into administration by focusing on lessons learned at Princeton.

Through concepts and stories, my study explores challenges and puzzles that arise when we seek to realize the idea of a distinctive university. Though I occasionally interweave literature on higher education and management as well as data, my analysis is based mainly on experience and reflection, including seventeen years in administration, six as a chairperson at two institutions and eleven as a dean. The tale interweaves the personal narrative, the idea of a distinctive university, and prominent structures of the American university, with examples taken from practice, into one larger story.

P‍art 1, "Vision and Change," links the historical development of the idea of a university with transformations in vision and argues for the value of distinctive vision even today. Chapter 1 provides a broader setting for the more specific narrative that follows. How have universities historically been led by a distinctive vision? How should we understand the two most significant changes in the history of the idea of the university, the German revolution in the early nineteenth century and the American transformation after World War II? In what ways do our universities today differ from what they should be? Recognizing gaps that need to be addressed is one possible way to move toward articulating a distinctive vision and effecting change. My second chapter emphasizes the advantages of vision and distinctive identity, offers examples of contradictory and compelling visions, and explores the ways in which vision can motivate change.

Part 2, " Embodying and Funding the Vision," shows that a vision without embodiment and resources is illusory. Chapter 3 exhibits the extent to which even a compelling intellectual vision must always be linked to rhetoric, support structures, and community. It also addresses contexts in which vision can only be realized by working through conflict. Chapter 4 addresses nuanced connections between vision and funding. Here, and in part 3, one finds firsthand reflections on the landscape and inner workings of the American university.

Part 3, "Structures, Strategies, Struggles," reflects on administrators' more pragmatic tools, which explain to some degree the distinguishing characteristics and indeed the success of the great American university. The overarching structures and strategies, each of which receives its own chapter, are flexibility, competition, incentives, accountability, and community. Each is a means to realize a distinctive vision, even if community is both a means and an end. The chapters conclude with the challenges and problems that arise with these otherwise attractive concepts.

Whereas I introduce my own story in the remainder of this section, in chapter 1 I look more broadly at the historical and contemporary context. All of the subsequent chapters interweave my personal voice with broader ideas and data.

Over the course of many years, I have experienced a wide range of American universities. Williams, my undergraduate alma mater, is a liberal arts college with just over two thousand students. I received my doctorate at Princeton, a private research university. Ohio State, where I taught for twelve years and was an administrator for five, is one of the country's largest comprehensive public universities and today has more than fifty-eight thousand students. For the past nineteen years I have been at Notre Dame, one of the nation's top-twenty universities and arguably America's leading Catholic university. My experience draws on the diversity of the American system, which, along with its liberal arts colleges, private research universities, and large public universities, also includes community colleges with relatively easy student access and modest fees. America benefits from this institutional diversity.

I have also had extensive experience at German universities. I studied for one semester at an American program affiliated with the University of Bonn and for two years directly at the University of Tübingen, where I completed a master's degree. Some years later I taught at the University of Dresden and at the University of Essen, where I also enjoyed a Humboldt Fellowship. In 2009, I served as Christian-Wolff-Professor at the Martin-Luther-Universität Halle-Wittenberg. At these universities, I developed great admiration for the distinctive strengths of a different tradition, including the students' remarkable independence, the high academic standards, and the strong sense for the intrinsic value of study and scholarship. Some of my criticisms of the American university include comparisons with German universities. One can learn from other universities' best practices, even when one's own system or university is superb.

W hen I was a graduate student at Princeton, those of us teaching German language and culture had an office together in a spacious and comfortable attic. My teaching developed in the context of sharing best practices with colleagues. Even today my greatest advances tend to come from speaking with colleagues about challenges they face and strategies they employ. We certainly do know, on the basis of empirical research, some basic principles of pedagogy: for instance, that students learn more when they are actively engaged in the learning process and when they can also learn from their peers. Teaching well means being attentive to such principles; beyond that, good teachers know their material, reflect on the match between learning goals and student performance, and ensure common sense and creativity, which are enriched by the sharing of best practices.

Administration is not radically different. The few absolutely essential principles are effectively complemented by the sharing of common challenges and best practices. Despite the name, best practices can become better still when they are shared with others, who make them their own and thereby enrich them further. No less important than best practices are mistakes from which we can learn.

When I was dean, we had monthly meetings of the twenty-one chairpersons, four associate deans, and three senior staff persons, who reported to me. The agenda had three categories: brief items, which I zipped through very quickly and summarized in a follow-up e-mail; discussion items, which took the bulk of our time; and best practices, which entailed chairpersons, usually but not always at my invitation, speaking about some innovative or productive activity in their departments, be it in teaching, mentoring, public relations, or any number of other areas. Chairpersons liked this part of the meeting the best, and so did I.

One of the challenges of being an administrator is that you are often alone. You wrestle frequently with personnel issues, which cannot be shared. Venting about complexities or frustrations with a colleague is inappropriate. Therefore, to have a window onto the experience of another administrator can be advantageous. Also, there is a natural human desire to see theory in the world, and practical examples can be inspiring to others. Administrators at diverse kinds of institutions often face similar challenges.

Some years ago I wrote a book about the idea of a Catholic university. I also gave talks that introduced audiences to the book. I was often asked about next steps, and my talks increasingly became focused not on the abstract idea of a Catholic university but on strategies to realize the idea, which drew on my experience as dean. Widening the circle some, I also gave talks to leaders of Christian colleges and universities about aspects of mission that were more formal and expansive, including plans for ensuring that chairpersons are encouraged, well supported, and given appropriate feedback. Then I wrote a book about the value of a liberal arts education, and similar practical discussions ensued. If we accept this vision of the liberal arts, how can we realize it on our campus? This book builds on the reception of those two books to address the following: how to bridge the normative (what we should be) and the descriptive (what we are now) through the strategic.

Further reflections on strategy emerged in the context of a series of talks I gave that led to a third book, this time for a German audience, on the distinguishing characteristics of American higher education and the following questions: What can Germans learn from the American university and what should they avoid? I realized that some of the stories I told to Germans might also have wide appeal in the United States.

Serving as a chairperson or dean is in a sense not that complicated. One needs to have a vision, some sense of strategy, a sensibility for structures, and a capacity to deal with people. The issues are basically the same, only larger and more intense, as one moves up the ladder. Certainly some handbooks can be useful, as several were to me when I would think out loud about how their thoughts applied to my own situation.

But even good technical books are of less value than the indirect insights one gains from reading philosophy and literature and exchanging stories and experiences. I often said to colleagues that you don't really need experience to become a chairperson: It is a matter of common sense. I still believe that, but I also learned that because extensive experience brings with it a certain kind of expertise, you become more efficient. We know from cognitive science that expertise and efficiency are linked (Neubauer and Fink); in an administrative context, experience accelerates decision making and gives you a wider range for your deliberations. Experience can also be vicarious; as we listen to the stories of others, we gain expertise.

This book is not an overview of American higher education, as Derek Bok offers in *Higher Education in America*, nor is it an introduction to a particular administrative role, like the many handbooks on being a dean or chairperson, though it contains elements of both. It is animated by ideas about the value of articulating and embodying a distinctive vision for higher education and is enriched by experiential reflection, which seeks to give life and color to the story.

The book was written partly for academic administrators, especially but not exclusively administrators at distinctive colleges and universities: deans and aspiring deans, who may be interested in learning from a former dean and his experiences; chairpersons, whose roles are not dissimilar and who may want to understand how a dean thinks; and other administrators, such as associate deans, associate provosts, and directors, who face challenges they will find mirrored here. I hope faculty members, whose interest in the inner workings of the university has increased dramatically, partly because of disturbing changes and new challenges, will also find reflections that engage them as they think about their own institutional cultures and strategies. Beyond its audience of American administrators and faculty members, the book may also interest global readers, who turn to the world's leading system of higher education for ideas and best practices, as well as to those American readers—from board members and donors to students and parents—who are curious about the functioning of higher education.

L et me turn now to some personal reflections. I begin my story at the end. After serving as dean for a decade and being very much ready to return to the faculty ranks, I anticipated several potential challenges.

The first was seemingly trivial but not unimportant. As dean, I had a superb staff. I never had to worry about mundane matters, but I knew that as a regular faculty member I would. Before I left office, I ordered a scanner and a dictation program for my computer and made sure that I knew where to make copies, how to place books on reserve, where to order supplies, and so forth. I anticipated as many practical needs as I could.

The second involved giving up the activity of shaping a college. A dean is the center of a great deal of activity, and one gets an adrenaline rush from making things happen. What would replace that dynamism, that sense of mission and accomplishment? Would I miss it?

Despite immersing myself in the larger enterprise, I found I was even happier when I could steal a few hours alone, usually on Sunday evenings, for thinking and writing. The intrinsic value of scholarship is great, and little, including higher administration, can trump the joy of doing something for its own sake.

Being dean means that you are always pressed for time. One has to juggle so much. When as a graduate student I juggled in the marketplaces of Germany, I had the freedom to choose how many balls, rings, clubs, and apples to send into the air; as dean, others often tossed me the objects, and they came unexpectedly and relentlessly, too many at once for me not to let a few drop. Often I would go for a swim in the early evening to wake myself up for the second half of the workday. One day I snuck in a quick swim during the afternoon. Racing to the office and entering through the back door, I was scurrying through the suite, ready to greet a donor, when my staff practically tackled me and told me in exasperation that my hair was heading in about sixty different directions. In rushing out of the locker room, I had neglected to comb my hair or look in the mirror. My colleagues quickly searched their drawers and purses to find a brush so as to rescue me.

Time and inattention were constant challenges. My wife and I had turned down a couple of invitations from a generous local donor, when I saw an invitation in my inbox. I glanced at it, called my wife, and told her that she didn't need to go but that I should, since we had been unable to accept the last few times. I wrote yes on the invitation and dropped it back in the outbox for my assistant. On the day of the event, the invitation was back in my inbox; this time, I looked at it a bit more closely. It was not a social event, it turned out, but a fundraiser at the host's home with one of Indiana's senators. I lived in Michigan. Oh, well, I thought, and headed out. There was a donation box for checks. I didn't have a checkbook on me, so I passed by the box and found myself getting my picture taken with the senator. I then proceeded on to a modest buffet and an after-dinner address. The next day, my assistant informed me that the host's assistant had called. Since there was no check from me, she wanted to know if I was planning to send my check in the mail. I said (of course) yes and looked now for a third time at the materials (this time very closely). There were various levels of giving suggested. I decided that being already late, I should probably not pick the lowest amount. Each Christmas after that, I received a picture of the senator and his family along with a note.

My wife called it my thousand dollar Christmas card.

Hurrying from one event or meeting to another and being so oriented toward fund raising, structural issues, and, often, long-term goals, a dean misses the kind of immediate personal satisfaction that comes from focusing more on teaching—seeing students smile, for example, as they get excited about a topic or grasp new insights. When as dean I would come home and be in an especially good mood, my wife would sometimes say, "You taught today, didn't you?" She could tell that being around students and engaging texts and ideas, as opposed to dealing with management issues and long-range university planning, led to a more immediate and visible joy.

My Christmas vacation each year consisted of carefully analyzing the promotion-and-tenure packets of approximately forty candidates; writing assessments of those cases, which at times were several pages in length; and then making my recommendations to the university promotion-and-tenure committee. In difficult cases I would meet with the departmental committees just after the holidays or in some cases before. For eleven years, that work pretty much consumed the entire holiday vacation. No, I would not miss it.

After being dean for such a long time, I realized my third challenge would be how I would react when someone new came in and started dismantling things I had created, without even asking why I had introduced them.

Still, I had stayed in the position long enough that most of the important structural changes had become part of the routine. I was superfluous, and the changes were no longer foreign innovations but had become the way Notre Dame did things. One of my goals as dean had been to institutionalize changes so that I personally would become irrelevant. Much of what we had done was now part of the fabric of the college. I wasn't needed, and that's exactly what I wanted. My successor, John McGreevy, had worked with me for five years as chairperson of one of Notre Dame's best departments. In becoming dean, he was sacrificing his scholarship to take a turn in administration because of his love for the institution, so he had no qualms about contacting me now and again, especially in his early years, when he wanted advice on a particular puzzle. Whatever he did change, I welcomed. After eleven years, I was eager to see someone else set new accents, address what was not working well, push new initiatives. I knew that a university benefits from fresh ideas, new personalities, and the ritual experience of new beginnings.

The fourth challenge was getting back to full-time teaching and re-search. I had continued to teach one course per year as dean, which had been good for my soul. It had also offered me a window onto current Notre Dame students and given me a shared topic with faculty members. I had always preferred the somewhat antiquated model, which I admired already as an undergraduate at Williams College, whereby an administra-tor is an active scholar-teacher, who serves for a period of time and then passes the baton to return to full-time teaching and scholarship. Having had the opportunity to serve so many years in administration, I also pushed that older model to its limit. I looked forward to serving as a full-time teacher and scholar. When I asked a former provost what advice he had for someone leaving administration, he recommended that I teach and do research in some new areas. So besides returning to German lan-guage teaching after many decades of other kinds of teaching, I added a course on German cinema and a year-long humanities seminar for first-year honors students, taking them in the fall from Homer to Dante and in the spring from Machiavelli to Woody Allen. Being back in the faculty ranks was more fun than I could have imagined.

On the research front, I had continued to publish as dean but, save for a very slim book on the idea of a Catholic university and an emerging book on the value of the liberal arts, I had not developed new research projects. I was leaving the dean's office intellectually empty. This is the predicament of long-serving, higher-level administrators. Frank Rhodes writes soberly of presidents: "Busy with this, preoccupied with that, dis-tracted by a dozen pressing issues, presidents develop an inner emptiness and personal hollowness; they are starved of the intellectual and spiritual nourishment which is the sustenance of the campus" (18). I was saved after I stepped down by a lengthy leave, which allowed me to develop a large number of new research projects. I now have three postdean books behind me, am overseeing a large multiyear grant, have another two books well under way, and have ideas for several more. The leave completely recharged me intellectually. It is difficult to think new academic thoughts when all of your time is consumed by meetings and memos.

The transition also brought with it some minor disadvantages. It is much simpler to tell someone outside the university that you are a dean than a professor. As dean, one goes to the office every day, and to the outside world, it looks much like real work. A professor may not teach every day and so may stay home, getting even more work done, but it doesn't appear that way. Americans still associate work with the office or the job site. One Friday afternoon, before I had become dean, my wife came home after a tough work week; she opened the garage door that faced onto our living room and saw me lying on the couch, seemingly watching TV, with a Coke on the table. She looked at me in disgust and said, "You never work!"

My defense—that I was watching a John Ford film, on which I was writing an essay—somehow didn't dispel the impression.

That Sunday afternoon I folded some wash, put it away, and then sat on the bed against a backrest and started reading. Shortly thereafter my wife came into the room, saw me reading, and said in exasperation, "You're always working!" I replied, "The two statements can't both be true!"

A professor's work is his hobby. Being dean, however meaningful the labor, is nothing like pursuing a hobby, so I actually looked in those years like an upstanding member of the community. After stepping down, I became, in the eyes of nonacademics, one of those professors who never works.

I can recall my wife many years ago telling a coworker in Columbus that I worked at Ohio State. "What does he do?" "He teaches German . . . and he does research." Silence. "Research? What kind of research does a German professor do?" "Well, he's a literary critic. He writes books about other books, you know, novels and dramas and such." "Oh, you mean, CliffsNotes."

I had to cut back on some scholarly activities as dean and I rarely attended disciplinary conferences. I felt a bit disconnected from my scholarly peers, especially the next generation, when I began attending again. It was as if I, as a German scholar, had been away for a few months, but the profession and its personnel had suddenly aged a dozen years. There were full professors who had been graduate students when I took my extended exit. A saving grace has been that much of my research had moved into broader areas, and I have different kinds of connections.

There have also been partly unanticipated advantages. When I left office, I knew each faculty member, and so have a different relationship to my colleagues and my environment than if I had not served in administration for many years. Walking the faculty halls as a former dean is like strolling through an expanded departmental space, where you know hundreds of colleagues, often quite well. Those colleagues greet you and engage in friendly conversations in ways that are quite different from the often hurried and at times agenda-laden exchanges I managed when rushing across campus as dean.

But there was one final challenge that awaited me, one that I had not in the least anticipated. I finished my term at the end of June 2008, but I worked until about six o'clock in the evening on July 3, trying to finalize the recruitment of two endowed chairs and postdating letters I had not had the chance to clear off my desk. At six that evening I turned off my computer, walked outside, clapped and rubbed my hands, and said to my wife, "I'm done."

But for the next eighteen months or so, my dreams were overwhelmingly and repeatedly related to my life as dean and the kinds of puzzles I had encountered. They were not amusing, as dreams sometimes are, but an extension of work: I discussed tenure standards with faculty members, gave a rationale for students taking four courses per semester instead of five, and offered reasons to fund a proposed social science building. So while my conscious mind was on to new activities, my body was telling me that the traces of all-consuming administrative work, one seventy-five-hour week after another for more than a decade, could not be washed away so easily.

Before becoming an administrator, I never dreamed of it.

Within a year of receiving tenure, I was invited to breakfast by my dean at Ohio State, Mike Riley. There, he explained that the recent search for a chairperson, which had led to both internal and external finalists, had not brought forward the candidate he thought would be best. I was that candidate, he said, and if I told my colleagues I would be willing to serve, he would take care of the rest. He knew they would support me. I protested that I was much too young, that it would not be fair, that there were better candidates—all to no avail.

My previous executive experience had consisted of running the kitchen of a restaurant one summer when I was seventeen. Five days before Independence Day weekend, the chef announced he was leaving. The owners saw no other option than to close until they could find a replacement. I had begun as a dishwasher two summers earlier, had moved up to fry cook and now assistant, and had learned most of the dishes. I told the owner that if he would bake the bread and if the chef, before leaving, would teach me how to prepare the sauces and broil the meats, I could take over the kitchen. I became the chef, preparing dishes from Chateaubriand to lobster thermidor. When unexpected requests came my way, I had to improvise. One customer ordered his sirloin "black and blue." I asked an older waitress what that meant. "Black on the outside and raw on the inside," she replied. I turned on the gas burner and stuck the steak in the flames. One afternoon I made some mashed potatoes with cheese and chives, laid them out in a hotel pan, and spread bacon strips on top. It seemed too long a description for the servers' blackboard. I thought of the odd circumstance that "shrimp scampi" means "shrimp shrimp" (*scampi* being the plural of *scampo*, prawn in Italian), so, armed with my high school knowledge of German, I wrote on the board "*Kart-offeln* potatoes." That night I sold about eighty-five *Kartoffeln* potatoes (potatoes potatoes) and, for the less curious and adventuresome, a few smatterings of Delmonico, Lyonnaise, baked, and fries.

In much the same way that I had gotten in over my head in the restaurant, I accepted the position of chairperson ahead of my time. Yet here I perceived a calling. Already while I had been an assistant professor, I had developed a sense of what the department most needed, but I was torn about serving as chairperson. On the one hand, as a newly tenured associate professor, I wanted to preserve my research time and thought the appointment was in principle inappropriately early. On the other hand, I knew the problems and had ideas about how to deal with them. We had been in difficult circumstances, and the first task, I determined, was to develop, with an internal advisory committee, a professional code of conduct that was later unanimously approved and ensured that relations remained civil and that graduate students, for example, would never be the victims of faculty strife. In all, those five years went very well. We implemented innovations of various kinds, and our department, along with a small number of others, was chosen for selective excellence funding. We developed a vision and set of priorities. We received external funding for a visiting professorship from Germany, a study abroad program in Dresden, visiting graduate students from Germany, and a beautiful Victorian home on the edge of campus, which was renovated and converted into a German house suitable for residency and events. We reformed both the undergraduate and graduate curricula, creating diverse tracks for majors and offering graduate students new opportunities for apprenticeships in teaching literature. Unanimous approval was given to a document on variable teaching assignments, with some faculty teaching more, some less.

Since I in many ways did not want to become chairperson, I was in a good negotiating position and was able to arrange for an acting chairperson during my first year, which I spent on leave, though I was still responsible for budget, promotion and tenure, and other weighty matters. In January, I was called into the dean's office; informed that the college had to come up with its share of a midseason budget cut, unexpectedly imposed by the state legislature; and told that I needed to make some drastic cuts of my own. Among other tasks, I had to call an eminent professor at Yale, who was slated to join us as a visiting professor and who had written a sterling review of my first book, in other words, someone I had imagined could become a mentor and writer of recommendation letters; that dream ended when I asked him if he could get back on Yale's payroll, since we no longer had any money for him. Welcome to administration!

But overseeing the budget also became an opportunity for creativity. We converted two departing faculty lines to fellowships so that we were able to fund graduate fellowships more generously and increase the number of graduate student research fellowships. I reasoned that we would likely have lost the lines in any case, but, more importantly, we did not need the courses offered by those departing faculty. We needed more competitive but fewer graduate students and stronger support, including top-off dollars, to compete with the best stipends nationally. We used funds to create an innovative visiting position for a two-week residency that involved regular breakfasts with students, a public lecture, and an intensive compact graduate seminar (for one-third of the price we had once paid to have someone fly in once a week for a ten-week quarter). Because it was a two-week instead of a ten-week commitment, we were able to obtain our first-choice candidate each time.

When, after three years, a new dean arrived, he asked if he could use me to pilot a review scheme for chairpersons. After reviewing the results, he told me that on his five-point scale, he had never seen evaluations like mine, which included numerous 5+ and 5++ scores—a great contrast to some of the scores I would later receive as dean. During my first term, I had the image of the recalcitrant chair, uneager to stay in the job but doing fine work, and that very much helped my reception. I was offered another four-year term, which I was inclined not to take. As part of the negotiation, the dean offered me either two or four years; the four-year term involved a much higher base salary, but the two-year one still included a welcome raise. I took the two years. I did not see myself as a long-term administrator.

W hen I moved to Notre Dame and the dean who hired me announced a week after my arrival that he was moving on, a search commenced. Someone nominated me, and I composed a letter saying that I preferred not to do it. I did not want to be impolite, so I did not send it. In January, when the search was presumably well under way, the provost called to say he had never heard back from me. I dutifully printed out the letter and brought it to his office. I trudged across the snowy campus in my boots and hand delivered it to his assistant. I had left the window a bit too open and I became for the second time a reluctant administrator. But here, too, and even more so, I sensed a mission and threw myself into the work.

In the process of deciding to come to Notre Dame, I had spent considerable time thinking about its strengths and weaknesses in comparison with Ohio State. I had developed a sense for what should be preserved and enhanced and what needed radical reform. These ideas ranged from a crisper vision and higher tenure standards to seemingly mundane matters of administration. Because I intended to get in and get out, I worked very quickly. I ignored the conventional wisdom about waiting a year be-fore undertaking any significant reforms. Instead, I waited a month, until I could meet publicly with the faculty. On the day before classes started, I called the faculty together and explained why I had grown to love the distinctive mission of Notre Dame, but I also stressed that we were not nearly as good as we could or should be. We had too many long-term associate professors and needed to introduce annual reviews and merit raises. We would change the practice of all departing faculty positions staying in the departments and would instead return them to the dean for reallocation. We needed to reduce underenrolled classes and the number of classes with too many students. Despite the strong rhetoric on my part, most of the faculty questions that day were about less controversial mat-ters, including the integration of academic and residential life and Notre Dame's distinctive interest in ultimate questions.

When I explained my plans in still greater detail a few weeks later to a group of about sixty donors, who formed our advisory council, they focused on the changes. They were both enthusiastic and deeply skepti-cal. One of them mumbled to another, "This guy won't last very long." Another, used to a dog-and-pony show about how great Notre Dame was, was taken aback not only by my sober assessment of our gaps but even more so by my intentions. "Does anyone else at Notre Dame know of these plans?" he asked.

My highest goal as dean focused on vision and my second on strate-gies of efficiency and accountability that I thought would also be neces-sary prerequisites for gaining more resources. I did not initially place much stress on the social element, which was for me not a natural strength and whose importance I had underestimated. At Ohio State that did not matter for several reasons. First, it was not expected of me, a young associate professor, who had been drafted into the job a year after tenure; and fortunately one of the senior faculty considered hosting social events for the department to be part of her vocation. Second, since we had only twenty or so colleagues in our department at Ohio State, I saw them on a regular basis, and additional social events were not a high priority. I spent all day Mondays, Wednesdays, and Fridays in the office; I taught on those days and my door was open all day long. The chair's door opened not only onto the departmental suite, which housed the assistants, mailboxes, and the like, but also directly onto the corridor.

Unless I was speaking with a faculty member or a student, both doors were always wide open. On Tuesdays and Thursdays I worked at home, preparing my teaching, doing more complex administrative work, and engaging in research. I told faculty not to hesitate calling me there. A short interruption was nothing. My wife worked, and we had no children, so knowing only I would answer, my colleagues called as needed. Third, the social dimension can mean different things in different contexts. For us, a department that had seen much strife in recent years, the social involved running meetings effectively and diplomatically, engaging in level-headed conversations with all, and creating structures and procedures that ensured civility and fairness.

As a dean with hundreds of faculty members, the social element was wildly different. The challenge and difficulty were exacerbated because I had come from elsewhere, and was not, therefore, known. Moreover I had inherited a very informal operation. Everyone had direct contact with the dean, and there were few or no procedures, faculty committees, and the like. Changing how everything functioned meant also changing the social fabric. In addition, I made multiple decisions, in terms of both structure and personnel, that went against tradition. One does not remain wildly popular, for example, by announcing that faculty lines are no longer owned by departments or by overturning positive tenure recommendations.

Beyond those factors one of my own personality traits created challenges. As a chairperson, one can be a modest introvert, but as a dean, that is impossible. I remember that the first time I taught, I was suddenly transformed from an introvert into an extrovert, but that was always only for an hour or so. As a natural introvert, I found my new role as dean difficult. In my family I was the youngest of three boys. When we were growing up, the neighbors jokingly called us "the vert-brothers." I was the "introvert," my middle brother was the "extrovert," and my oldest brother was awarded the name, well, I'd better not say.

To succeed as dean, I had to become an extrovert, and the number of years I spent in the role fundamentally changed my personality. I say to my students, "You have to play the role of an articulate intellectual, and over time you will become increasingly articulate and intellectual." As dean I played the role of the extrovert, who increasingly reached out to experience and enjoy other people's company.

In fact, after my five-year review as dean, one of the faculty members on the committee told me that she had pegged me on the Myers-Briggs scale as intuitive, thinking, and judging, but she was not sure whether I was introverted or extroverted. I had heard of the scale but I had never taken the test. When I took several versions of it, I saw that she was right on the first three, and the results were mixed on the scale of introversion/extroversion. I was indeed in my history and core introverted, but as dean I had become extroverted. I had almost managed to become someone else. In the overall scheme I had moved from what David Keirsey calls the "Mastermind" (encompassing less than 1 percent of the population) to the "Fieldmarshal" (encompassing less than 2 percent of the population). I kept retaking the test to try to come out with a more innocent and appealing title like "Healer" or "Teacher," but I failed each time. In truth, some of what seemed to be the strengths and weaknesses of the Doctor Mabuse and Erwin Rommel types had in fact surfaced in my review, a rather bracing and sobering experience to which I return later in the book.

Since I still saw myself in some sense as a faculty member, who thinks independently, and not yet as a dean, who has a greater administrative and social identity, I also fell into the trap of underestimating the role of simple and innocuous ritual and overestimating the value of engaged intellectual discussion. When asked in the first weeks of my tenure as dean if I would give some opening remarks for a gender studies panel and reception, I said yes, and offered some thoughts about gender studies that went beyond, "Gender studies is essential to our flourishing as a college, have a great year, and enjoy the refreshments!" I reflected out loud on the strengths and weaknesses of gender studies as a discipline and on strategies for its distinctive flourishing at Notre Dame. I suggested that it not isolate itself from the departments but instead reach out to and seek to influence the more traditional disciplines; that its scholars write in a language intelligible to colleagues and students from all disciplines; that it weigh the self-cancelling structure of any reduction of values to power alone and instead embed itself within a tradition that makes strong, rational arguments for the validity of universal human rights; and finally, that it continue to bring its appealing existential component to scholarship and teaching but be wary of restricting justice to identity politics, thereby overlooking broader issues of neglected justice, such as those involving future generations.

It was not a smart move.

The halls were abuzz about what hidden messages I was trying to convey. I received letters, e-mails, and requests for meetings. I told the provost that my tenure might be shorter than he intended. But in the end, the commotion was calmed. I met with several people one-on-one over lunch; they immediately saw that I was still thinking as a scholar, not as an administrator, and that my arguments were not absurd. Inadvertently, I had initiated a not uninteresting public debate on complex puzzles that continued in one of the campus newspapers. I had learned in a surprising way that being a dean meant people really listened to what I had to say, and I quickly became aware that if I was going to think out loud, not as a scholar, but as an administrator, I would need to consider the occasions very carefully. Since one of an administrator's goals is to cause a rupture only when it serves an important and targeted purpose, gaining a deeper understanding of the value of occasionally innocuous talking points was valuable.

I was also modestly surprised at how often, at times on unexpected occasions, I was asked to speak. In my first weeks I was invited by one of our centers to an award ceremony, and, after a pleasant dinner with faculty and guests and a few minutes of comments by the director, I unexpectedly heard, "And now Dean Roche will tell us how important the such-and-such center is to the life of Notre Dame." I did not know that I was on the docket. I somehow managed to hit the right notes, even after wondering in the back of my mind whether I had even internalized the names of the two honorees. From that point onward, when I was on my way to any event, I always thought of a word or two to say, should it be necessary or appropriate.

Another challenge for the scholar-teacher as dean involves suddenly giving up research projects, when one is, let's say, in the middle of a book. I had accumulated significant research time from my days at Ohio State, and I insisted on taking a year's leave, even though I would continue to be involved with important issues, such as promotion and tenure, senior hiring, budget, and fund raising. I took that partial leave during my third year as dean. I was still involved in administrative work about a third of the time, but I was able to finish two books that were well under way when I entered the dean's office and to write another very short book. That was very important for my identity as a faculty member and scholar.

Although some faculty told me they appreciated having an active scholar-teacher as dean and no faculty member ever said a negative word to me directly, I was told in my five-year review that a good number of faculty members had complained about the leave. A dean, they said, should be first and foremost a dean. In truth, if the leave had not been granted, I would have declined the post and had a much different story to tell.

When I was asked by the provost to stay for one additional year beyond ten, I was not keen on the idea. I could have imagined stepping down after about eight or nine years. But several factors—the arrivals of a new president and a new provost and my desire to see multiple internal candidates for dean develop, and ensure they had some leave time before I announced my departure—resulted in my deciding to finish my second term. I had certainly not paced myself for more. As it turned out, however, I stayed on for an eleventh year, which meant I ended up serving as an administrator for seventeen of my first eighteen years as a tenured faculty member. The provost and I agreed that in the second semester of year ten, I would take a partial leave to work on another book. That spring I was on 90 percent of the time, which still represented a break but demonstrated how quickly administrative positions can become complex. Fortunately, as I went into my final year, the provost made clear to the faculty that nothing would go on hold: He had full confidence in my work, and I would lead as if this were not my last year as dean, so that no time would be wasted in a transition. Just as I did not hold back in my first year, I did not hold back in my final year.

Faculty members tend to have an intuitive reluctance to serve as academic administrators; most faculty members were drawn to the profession through a love of teaching or research and were then socialized into an atmosphere whose default rhetoric expresses unease about administration. My initial reluctance about moving into administration shifted over time to ambivalence: I remained eager to return to the faculty ranks even as I enjoyed the different puzzles and positive effects of being an engaged administrator. There were also clear moments of fulfillment, as I worked with others to realize a vision and enhance a community of scholars and learners. An academic administrator with even a modest vision and a modicum of formal capacities, I saw, can address inadequacies and make a positive difference; in that sense, administration is worth the time and effort. I grew to embrace what had seemed foreign and uninviting. I saw more and more positive changes, developed an entirely new cohort of colleagues and friends beyond the department and later the college, and learned to appreciate more fully the ways staff persons, often behind the scenes, provide effective support for faculty and students. Further, administration allowed me to develop different sides of myself. The unusually quick pace sharpened various of my capacities and was in its own way energizing, even as it pulled me away from otherwise preferable pursuits. I developed a broader horizon, learning much more about the detailed workings of a university as well as about broader issues that affect higher education. And I gained a much stronger sense of collective identity: I realized in new ways that faculty members who had administrative experience were able, if they returned to the faculty ranks, to bring new perspectives to the local collective and help break down the automatic divide between faculty and administration.

PART I

Vision and Change

The two great revolutions in the history of the idea of the university flowed from new visions of what a university could and should become. How are we to understand these visions and their capacities for inaugurating change?

Despite these revolutions, first in Germany and then in the United States, the gaps that remain in the contemporary higher education landscape are staggering and sobering. How might recognizing and addressing these gaps trigger yet new aspirations and new visions of what a university could and should become?

Vision is central not only for the idea of a university as such. It is the driving force in the collective identity of any particular university or college. What strategies exist for developing a vision? Why is distinctive vision so significant and at the same time so difficult to sustain? How can vision work effectively today, and how can it go awry? Finally, in what ways can vision be a vehicle for both solidifying tradition and inaugurating change?

CHAPTER ONE

The Idea and Reality of the University, or How We Got Where We Are

The history of the university has seen three paradigm shifts. In the early nineteenth century, German universities, with their signature integration of teaching and research, changed the landscape of universities across the world and remained preeminent for well over a century. In the second half of the twentieth century, the American university, with unprecedented resources and enrollments, further transformed the idea of the university. Today we are undergoing a third paradigm shift characterized by increasing internationalism, including global competition for faculty and students, new technologies that allow universities to reach international audiences, collaboration of scholars across countries and of universities around the world, and the emergence and importance of international rankings.

My brief account of the idea and reality of the university focuses on the first two transformations, both of which were animated by compelling and distinctive visions: the German revolution in the early nineteenth century and the American transformation in the mid-twentieth century. One can learn a great deal, both on the formal level and in terms of content, by understanding other models and one's own past.

A vision for a university can emerge from an ideal of what should be, which then triggers action to realize that vision. But a vision can also arise by analyzing the deficiencies of the existing university and seeking to address them, making their reversal the focus of the vision. I conclude this chapter with a brief account of gaps in the American system. Both strategies—the ideal and the critical—presuppose that the university is not yet what it should and could be.

The German Revolution in the Idea of the University

The general view of the universities in the eighteenth century was not positive. The university was viewed by many as sterile, with knowledge understood to be fixed and professors considered to be simply transmitters of that knowledge to students. Most universities offered their students little more than an extension of secondary education, with emphasis on training in ancient languages and the interpretation of classical works. Mastery of the classics was viewed as a test of intellectual ability. But there were other, more practical tests of good thinking, and advances in astronomy and physics had rendered many of the classical scientific texts outdated. Unease arising from the lack of practicality and the nonintegration of modern science led to research, often done by amateurs, outside the universities, as well as to the creation of independent institutes to train professionals, including engineers. Some argued that utilitarian, practical knowledge, which was in high demand, could best be obtained elsewhere. Most of the great thinkers of the seventeenth and eighteenth centuries—Francis Bacon, Thomas Hobbes, René Descartes, Baruch Spinoza, John Locke, Gottfried Wilhelm Leibniz, Voltaire, and Jean-Jacques Rousseau, among others—developed their work outside the universities.

In addition to having few students, the universities were inadequately funded. The poor reputation of the universities was not aided by student dueling and rioting. Further, the universities were perceived as perpetuating past privileges. Thus in 1793, in the wake of the French Revolution, the French universities were abolished. To take their place, France created specialized institutions, with independent faculties, focused on the professional education of doctors, engineers, lawyers, and teachers.

Germany developed a different model. By the 1740s, Germany had begun to see some changes. At the time, Halle, which was a center of both the Enlightenment and Pietism movements, enjoyed the best reputation among German universities; it was also the largest, with more than a thousand students (Ellwein 332). Göttingen, which became the most prominent after 1750 (Turner 504), introduced new subjects, such as history and philology, and invested heavily in mathematics and science as well as in law, for which it became famous. Jena also gained a flourishing reputation, having become renowned in philosophy and aesthetics and for numbering such luminaries and younger intellectuals as J. G. Fichte, Friedrich Schiller, F. W. J. Schelling, G. W. F. Hegel, and the brothers Schlegel (August and Friedrich) among its teachers. Johann Wolfgang Goethe was close by in Weimar.

Both Halle and Jena were closed during the Napoleonic Wars, but their revolutionary advances bore fruit in 1810, with the founding of the University of Berlin, which sought and, in many cases, obtained the best faculty and whose early teachers included Fichte, Friedrich Schleiermacher, Hegel, and Schelling. Halle, Göttingen, Jena, and Berlin set the stage for what became the first towering achievement of the modern university. The German universities not only ascended in quality, they transformed the idea of the university.

Instead of having different faculties focused on professional education, the German university, animated by idealistic thinking, embraced the unity of knowledge across disciplines. No longer subject to direct oversight by the government as the French institutes were, German universities secured autonomy. In France the new curricular model was animated by the professional schools, whereas in Germany the driving force was research, including new scholarly and pedagogical methods. The educational reforms in Germany integrated the French abandonment of past privilege: status was to come not from tradition and social rank but from the meritorious achievement of faculty in scholarship and of students in examinations, each bolstered by freedoms along the way.

Very quickly the new ideas spread. At the German research university of the nineteenth century, the discovery of new truths, rather than the transmission of knowledge, became the animating principle. The German idea was that professors should not be giving textbook summaries of what others thought but should instead be scholarly models themselves, showing students how one arrives at new knowledge. As Schleiermacher described it, "The teacher must let everything he says emerge in front of his listeners; he should not recount what he knows but instead reproduce his coming to know, the act itself, so that the listeners are not constantly gathering in mere bits of knowledge but should instead see immediately before them the act of reason itself in bringing forth knowledge and intuitively emulate it themselves" (62–63).[1]

In contrast, Cardinal Newman's *Idea of a University*, published in 1852, still held to the idea that the university should be primarily oriented toward teaching, even if the German thinkers shared with Newman the value of learning and knowledge as ends in themselves. At the German universities, the teacher and scholar were one; it was considered important that students have the personal experience of encountering great scholars. A primary educational goal was to draw students into research and guide them toward autonomy. For Fichte, "the formation of the capacity for learning" was more important than learning itself (131). The concept of the seminar, which engaged students as active learners, was introduced, initially in philology and then in history, becoming a distinctive and essential part of the German university. Spread from Göttingen already in the 1770s, it had become central to the pedagogy of the German university within one or two generations. The seminar was given a philosophical defense by Fichte as a supplement to lectures and merely receptive learning (13–34). Examinations and student essays, Fichte argued further, should not parrot back information but instead exhibit the self-activity of the student's mind, the capacity to take what one has learned and extend it in a variety of areas (130–34).

New subjects were added to the university, led by the work of Alexander von Humboldt, brother of the founder of the University of Berlin, Wilhelm von Humboldt. The early nineteenth century had seen considerable expansion in the humanities. In the second half of the century, the construction of modern research facilities, including scientific laboratories, led to widespread development of the natural sciences. Here Germany left behind France and England, which were still making piecemeal scientific advances on the basis of makeshift laboratories and amateur

---

1. Unless otherwise noted, all translations are by the author.

activity. Germany in contrast offered first-rate laboratories. Luminaries in science, such as Justus Liebig in Gießen, whose chemistry laboratory lasted decades beyond its founding in 1826, and the great mathematician Karl Friedrich Gauss in Göttingen, advanced the reputation of the German university. This asymmetry continued for generations. In the early twentieth century, Berlin enjoyed the presence of two of the greatest physicists of all time, Max Planck and Albert Einstein.

By the 1830s, the German model had become solidified and was supreme. It was adopted not only by the other German-speaking countries but throughout parts of northern, southern, and eastern Europe, including Scandinavia, Greece, and Russia (W. Clark 28–29). By the end of the nineteenth century, the German model had triggered changes in England and America. Eventually France, too, fell under German influence. Even Japan, despite, like France, having a strong central government, opted for the German not the French model. Students from around the world came to study with master teachers in Germany, where new methodologies were pioneered in classical and comparative philology, biblical criticism, history, and the sciences. Bliss Perry wrote, "That Germany possessed the sole secret of scholarship was no more doubted by us young fellows in the eighteen-eighties than it had been doubted by George Ticknor and Edward Everett when they sailed from Boston, bound for Göttingen, in 1814" (88–89). The German concept of *Wissenschaft* had almost magical meaning for Americans at the time. James Morgan Hart, reminiscing on his experiences of German universities, wrote, "By *Wissenschaft* the Germans mean knowledge in the most exalted sense of that term, namely, the ardent, methodical, independent search after truth in any and all of its forms, but wholly irrespective of utilitarian application" (250). In one discipline after another, the Germans towered above others, distinguished, for example, by teachers such as Leopold von Ranke and Theodor Mommsen in history, Ulrich von Wilamowitz in philology, and Max Weber and Georg Simmel in sociology.

What made the German universities so distinctive? At least five principles are essential to the idea of a university. Two of them—the unity of knowledge across disciplines and the value of knowledge for its own sake—were strengthened and redefined during the long era of greatness at the German universities. Three of them—the integration of research and teaching, academic freedom, and *Bildung* or self-formation—were invented by the Germans.

The first principle originated in the medieval idea of the unity of being and knowing and was reinforced by the striving of German idealism for an understanding of the organic relation of all knowledge. It holds that the university should be characterized, first, by the integration of disciplines and the search for not only specialized knowledge but also the relation of the diverse parts of knowledge to one another. This is what animates the pursuit of ever-more simple but comprehensive theories, and this is why the various disciplines—mathematics, science, the social sciences, the arts, and the humanities along with architecture, business, engineering, law, and medicine—are housed within a single institution. In this sense, the university differs from institutes that focus on individual disciplines, such as the arts, business, or technology, which was the practice in France during the ascent of the German university and which has become increasingly common in developing countries and at for-profit institutions as unity gives way to isolated applications. In contrast, the relation of the disciplines to one another and the search for unity, however difficult, still belong to the idea of a university.

The second principle of the university, drawing on the ancient and medieval elevation of the value of contemplation, recognizes knowledge as an end in itself. It therefore encourages basic science, independently of its applications. The German university elevated pure research and the centrality of the arts and sciences. This reevaluation reversed the hierarchy of the faculties that had held sway at the medieval universities, where the arts and sciences were merely preparatory to the higher study of law, medicine, and theology. In the wake of the German revolution in higher education, application took a secondary position in relation to the search for truth, a search that remains central to the idea of the university.

As stated above, the first two principles, advancing the unity and the intrinsic value of truth, were strengthened and redefined at the German universities. The next three originated with the Germans and revolutionized the concept of the university in fundamental ways.

The third principle is that, for universities to compete with one another and for faculty to attract students, classes should integrate new and interesting material; the rote transmission of past knowledge and second-hand material virtually disappeared from the German lecture halls and seminars of the nineteenth century. The idea of the teacher as a scholar has since become an essential part of what we call a university today. Oxford and Cambridge along with Harvard, Yale, and Princeton would today be unthinkable without the principle of the unity of teaching and research. Faculty endeavor to impart knowledge to students through teaching, thereby preserving and interpreting the cultural documents of the past and making transparent the most recent advances and still unresolved questions in their fields, but they also attempt to make new discoveries through their scholarship and creative activity. In short, the university elevates both the transmission of knowledge and the discovery of new knowledge, and it seeks to awaken among its best and most advanced students not simply a reception of knowledge but an active interest in research. The research laboratory and the research seminar are essential parts of the university's teaching function. By integrating teaching and research, the university also fosters community among students and faculty.

The fourth principle concerns academic freedom. German universities, though dependent on the state for funding, retained their autonomy in scholarship and curriculum. Academic freedom prevented invasive state interference and guaranteed the university's freedom from the church. Academic freedom also involved the autonomy of the scholar, who was now free to consider all positions in the search for truth, no longer weighed down by the power of tradition and more likely to inspire students because he was teaching what he was actively discovering; the concept of academic freedom remains core to great universities today. Germany invented the concept of *Lehrfreiheit*, according to which scholars have the right to select topics for teaching along with the corollary freedoms to follow investigations wherever they might lead and disseminate the results as they wish. The state retained financial authority, control over some of the more professionally oriented examinations, and final decisions on appointments to chairs. *Lernfreiheit*, also a German invention, placed little stress on required courses and emphasized the student's freedom to choose various courses and teachers, to transfer from one university to another, and to learn independently, without interim exams. In reflecting on the independence of students, Schleiermacher argued, "that a whole new life, a higher, truly scientific spirit should be awakened," which could not succeed "under external constraints; instead, the attempt can be carried out only in a climate of complete freedom of spirit" (110).

The student was free to pursue his path until it was time for graduation-related examinations: "freedom and independence" along with an awakening "longing . . . for science," recognized only from afar during the school years, should guide the university student (Humboldt 4: 261). *Lernfreiheit* or freedom of learning thus created "the primary social constitution of the Humboldt university, one that united professors and students in social parity" (Schelsky 92). Through the middle of the twentieth century, outside of a small number of fields, such as medicine, few compulsory lessons existed. The idea behind this freedom was that students needed to be educated to autonomy. Moreover, the very idea of the seminar was that the common striving for knowledge animated faculty and students and united them in a common pursuit; not only were faculty there to help guide students, but students were there, according to Humboldt, to help faculty in their search for new knowledge: "It is further a distinction of institutions of higher learning that they always treat science as a problem that has yet to be fully solved and therefore remain constantly engaged in research, whereas the schools deal with, and teach, only completed and agreed-upon bits of knowledge. The relationship between teacher and student becomes in this way a thoroughly different one than before. The former is not there for the latter; both are there for science" (4: 256).

Central to the concept of *Bildung* or formation—the fifth principle—was the elevation of active thinking, the creative mind, and the individual. Engagement with scholarship presupposed the student's independent activity, and this activity was directed also toward the formation and cultivation of self. Not simply scholarship or future employability but the development of character and a well-rounded person were central to the idealist concept of education. Broad exploration of the world as it is and as it should be were considered central to the concept of the educated person, as defined by the idealists. Although universities and students have increasingly elevated scholarly inquiry and job preparation over the development of the well-rounded person, no university education that earns the name can involve only training; it must also involve education and to some extent formation (Roche, "Should Faculty?").

The intellectual superiority of the German universities from the early nineteenth century through the Weimar Republic was universally acknowledged. From 1901 through 1932, Germany received over thirty Nobel prizes in the sciences, more than the next two countries, the United Kingdom and France, combined.

What has happened since then? The most important change was the decimation of the universities and intellectual life under the Nazis. The loss of Jewish scholars and scientists as well as critics of the regime, overwhelmingly to America, was enormous. Some 25 percent of the pre-1933 physicists and twenty current or future Nobel winners, including eleven in physics, were displaced (Beyerchen 47). The names of those in the humanities and social sciences who were dismissed or who fled reads like a who's who of modern German letters and includes Theodor Adorno, Hannah Arendt, Rudolf Arnheim, Erich Auerbach, Walter Benjamin, Ernst Bloch, Martin Buber, Rudolf Carnap, Ernst Cassirer, Erik Erikson, Sigmund Freud, Erich Fromm, Max Horkheimer, Karl Jaspers, Hans Jonas, Erich von Kahler, Siegried Kracauer, Paul Oskar Kristeller, Karl Löwith, Karl Mannheim, Herbert Marcuse, Erwin Panofsky, Leo Spitzer, Leo Strauss, Paul Tillich, and Alfred Weber.

Not only the scholars of this generation but many of the children of émigrés who settled in the United States went on to achieve illustrious university careers; these children were fifteen times more likely than the average American to be listed in *Who's Who*, and at least four of them— Eric Kandel, Walter Kohn, Arno Penzias, and Jack Steinberger—received Nobel prizes in science (Sonnert and Holton 2–3, 66). Also among these children one can include Henry Kissinger, the eminent intellectual historians Peter Gay and Fritz Stern, and the author of one of the best books on American higher education, Henry Rosovsky.

Germany of course struggled to get beyond the rubble: the loss of faculty, the compromised position of many who remained, and the loss of continuity all made the German situation difficult, but three additional factors were at play.

First was the conflict between two competing visions: on the one hand was the vision of an elite university that educated the best students in research, that is, the heritage of the Humboldt university, as the traditional German university increasingly came to be called (*Lange-wiesche*), while on the other hand was the vision of a mass university that had increasingly sought to educate a majority of young persons. In 1950, only 4 percent of the German cohort went to the university. By 1960, this had increased to 8 percent, by 1970 to 15 percent, by 1980 to 20 percent, by 2000 to 33 percent, by 2010 to 46 percent, and by 2013 to 53 percent (Heinzel 26; *Bildung und Forschung* 52). Unlike the United States, Germany does not have elite universities with selective admissions, and the ideals of the traditional German university are not easily achieved at the mass university.

Second was the insufficient funding that led to abysmal student–faculty ratios. Even the creation of new universities and the expansion of faculty could not keep pace with the rise in student numbers. In 1875–76, Tübingen had a student-to-professor ratio of 14 to 1, and in Bonn the figure was 9 to 1. In 1980–81, the figure in Tübingen had risen to 94 to 1 and in Bonn to 117 to 1 (Ellwein 338–39). No German university comes close to having the premier funding enjoyed at America's top universities. The expenditure per student at an Ivy League university such as Princeton is more than eleven times the German average (*Report of the Treasurer* 27). Princeton is an exceptional institution of course, but even lesser-endowed American universities have better student ratios and on average more funding than their German counterparts. A study by the Organization for Economic Co-operation and Development (OECD) found that German universities are funded at a per-student rate of only 64 percent of the US average (*Education at a Glance 2015*, table B1.1a). The recent Excellence Initiative, designed to advance dozens of German universities with a variety of projects, has a projected investment of approximately €1.9 billion from 2006 to 2012 and €2.7 billion from 2012 until 2017. On a comparative scale, the larger second installment is a bit less than the amount of research support the United States allocated in fiscal year 2011 to four leading American universities (*Chronicle of Higher Educ., Almanac 2013–14*, 58).

Third was a set of cultural parameters that do not foster excellence: little competition among universities, especially for students; little room for flexibility and initiative on the part of university administrators; an inconsequential concept of accountability; and a lack of attention to student centeredness and community, which will mean few serious donations from alumni for generations to come. This differs from the United States. Even underfunded state colleges and small private ones that struggle with their budgets operate with a good deal of flexibility and are engaged in a market environment that rewards initiative. Although the German university had developed an extraordinary vision, it failed to grasp the significance of conflicting identities and lost sight of strategies to make its vision a continuing reality (Roche, *Was die deutschen*).

The Distinction of the Great American University

The premier standing once held by Germany is now occupied by the United States, whose universities were radically transformed in the second half of the twentieth century. How was this transformation possible and what distinguishes the greatness of the American university?

First in the eyes of the world is the dominance in research. In the 2016 *U21 Ranking of National Higher Education Systems*, the United States places first (Williams et al. 7). The overwhelming percentage of Nobel prize winners each year consists of scholars trained or working at American universities, many of whom were not born in the United States. Of the Nobel prizes for research from 2000 to 2015, for example, 100 of 155 went to scholars working in the United States (70 of these went to individuals who were born there), 14 to scholars in the United Kingdom, and 12 to scholars in Japan. No other country had more than 8. In the *Academic Ranking of World Universities 2015*, fifteen of the seventeen top-ranked universities are American (Cambridge and Oxford are the other two).

America's research trajectory benefited immeasurably from the nineteenth-century importation of the German research university model and the postwar influx of federal research funding, private gifts, and tuition dollars. The early American universities were for the most part small and focused on educating students to the baccalaureate. Four years after the first graduate programs appeared at Harvard, Johns Hopkins University was founded in 1876 as an American version of the German research university. A large number of the faculty had received their degrees from German universities, so that Johns Hopkins was informally called the American Göttingen (Röhrs 80, 83). Virtually all of the leading university presidents of the late nineteenth century, including Charles William Eliot, who introduced doctoral studies to Harvard, had studied in Germany (Lucas 177; Rüegg 3: 169). Already in the 1850s, the German model was much discussed, and by the 1870s Americans had begun to imitate it. Tremendous competition developed, especially among private universities. This was foreign to the German climate and indeed to the overwhelming number of public universities elsewhere in the world. Universities competed with one another for the best graduating PhDs and the best advanced scholars. Reputations rose or fell with the results. Clark University never recovered its standing after the University of Chicago raided almost its entire faculty in the early 1890s (Hall 295–98); both universities had been founded, like Johns Hopkins, for graduate study.

But the great unleashing of American research came much later. Scientific advances, including the development of the atom bomb, aided the American war effort in World War II. At the time, many university professors became government workers. Scientific research for military purposes was conducted by government personnel. After the war, a new paradigm was proposed. President Franklin Delano Roosevelt asked Vannevar Bush, former dean at the Massachusetts Institute of Technology (MIT), to make a recommendation on how university research could aid the nation also in a time of peace. During the war, Bush had directed the US Office of Scientific Research and Development. Bush had the idea of contracting out this research to universities and other scientific institutes. His report *Science: The Endless Frontier*, published in 1945, advocated university science as useful to advances in public health, national security, standard of living, job creation, and cultural advancement, as well as to the development of future talent. Not simply applied but also basic research was to be supported, as basic science could lead to unanticipated applications. Grants would be awarded on the basis of merit; geographical distribution would play no role.

After much discussion in Congress, these recommendations led to the expansion of the National Institutes of Health (NIH) in 1947, the creation of the National Science Foundation (NSF) in 1950, and the allocation of significant financial resources from the federal government to universities. In some ways this was a continuation of the German conceptual model—that original research and education should work in tandem—and a rejection of the most recent American development, which involved scientists leaving their universities to work directly for the federal government. The result was tremendous federal support of university science, from faculty salaries and postdoctoral scholars to graduate stipends, travel, project-specific equipment, and administrative costs in support of research.

After the Russians launched Sputnik in 1957, America resolved to subsidize education even more. In effect, competition meant the release of more resources. National Science Foundation funding for fiscal year 1959 was increased from $40 million to $130 million (Geiger, *Research* 174). Another consequence was the National Defense Education Act of 1958, which involved direct subsidies of higher education, not simply contracted research. In the 1960s, federal support was extended to the arts, humanities, and social sciences. Besides continuing to support an already-existing elite set of institutions, President Lyndon B. Johnson set the goal of increasing the number of very good research universities, expanding the range of institutions that could successfully compete for funding (Graham and Diamond 40).

Today multiple federal agencies support research. According to the *Chronicle of Higher Education's Almanac 2011–12*, total spending on research by colleges and universities in 2010–11 was $54.9 billion, with 59 percent coming from the federal government, 20 percent from the institutions themselves, 7 percent from state and local governments, and 6 percent from industry (4).

But ascendancy in research was not the only bringer of resources to the American university. Tuition from ever-expanding numbers of students and the gifts of alumni and other supporters were also sources of support. The English model of the importance of residential life had become no less prominent than the German emphasis on research. In the United States, one found residential halls, student unions, athletic teams, academic clubs, counseling centers, and the like. With their students having a special undergraduate residential experience, colleges found themselves the beneficiaries of financial support, which also funded research, from those who fondly recalled their alma maters. A cycle served to establish the preeminence of a smaller set of universities: the more resources, the better the faculty and the greater the investment in student life; the better the undergraduate experience, the more abundant the donations from alumni.

The United States developed a unique institutional structure: a residential undergraduate college of arts and sciences coupled with a graduate school and professional schools in fields such as architecture, business, education, engineering, law, and medicine. Even undergraduates majoring in professional disciplines such as business were and still are required to take arts and sciences courses, which develop liberal arts skills. America imported the German model of the research university, with its stress on graduate studies and research, but transformed it by creating a split between undergraduate and graduate education that was foreign to the German landscape (Turner and Bernard). Faculty who taught graduate students and conducted research also taught undergraduate students, including students not pursuing degrees in their fields. As much as the Americans were enamored with the German research university, they found some aspects wanting, and they sought on American soil something other than a direct imitation (Axtell 244–56).

The distinction of the American college did not only involve a rich undergraduate life and a liberal arts curriculum; America became the first country to move to more and more students, a development that culminated in the mass university. These huge student numbers, unlike those in Germany and elsewhere, were not a burden but rather a boon to finances. The students, aided by federal grants and loans, paid tuition. Not until after World War I did the demographics begin to change. In 1914, the average liberal arts college had only fourteen instructors and 165 students (Levine 38). It is a wistful memory that, before the advent of World War I, the president of a college, who still taught classes and knew all the faculty and students, might board a ship for Europe in May and not return until August. The twentieth century saw a radical expansion of the number and variety of institutions, along with raised standards for admission, diversification of the curriculum, increasing professionalization among the faculty, and greater opportunities for college graduates, all of which have continued to the present day. As recently as 1910, only about 2 percent of young Americans went to college, but by 1940, the result of a postwar boom that stretched through the 1920s, the figure had risen to around 12 percent. In 1925, the American population of 117 million was only 1.7 times greater than the German population of 63 million, but the US student population of some 800,000 was a remarkable 11.7 times greater than the German student population of some

68,000 (Levine 42). America was moving from an elite system of higher education toward a mass system of higher education.

The two decades after World War II saw still more dramatic growth, which fueled all kinds of economic activity in the United States, including at universities. The student population skyrocketed. The Servicemen's Readjustment Act of 1944 (G.I. Bill) subsidized tuition and books and supported living expenses at each veteran's college of choice. In 1947, 69 percent of the male students and 49 percent of all college enrollments were veterans (Olson 26). Further factors were the baby boom, so called for the unusually high number of births from 1946 through 1964; increasing inclusiveness, resulting in more and more women attending college; and an enhancement of the American dream, which included the expectation that an ever-greater percentage of the population would attend college. President Johnson played a significant role in expanding federal financial aid, which in his mind was linked to the war on poverty and unemployment. Between 1963 and 1966, federal aid to colleges increased from $1.4 billion to $3.7 billion (Loss 169). What the G.I. Bill did for a select group, Johnson's Higher Education Act of 1965 accomplished for all. These transformations resulted in growth in campus size, faculty, and support staff. The majority of American universities benefited from the increase in tuition dollars paid by students and the greater state subsidies, which were in many cases tied to enrollment. The numbers are staggering: fewer than 250,000 college students at the turn of the century, 1.1 million in 1930, 8.5 million in 1970, 15.3 million in 2000, 17.4 million by 2005, and more than 21 million by 2010 (Natl. Center for Educ. Statistics, *Digest*, table 303.25). Today, some 71 percent of America's youth enter college (OECD, *Education at a Glance 2014*, table C3.2.a).

To deal with these numbers, America invented another unique phenomenon, the community college. Over 90 percent of Americans live within twenty-five miles of a community college, and close to 50 percent of students attending community colleges live within 10 miles of their campus (Cohen and Kisker 447). Community colleges offer remedial education, which is needed by an estimated 60 percent of their students (Esch). The community colleges have helped immeasurably in expanding access to higher education. Instead of viewing the new community colleges as competition, the premier colleges and universities, both private and public, welcomed them. Part of the thinking, though incorrect, was that community colleges would free up four-year colleges and universities from the first two years of college instruction; traditional colleges would then accept transfer students and focus on advanced undergraduates and graduate students. University educators did, however, correctly understand that community colleges would help them avoid being drowned in large numbers of students. And between the community colleges and the research universities is an incredibly diverse range of colleges and universities.

Along with federal funding came ever-more private gifts. Private spending, including both tuition and gifts, towers above what one sees in other countries. Between 1890 and 1930, the premier universities wanted to ensure stability, autonomy, and competitiveness and so became active in increasing and shepherding their endowments (Kimball and Johnson). The United States invests 2.8 percent of GDP in higher education, a greater percentage than any other country (OECD, *Education at a Glance 2015*, table B2.3). Only three other countries reach 2 percent: Canada and Chile at 2.5 percent and Korea at 2.3 percent (table B2.3). The OECD average is 1.5 percent (table B2.3). The United States also invests more in higher education per student than other countries with the exception of Luxembourg, which, after having not reported data for some years, comes in at a surprisingly high $32,876 per student (OECD, *Education at a Glance 2015*, table B1.1a). *Education at a Glance 2015* shows the US investment to be $26,562 per student (table B1.1a). The OECD average is $15,028, and the only other countries that come close to the United States are Switzerland at $25,264, the United Kingdom at $24,338, Sweden at $22,534, and Canada at $22,006 (table B1.1a). According to the annual survey of the National Association of College and University Business Officers and Commonfund Institute, in 2014, ninety-two American universities had endowments of $1 billion or more, and an additional eighty-one had endowments over $500 million (*Chronicle of Higher Educ., Almanac 2015–16*, 52–53). The Council for Aid to Education reported that in 2015 American universities received almost $40.3 billion in private donations.

T he American university landscape has yet a third distinctive element. The country invested in public universities in order to foster applied fields and public service. Although federal money for universities was essentially a post–World War II invention, the federal government had already played one major and truly decisive role in the nineteenth century. The Morrill Land-Grant College Act of 1862, passed by the wartime Congress and signed into law by Abraham Lincoln, granted federal land to the states. They in turn were given the incentive to sell the land, with the obligation that the proceeds would be used to establish and advance public colleges and universities for liberal and practical education, as well as for outreach extension programs for persons not in college (Thelin 75–79). The goal was to ensure the country had well-educated engineers and farmers and to add a public-service component to the teaching mission of colleges.

Americans did not see a conflict between pure and applied scholarship, and so universities quickly integrated scientific and clinical scholarship with university hospitals and introduced applied scholarship in agriculture, engineering, and education. Whereas the German universities kept engineering at bay (the technological institutes did not receive the name university until 1899) and did not integrate practical fields such as agriculture, business, and social work until the 1960s (Ben-David 48), American universities readily combined pure and applied scholarship. However passionately American academics had received the German model, they transformed the idea of specialized research to fit into an environment that was no less responsive to the integrative liberal arts ideal and the value of utilitarian learning, both of which were foreign to Germany.

One could say, then, that the modern American university integrated three dimensions: a focus on scholarship and advanced study, which came from Germany; the elevation of undergraduate student life and the development of the whole person, which partly drew on the British model; and the land-grant tradition of applied scholarship in areas such as farming, manufacturing, and veterinary medicine, which was distinctly American. Some universities sought fully to integrate all three elements. Others integrated one or two elements, research and liberal education or research and public service, while still others focused on one of the models. Whichever model was adopted, the landscape of American higher education collectively fostered all three elements and became thereby distinctive.

Whereas other countries have begun to catch up with America's mass education, no country has anything that resembles our diversity of institutions. I devote the first two parts of my book to the idea and reality of the distinctive university. American universities have furthermore interwoven a set of structures and strategies—flexibility, competition, incentives, accountability, and community—that differ from what one has traditionally seen in other countries. I devote the third part to these concepts.

Contemporary Gaps between the Ideal and the Real

Although the United States now has an overwhelming percentage of the world's premier universities, gaps remain. Whereas educational attainment in the United States rose dramatically for the first seventy-five years of the twentieth century and towered above other countries, it has grown only modestly since then. Other countries have seen their higher education completion rates increase, so that the United States has lost its first-in-class status. To remain the best, one must do more than congratulate oneself on having an exceptional history; one must focus on addressing weaknesses.

A comprehensive plan for improvement requires not only an idealistic vision of the future but also a sober assessment of contemporary reality. What are the most significant gaps in the American college landscape?

College Preparation

Although some young Americans receive a superb school education that is second to none, the average quality of an American high school education is so weak that many students are inadequately prepared. In a 2011 survey, 58 percent of American college and university presidents said that public high schools were doing a worse job than a decade ago in preparing students for college (Pew 73). Universities make few efforts to address the problem, as they are focused on their own challenges, and many states do an inadequate job of working toward an articulation of the two systems.

This widespread unpreparedness is certainly one explanation for the United States' not producing enough strong American prospects for graduate study. Large numbers of graduate students come from Asia and elsewhere. While such students greatly enrich the United States, the high numbers mask the problem of insufficiently prepared and interested Americans. In 1977, 82 percent of doctoral degrees awarded in the United States went to American citizens; by 2007, the figure had dropped to 57 percent (Wendler et al. 21). In 2007 only 29 percent of engineering doctorates went to US citizens, whereas thirty years earlier the figure was 56 percent (Wendler et al. 21). During that span the percentage of US citizens obtaining doctorates in the physical sciences dropped from 76 percent to 43 percent (Wendler et al. 21).

Opportunity Gap

Whites graduate at a much higher rate than African Americans and Hispanics. Between 1975 and 2010, the gap in degree attainment between African Americans and whites increased from 13 percent to 19 percent, and the gap between Hispanics and whites increased from 15 percent to 25 percent (Aud et al. 74). Although the number of Hispanics and African Americans among first-year students enrolling in college grew by 107 percent and 73 percent, respectively, compared with 15 percent for white Americans, between 1995 and 2009, 82 percent of the additional white students attended the 468 most-selective and best-funded four-year colleges, compared with just 13 percent of Latino Americans and 9 percent of African Americans (Carnevale and Strohl 9, 16).

Even greater than the racial gap is the economic gap (Reardon). Despite the considerable resources of the American universities and the professed desire of the elite universities to enroll students from less privileged backgrounds, the results have been poor. A study from 2003 showed that at the 146 most selective colleges and universities, more than 90 percent of first-year students came from the top half of the socioeconomic ladder, with 74 percent coming from the top quartile and only 3 percent from the bottom quartile (Carnevale and Rose 46). Even as students from lower-income families have improved their academic credentials, so have students from higher-income families, thereby ensuring the latter's competitive advantage for the limited slots at the premier colleges.

As a result, the net gain in access for lower-income students has been modest (Bastedo and Jaquette). The gap, based on family income quartile, between those who graduated from college and those who did not has grown remarkably. In 1970, the gap between the bottom and the top quartile in attaining a four-year college degree was 33 percent (22–55 percent); in 2011 it was 64 percent (23–87 percent) (Mortenson 13). Persons with lower incomes are less likely to attend college and when they do, they tend to land at the local community college. These differences apply independently of test scores. In a 2015 study by the National Center for Education Statistics that divided students into three groups on the basis of parents' education, income, and occupation, students who scored in the top quartile in math but came from the lower socioeconomic group graduated college at a rate of 41 percent; their counterparts in the highest socioeconomic group graduated at a rate of 74 percent (*Postsecondary Attainment* 6). The other group to graduate at 41 percent consisted of those from the highest socioeconomic group who scored in the second quartile in math (6).

The issue of access for poorer students has much to do with the students' environment in the earlier years—at home, in school, and in the neighborhoods. Quality of student preparedness correlates closely with parental income.[2] Better schools operate in wealthier districts, and in certain areas young persons must contend with drugs, violence, and other challenges. Sobering is the comment of Gladieux and Swail: "The data suggest that the die is cast for many students by the eighth grade. Students without the appropriate math and reading skills by that grade are unlikely to acquire them by the end of high school" (186). Arguably the greatest factor is the home environment: college-educated parents spend 50 percent more time talking, reading, and playing with toddlers than other parents, which creates differences in preparedness for learning and reinforces the opportunity gap (Putnam).

2. Mean scores on the Scholastic Aptitude Test (SAT) rise on average, and without exception, at each $20,000 income-level shift from under $20,000 to over $200,000; mean scores also consistently rise with parental degrees, from high school to associate to bachelor's to graduate (*2013 College-Bound Seniors* 4).

Undermatching

Universities have collectively been unsuccessful in marketing their financial aid opportunities to lower-income students who have college potential, and too many such students are insufficiently informed about college selection and resources, such that they enroll at colleges below their capabilities. Students in less competitive colleges, that is, students who are underplaced, tend to graduate at lower rates than students placed in more ambitious universities, as these institutions have better educational resources and more financial aid, as well as a more positive peer effect and a stronger aspirational climate (Bowen, Chingos, and McPherson 233–34). The lower the family income, the more likely students are to suffer from an undermatch, and the lower the level of parental education, the more likely they are to experience an undermatch (Bowen, Chingos, and McPherson 103).

Admissions

American universities take into account the whole person and do not simply accept students on the basis of grade point average, as is the case in some other countries, which have no understanding that test scores are not the only predictors of success. Nonetheless, adjustments are made for children of donors and even potential donors, children of alumni, and children of the famous and politically well connected (Golden). Whereas state universities were traditionally known for their commitment to access, we now see an ever-greater effort to recruit students, including out-of-state students, who can pay full tuition and don't need financial aid (Green 7). The unintended result is a reduction in underrepresented minorities (Jacquette, Curs, and Posselt). An analogous situation exists at less endowed private universities, where students who can pay may receive preference in admissions, even if they have weaker credentials (Green 10). The university knows what its budget will permit, and it accepts a certain percentage of students who can pay and a certain percentage who need financial aid, which increases the chances of acceptance for wealthier students and diminishes the prospects for students who need financial aid. Some Americans accept these trade-offs as inevitable, but admitting students on the basis of parental income and personal connections would seem to counter basic principles of justice;

indeed, in some countries, such as Germany, the practices would be unconstitutional.

Scholarship Deficit

Private universities fund scholarships from one of two sources: either endowment or general operating costs, so-called tuition discounting. When the endowment is the source, tuition is actually paid; the payout from the endowment becomes part of the university's operating budget. When significant levels of financial aid come from the endowment and when the endowment payout is low at the same time that tuition continues to rise, the university must essentially cut its budget or reduce its commitment to financial aid.

If financial aid comes from so-called tuition discounting, that is, waiving all or part of that obligation for selected students, then a more needy student body means less funding is available to address the university's needs and ambitions, including programming support for students. When the endowment drops or student need increases, cuts are necessary elsewhere in the university to subsidize financial aid. To offset the cuts, some universities raise tuition even higher, but much of that increased tuition disappears because it is used to subsidize financial aid (McPherson and Schapiro 68). There is no easy way out of the cycle. The higher tuition leads to public unease about the price of higher education, and the reductions in the general operating budget tend to weaken academic quality. Only a small number of colleges are fully need blind, that is, they admit students independently of their ability to pay, and cover the costs of anyone who cannot. Precisely when the economy is weak and students need more support, states have tended to reduce allocations for public universities, thus forcing them to raise tuition and thereby making access to public universities more challenging. Since the Great Recession of 2008, states have reduced spending on public higher education by 17 percent, while tuition at state universities has risen 33 percent (Mitchell, Leachman, and Masterson 2).

Merit Aid

Not only are most colleges unable to be fully need blind, universities have been increasingly awarding merit scholarships to attract students on the basis of academic quality, irrespective of their financial situation. This, in turn, reduces the pool of funding for poorer students. Although need-based aid to students increased from 1995–96 to 2007–08, merit-based aid increased more dramatically. In 1995–96, 8 percent of full-time undergraduates at public colleges received merit aid; by 2007–08, the figure had risen to 24 percent; meanwhile, merit aid for full-time undergraduates at private universities increased from 24 percent of students to 44 percent (Woo and Choy 9). Merit aid is especially widespread at less selective colleges, which try, as it were, to buy the best students. According to a College Board study, from 2007–08 through 2010–11, selective institutions awarded 7 to 10 percent of their grants for merit, whereas less selective colleges and universities allocated 25 to 30 percent of theirs for merit (*Trends in Student Aid 2011–12*, 27). Also, state governments have increasingly chosen to expand politically popular merit-based aid at the expense of need-based aid (Advisory Committee on Student Financial Assistance, *Empty Promises* 37).

College leaders defend merit aid by noting that modest additional support helps them compete with other institutions by attracting students who can raise the college's intellectual atmosphere as well as its standing. Moreover, since merit funding often comes in smaller amounts than need-based aid, such students pay most of the tuition, some of which can be redirected to support needier students. The arguments, then, are not insignificant, but when financial aid is scarce, widespread movement of funding from need-based to merit aid means that in many cases poorer students are unable to afford a good education.

Athletic scholarships are merit scholarships as well. One can understand awarding athletic scholarships for revenue sports such as football and basketball, since good teams can bring resources to the university, but defending the idea for the dozens of other sports in which colleges compete and which are also subsidized is difficult. Is athletics more central to the core of the university than biology or philosophy? Some universities will admit (and support) a B-level student who is an A-level hockey player over an A-level student who is a B-level hockey player. That is difficult to defend in terms of putting resources behind the university's highest priorities. Instead, it is more like competition run amuck; yet once a university has invested in facilities and coaches, begun recruiting student-athletes, and raised alumni expectations, retreat is difficult.

Burdening Expenses

For many American families, tuition is the second-largest lifetime expense, after the purchase of a house, and thus, not surprisingly, is a major concern for parents (Clotfelter 1). Even though the total amount of student loans has finally begun to decrease, the figures remain high (College Board, *Trends in Student Aid 2015*, 16). Loans were held by 64 percent of private college students who graduated in 2013–14 and averaged $30,200; for public college graduates, the figure was 60 percent and the loans averaged $25,500 (College Board, *Trends in Student Aid 2015*, 24). In the 1970s, funding from the federal government was overwhelmingly in the form of grants, which do not need to be repaid—at one point they covered as much as 70 percent of student financial aid—with federal loans as low as 20 percent; by 1990, federal grants constituted only 15 percent of financial aid and federal loans had risen to 60 percent (Vest 61–62). The remainder of student financial aid in both cases was being absorbed by institutional grants or loans. Although the country has slowly been moving from loans as a mortgage-like obligation, which must be repaid on a fixed schedule, to income-based repayment, stories remain fresh of persons struggling when the loans come due. Moreover, the federal government has increasingly shifted its support for educational expenses to tax benefits, which for the most part aid politically important middle-class and upper-middle-class families instead of the lower-income families who most need the help (Russo 87).

Some 45 percent of American students at four-year colleges work twenty or more hours per week to help cover costs (Johnson and Rochkind 4). Although the figure is affected by the 62 percent of part-time students who work more than twenty hours, a still high 23 percent of full-time students work twenty hours or more (*Almanac 2011–12*, 38). The stress of combining work and study dilutes the quality of education and contributes greatly to the dropout rate at American universities.

Temporary Faculty

Increasingly, at many universities, teaching is being done by part-time faculty members, adjuncts, or other persons not on the tenure track. The national average for faculty who are either working part-time or are on fixed-term appointments is, according to the American Association of University Professors, 65 percent (*AAUP Contingent Faculty Index* 5). The figure is misleading in the sense that the AAUP counts not classes or credit hours but individual instructors, so if a university hires a business-person or a journalist to teach a single vocational course, that person counts as much as a tenured faculty member with a normal load of two to eight courses annually. Similarly, when a faculty member takes a one-year sabbatical and is replaced by a visitor, the visitor is recorded. Still, whatever figure one settles on, it is high and unappealing, the result of a steady climb over the past forty years (Schuster and Finkelstein 233). The trend is the consequence not only of efficiency and cost cutting but also of other, often complicated factors, such as reducing teaching for the best researchers; giving temporary positions to former doctoral students, who have difficulties locating positions; extending teaching opportunities to retirees; and wanting to include professionals, who can integrate their experiences into their teaching (Cross and Goldenberg 30–32). The problem is especially acute in cities, where abundant temporary help is available. New York University, a majority of whose classes are taught by adjuncts, employs more than three thousand part-timers per year (Washburn 200). The ideal of the scholar-teacher is being further eroded by more and more faculty becoming specialists in either teaching or research (Schuster and Finkelstein 232–33), with the former teaching more credit hours at lower pay (since the competition for such persons is less intense).

Uneven Quality

The diverse landscape of American higher education means that some institutions are much weaker academically than others. The range of quality is advantageous in serving a diverse student clientele; however, this diversity also means that an American college education can be relatively mediocre. Some college graduates are simply not well educated, and the integration of teaching and research exists only at the better colleges and universities. Moreover, not all students recognize the differences, including some of the disadvantages of for-profit universities, between better and weaker institutions. Students are often unaware of the best potential fit for their academic qualifications and aspirations. The twofold puzzle here is the uneven quality, even if that diversity also serves positive ends, and the often unmet need for students to be sufficiently informed so that they are able to find the right fit.

The current graduation rate in the United States is wildly diverse across institutions, depending on quality and selectivity, and the 59.2 percent average for graduation within six years is less than ideal (Natl. Center for Educ. Statistics, *Digest*, table 326.10). At the doctoral level, the graduation rates are still lower: universities rarely provide financial support for graduate students beyond five or six years, but the graduation rates for five and six years are 22.5 percent and 36.1 percent, respectively (Sowell, Zhang, and Redd 15). Even the ten-year graduation rate of 56.6 percent is low (15). The result is a considerable waste of faculty investment and financial resources, since most graduate students require intensive faculty engagement and many receive generous financial aid. This sobering figure contrasts with regularly reported graduation rates of higher than 95 percent in medicine and attrition rates of lower than 15 percent in law (Caulfield, Redden, and Sondheimer; American Bar Association).[3]

Research versus Teaching

There is a widespread sense in the United States that undergraduate learning takes a backseat to research. Although this is often the lament of outsiders, who criticize the academy, the concern has also been raised in academic circles (Kronman; Lewis; Sperber; Deresiewicz). It is perhaps not surprising that Jonathan R. Cole's *Great American University* is devoted almost exclusively to research. At some universities, one can get tenure on the basis of research alone. I have seen that from some

---

3. Surprisingly, no organization tracks or publicizes law school graduation rates. The focus instead has been on employment outcomes and bar passage percentages. Attrition data do exist, however, and one can use the attrition data reported by law schools to the American Bar Association to calculate attrition rates per class. The attrition figures for the entering classes from 1999–2000 through 2009–2010 hover between 12 and 14 percent. The figures are only approximations, for they do not capture students, including part-time students, students who step out for a couple of years, and dual-degree students, who might leave after four years (attrition data stop after four years).

of the faculty members I refused to hire, even though they would have been coming from higher-ranking universities. America's preparation of graduate students for teaching is less than ideal. In graduate school, research is the focus, and when younger faculty are hired, they often resist teaching general education courses, which ask them to stretch beyond their disciplines or teach their disciplines to students majoring in other fields. As the philosopher Alasdair MacIntyre quipped, at a Notre Dame gathering to celebrate his eightieth birthday, "If you have a doctorate, you must work very hard to become an educated person." Specialization cuts against the breadth elevated in the liberal arts tradition. One of the weakest areas nationally is the teaching of science to nonscientists (Bok, *Our Underachieving Colleges* 260–61). One cannot awaken the highest levels of learning without teachers who are also active researchers, but the more research gains the upper hand, the more teaching and mentoring can be neglected. A recent Gallup poll indicated that only 14 percent of college graduates had one or more professors who cared about them as a person, made them excited about learning, and encouraged them to pursue their goals and dreams (*Great Jobs* 10).

Narrowness

Although students in the United States receive a broader undergraduate education than those in other countries, they tend to study only one subject at the graduate level, whereas advanced students in a country such as Germany have traditionally taken a second major or two minors; this has tended to make academics in the United States narrower in their outlook. The breadth continues even beyond the doctorate. The habilitation, a second book beyond the dissertation that must be written to qualify for a professorship in Germany, is normally expected to be in an area different from the first. In literary studies, for example, that would be a different century and genre.

Faculty in the United States, at least outside the sciences and engineering, have tended to view any doctoral student who wants to pursue a nonacademic career as a second-class citizen; this is disadvantageous not only for society but also for graduate students, who may encounter difficulties finding an academic position or may prefer to pursue careers at other kinds of institutions, such as museums or archives, or in other realms, such as journalism, publishing, business, or politics (Bender). Even as the situation is starting to change here, led partly by academic leaders in the discipline of history, we are behind on this issue (Grafton and Grossman). A recognition of the broader worth of the intellectual to society exists in other countries that runs counter to, and is a much richer tradition than, the narrowness of the academic track one tends to find in the United States. Whereas America has had, in its entire history, only one president with a PhD, nine of the nineteen politicians who have led postwar Germany as chancellor or president have had a PhD. Related to this problem is the narrowness of the categories by which graduate programs are ranked. In political science, for example, books, policy-relevant essays, and essays published in related fields but outside the discipline proper carry little weight (Campbell and Desch).

Scholarship in the United States tends to be more local and national than international compared with other countries, including even England (Evans). The percentage of faculty members in departments of history and sociology and political science who are working primarily on America or in philosophy departments who are focusing on work written in English is remarkable. In a comparison from the 1990s, 91–99 percent of professors in every country surveyed except for one agreed with the statement that in order to keep up with developments in his or her discipline, a scholar must read books and journals published abroad; the figure for the United States, the one outlier, was 62 percent (Altbach 42). Comparisons of citations in a major American sociology journal and a major German one reveal that the publications in the German journal are much more likely to take account of, and cite, scholarship from other countries. In this sense, they represent a richer international standard (Münch 134). Reasons for the narrowness of American scholars are multiple and include, among others, a greater sense of the importance of our own country and its traditions and less facility with other languages. Narrowness is not ideal for future global competitiveness.

We also see a confining instrumentalism. Neither the intrinsic value of knowledge nor engagement with great questions but practical ends dominate in American higher education. Although some American educators argue for more idealism in education (e.g., Kronman; Delbanco; Roche, *Why Choose?*; Edmundson, *Self*), faculty tend to focus on disciplinary knowledge and critical thinking. Students, who may not grasp the full potential of college for them as persons, often see higher education as little more than job preparation; this view can be easily reinforced by politicians unsympathetic to the liberal arts model.

The American tendency to value the instrumental over the intrinsic and idealistic is evident in our federal budget for research and scholarship. In fiscal year 2012, the National Endowment for the Humanities (NEH) received $146 million compared to $30.9 billion for the National Institutes of Health (NIH) and $7.033 billion for the National Science Foundation (NSF). The NEH figure represents 0.38 percent of the federal allotment to these three agencies and 0.1 percent of the total 2012 federal funding for research and development, including that for such agencies as the Department of Defense. In Germany, in contrast, during the same year, the humanities received 9 percent of federal funding (Deutsche Forschungsgemeinschaft 158). This was no aberration: the humanities figures for Germany for 2013 and 2014 were 9.2 percent and 9.6 percent, respectively (158).

Student Culture

The student culture in America is weakened by the social element, careerism, the sports culture, and cheating. Students are sometimes attracted to the premier colleges as avenues to success and the fostering of social connections instead of being driven by opportunities for learning (Douthat). In student surveys, making a living scores especially high compared to developing a meaningful philosophy of life (Pryor et al. 72–73). Because where one studies is more important than what one studies, the pressure to get into an excellent university leads to a focus on grades, an accumulation of extracurricular activities, and, for wealthier families, even the hiring of coaches to assist with preparation for standardized examinations and college application essays. The competition to get into the best colleges and universities and the pressure to do well once enrolled have led to an increase in student mental health problems, including eating disorders, the result of a wider cultural fascination with success and prestige that seems to be most visible and exacerbated in the lives of undergraduates.

The burden of carrying loans sometimes leads students to elevate practical over intellectual pursuits. Whereas only 8.6 percent of students in Germany major in business, in America the figure is 19.6 percent, higher than for any other subject and double the next highest major (Statistisches Bundesamt, *Bildung und Kultur* 36; Natl. Center for Educ. Statistics, *Digest*, table 322.10). Of all students, those majoring in business spend the fewest hours studying; as a result, they tend to be less engaged in substantial learning (Arum and Roksa), further diminishing the intellectual climate.

America has a long tradition of focusing on campus activities—social and extracurricular events, including athletics—that can overshadow learning and research. This was the case also in the Ivy League from the 1880s to World War I. When asked early in his presidency at Princeton University how many students there were at Princeton, Woodrow Wilson replied, "about 10 percent" (Oberdorfer 102). Slowly throughout the twentieth century, the better American colleges and universities moved away from an overwhelming orientation toward social clubs, campus life, and athletics to a primary focus on academics. Still, the appropriate balance is not always met. Student abuse of alcohol, hazing in student fraternities, and sexual assault are problems and are rarely dealt with outside the confines of the campus, which has a built-in incentive to keep stories quiet.

Athletics, the most prominent nonacademic activity on many campuses, brings substantial resources to a small number of the most successful programs, yet a majority of universities do not make a profit but instead pour funding into athletics that could otherwise go to academics. Indeed, fewer than twenty universities regularly bring in net revenues through athletics (the others, hundreds of them, lose money), and even the figures for those whose revenues exceed their expenses may be inflated, given the often hidden costs associated with buildings and overhead. Academic leaders who see the budgetary and other problems can easily get caught up in what Howard Nixon has labeled "the athletic trap": the lure of apparent advantages, such as institutional prominence, outweighs the political costs of scaling back. In 2014, the universities in the Southeastern Conference spent twelve times as much on athletics per student-athlete as they did on academics per student (Knight Commission). The work of Bowen and Levin has revealed the remarkable advantages student-athletes have in gaining admission, even at premier colleges and universities. The claim that athletics helps to build character, a sense of teamwork, and a competitive spirit, while true in many cases, can also be challenged; athletic experience can be linked with less desirable traits, such as lack of compassion and an overly black-and-white worldview (Edmundson, "Do Sports?").

Cheating is widespread. Some 75 percent of college students admit to one or more acts of academic dishonesty (McCabe, Trevino, and Butterfield 220–21). The causes are presumably multiple: fear that others may also be cheating and gaining an edge, a relative confidence that one will not be caught or that the penalties will be light, the admission of students who are not prepared to do the work, pressure to do well, institutional apathy or student indifference toward the institution's values, poor instruction and unclear expectations, carelessness, lack of integrity, and lack of student effort and interest in learning.

Grade Inflation

Students can be more concerned about grades than about learning, and grade inflation by faculty members, who do not want to exert the effort to make distinctions among students, do not want to deal with student complaints, and do not want to receive poor student evaluations, only exacerbates the problem. While some might argue that higher grades result from better students and better teaching, grades have risen at a time when students report that they are studying less (Arum and Roksa) and faculty are lamenting that students are not as strong in critical thinking, cultural literacy, or communication skills as they would like them to be. Yet grades have risen over the past thirty years, and A is now the most common grade assigned on an overwhelming majority of campuses (Rojstaczer and Healy).

There are several reasons to address grade inflation. First, not differentiating among students' levels of performance is unfair to the best students. Second, a failure to communicate meaningfully through grades means that we place greater reliance on test scores and informal avenues of recommendation. Third, undifferentiated grading does not signal to students the areas in which they truly excel. Fourth, and most importantly, grade inflation does not support good learning, because it does not send a clear signal to students that they could improve their work and stretch their capabilities.

Fragile Finances

The heralded financial strength of the American university is fragile. At least three issues loom as challenges. First, private universities are heavily dependent on endowment assets, which have undergone market fluctuations. As a result of occasional drops in endowment, many American universities have had to scale back staff, cancel faculty searches, and freeze salaries. Paradoxically, the wealthiest, those with the highest endowments, have been among the most adversely affected, since a greater percentage of their annual budgets come from the endowment payout, which, unlike tuition at most universities, saw decreases, not increases. Every Ivy League university has had to deal with cuts (including 19 percent over two years in arts and sciences at Harvard, whose problems were especially severe), layoffs, generous early-retirement buyouts, salary freezes, or delayed construction projects (Munk; Kaplan).

Second, state universities have seen their allocations drop dramatically. State funding per full-time public student, adjusted for inflation, dropped 26 percent nationally from 1990–91 to 2009–10 (Quinterno, *Great Cost* 2). Although 81 percent of millennial voters support increasing state funding for public colleges, 96 percent of states saw reductions between 2008 and 2014; meanwhile, tuition and fees at public colleges rose 28 percent during that same period (Young Invincibles 5–7). Public universities are invariably affected by the health of the state budget, and when budgetary crises arise, as they have recently, public universities have to contend with the fallout, including budget cuts resulting in layoffs; reduced salaries; the dissolution of vulnerable programs; increased teaching loads; frozen positions; and, for the students and their parents, significant tuition increases. Over time, state universities have seen consistent cuts in education. Other state needs, such as prisons, schools, and Medicaid, compete for scarce resources. Investing in prisons instead of education is not the most forward-thinking strategy, especially given the US's already-high prison population compared with the rest of the world. Still, between 1985 and 2000, state spending on prisons grew six times the rate of higher education (American Council on Educ., *Putting* 5). In California, the largest university system, 9.5 percent of spending in 2010 went to prisons, up from 4 percent in 1985; during that same stretch, spending for universities dropped from 11 to 5.7 percent (*Economist*).

The net result has been less per-student funding for the university, tuition increases, or both.

Third, federal funding for research and student loans will likely not keep pace with university and student expectations unless the federal government is able to increase revenues, cut spending, or reallocate resources. With competing demands in defense, health, infrastructure, and other areas, federal funding for research has not seen substantial increases in years, and most recently we have seen a decline. According to the National Science Board, during the five-year period 2004–9, when adjusted for inflation, the annual average increase in federal research funding was 0.8 percent (*Science and Engineering Indicators 2012*, ch. 5, p. 9). In the years from 2010 to 2014, levels of federal support for research dropped 11 percent, and when adjusted for inflation the drop was 17 percent (*Science and Engineering Indicators 2016*, ch. 4, p. 6). The major federal grant for low-income students is the Pell Grant. Created in 1972 to encourage more low-income students to attend college, Pell Grants are based entirely on financial need. In 1976, a Pell Grant covered almost 90 percent of the cost of attending a four-year public college, but by 2004, it covered a mere 24 percent (Sacks 178). With the federal budget strained from many angles, the amount of funding that would be needed to continue the program in accordance with its original intentions appears to be unsustainable.

Unseemly Incentives

The increasing prominence of money in the academy has affected behavior in ways that contradict the ideal of disinterested scholarship. The search for dollars can lead to overly close, potentially even unethical, collaboration between research and industry, in such a way that the hunt for grants and patents takes precedence over the search for and communication of truth (Washburn). Not only is there a widespread concern about conflicts of interest arising from the funding of research, but funding from industry seems to affect research: for example, 83.3 percent of independent studies concluded that sugar-sweetened beverages could be a potential risk factor for weight gain, whereas 83.3 percent of studies in which a potential financial conflict of interest was disclosed concluded that the evidence was insufficient to draw any such conclusion (Bes-Rastrollo et al.).

The 1980 Bayh-Dole Act, which allowed, and in a sense encouraged, universities to patent discoveries made by researchers whose projects are funded by federal dollars, has led to such close partnerships between universities and industry that concerns have been raised about publications delayed or embargoed to give industrial sponsors time to obtain patents, about faculty adjusting their data and conclusions or holding back on publications to serve their sponsors' and their own commercial interests, and about universities becoming more interested in relations with industry and in the accumulation of new resources than in ensuring quick access to data and avoiding conflicts of interest. Increasingly, universities have a stake in the outcome of research; disinterested inquiry stands in tension with continued financial support and potentially large income opportunities, especially in medicine.

Peer review is the appropriate method for the evaluation of research proposals, but not all research funding is distributed this way. Allocations in the form of "earmarks" or "pork" bypass the peer review system and are an ineffective way to advance the worthiest projects. Beginning in the 2011 fiscal year budget cycle, Congress forswore earmarks, but they could return in force, and in the interim, modest special interest provisions have made their way into spending bills. In the 2010 fiscal year, the last before abundant earmarks were curtailed, $1.9 billion was allocated this way. The universities having the best-placed connections brought in the most money. The University of Alabama at Tuscaloosa led the way, garnering $58.7 million in grants; three Mississippi universities were among the top twelve; and none of the twenty-five leading American universities were among the top twenty-five recipients (Lederman).

This brief account of gaps makes evident that the premier American model is not without problems, and with movement to ever-more international competition, the gaps loom even larger. At the end of each chapter of part 3, I outline further challenges and problems that exist even in areas where the American university otherwise shines.

Vision, or What No Administrator Can Do Without

Motivation is central to success in any enterprise. The most powerful motivation is identification with a vision. When we act because we identify with an appealing ideal, our actions are internally driven and voluntary. Rev. Theodore M. Hesburgh, in his classic essay on university leadership, argues that a president "may be the best administrator in the world, but without a clear and bright and, yes, beautiful vision, he is leading nowhere" (12). The ultimate criterion for evaluating a vision is intellectual; rhetoric and communication presuppose sound arguments. Ideas are thus the first presupposition of effective leadership. A coherent and multifaceted vision interweaves such diverse areas as the purpose of scholarly research, pedagogical values, ethical principles, institutional history, and pragmatic considerations.

A compelling vision attracts future students; forms the community of current faculty and students; and inspires graduates, donors, and other supporters. A compelling vision can also serve as a distinguishing alternative in relation to other institutions. Every vision has a negative, polemical side, even if it must be respectfully and diplomatically articulated. We want to be this and not that. Departing from a widespread tendency to shy away from distinctions of any kind, a university that wants to be different must be guided by distinction as well as by the reasons why this or that alternative has not been chosen. A vision and the arguments for it, as well as the capacity to articulate it, come not only from the president but also from every member of the university who is invited to contribute to the formulation and articulation of vision, albeit at varying levels of intensity and with varying levels of knowledge, experience, and authority.

Literature on leadership regularly places vision at the top of its scale of essential attributes (Bolman and Deal 340; Bennis 39; Fisher and Koch 68). Hesburgh, president of the University of Notre Dame from 1952 to 1987, stated, "The very essence of leadership is you have to have a vision. It's got to be a vision you articulate clearly and forcefully on every occasion. You can't blow an uncertain trumpet" (Bowen and Dolan 68). In books on higher education, a sentence such as the following is not at all uncommon or untrue: "The hallmark of any individual dean is his or her vision for the college and plan for realizing that vision" (Bright and Richards 20).

Vision is essential to the all-important tasks of setting priorities and allocating resources. It is also a necessary condition of what James MacGregor Burns calls transforming as opposed to simply transactional leadership. Transforming leadership leads to inspirational and meaningful change, thus elevating expectations and aspirations; moreover, it fosters its continuation by energetically ensuring that the vision is embedded in the communal culture and that new leaders are developed, who can carry the vision forward.

The vision and resulting priorities should guide all action. As Yogi Berra once said, "If you don't know where you're going, then when you get there, you'll be lost." Only after a vision and corresponding goals have been formulated do questions of budget, strategies of motivation, and organizational principles come into play. For that reason it is not surprising that a recent survey of trustees revealed that the most important criterion in evaluating presidents is their promotion of the institution's mission (*Chronicle of Higher Educ.*, "Trustees" A21). Of course trustees, the evaluators of the president's efficacy in realizing vision, must themselves be attuned to vision and the institution's highest priorities. Cole wisely suggests that trustees take, partly through digital technology, an extensive course on the history of higher education; the history of their own university; and their university's core values, inner workings, and contemporary challenges (*Toward* 286).

Identity and Identity Crises

What would be an example or two of institutional distinction or identity? When I entered the job market as a graduating PhD, I had to make a weighty decision: I turned down positions at two premier private research universities, as well as one at an excellent liberal arts college, to work at Ohio State. My decision was difficult and complex, but involved, among other factors, a commitment to the project of public higher education and a recognition that I might learn more at this very large, interesting, and different institution. I had a wonderful experience there, but one issue bothered and perplexed me. Because Ohio State had two identities in tension with one another, an internally contradictory vision had developed.

Ohio State was, on the one hand, the state's flagship research university, attracting the best faculty and overseeing the most and, in almost all cases, the strongest graduate programs. On the other hand, it was a university with very low tuition, a figure regulated by the state, and open admissions. When I arrived, the standard for undergraduate admissions was essentially first come, first served, so long as the prospective student had a minimal level of competence. Over time Ohio State became modestly competitive, but even so, most of the students who applied were admitted; when I left, the graduation rate (below 60 percent) was still modest enough that faculty had the sense they were investing in many students who would never graduate. The faculty for the most part was not the right faculty for that student body. The vision dictated that it be at one and the same time Ohio's flagship research university and its open access university. Many of the undergraduates would have been better served at community colleges, which have appropriate support structures for students who are less prepared. When the president wanted to introduce more selective admissions, he ran up against legislators who wanted the B and C students from their districts to be able to attend the premier state university.

There was much to admire about Ohio State. It provided an open avenue for students from all kinds of backgrounds. Almost every department had a large faculty with many strong performers. The emotional attachment to the university was not restricted to students, but encompassed, partly through the university's extraordinary success in athletics, the entire state. Faculty often worked in heroic ways to overcome the contradictory vision by, for example, developing honors courses for the best students. The very scale of the institution forced its leaders to introduce efficiencies and accountability.

When Notre Dame approached me about a position after I had been at Ohio State for nearly a decade, I was initially uninterested. Notre Dame was smaller, and it had virtually no graduate program in my field, simply a tiny and mediocre master's program. When I agreed to give a lecture there, I slowly became intrigued. What became evident to me was that Notre Dame had an even more complex, but more coherent, identity than Ohio State. I can recall a few years later explaining to Notre Dame's provost my sense of the university's distinction. He was existentially intrigued by the question of Notre Dame's identity. Notre Dame, I said, was at one and the same time a residential liberal arts college with a traditional emphasis on student learning; a research university that had become increasingly dynamic and ambitious; and a Catholic institution of international standing. When I chose to join the faculty in 1996 and become, a year later, dean of its largest college, several factors were involved, but the most important was my sense that Notre Dame had a fascinating and complex identity and the aspiration to come ever closer to realizing its highest ambitions. In one respect after another, the three parts of Notre Dame's triadic identity enriched each other.

My inaugural address as dean focused entirely on Notre Dame's triadic identity and was an attempt to sort out for myself and for the faculty how important these three elements were and how they could be interwoven so as to make the whole greater than the sum of the parts ("Notre Dame's Triadic Identity"). At the same time, I did not hesitate to note challenges, such as anti-intellectual currents in American Catholicism, inadequate funding of the research enterprise, or insufficiently differential decisions concerning faculty quality. I was open in my criticisms of Notre Dame for failing to realize the lofty aspirations inherent in each of these identities. We could strengthen each one, I argued, and we did over time.

A vision should be clear, and it can and should be repeated again and again. I articulated the concept of Notre Dame's triadic identity on one occasion after another until it could not be forgotten or overlooked. What I saw in Notre Dame has since become in many ways the self-understanding of Notre Dame and its current leadership. As an outsider I was in a good position to name what was already inherent in the institution but had not yet been fully brought to the level of the concept.

Whereas some research universities had let slide the importance of undergraduate learning, Notre Dame had never relinquished its traditional focus on students, which elicited strong alumni support. The liberal arts ideal remained vibrant in the residential campus, the core curriculum, and the education of the whole person. Spirituality in general and Catholicism in particular enriched the liberal arts experience. In a setting both academic and religious, no questions were bracketed, and ultimate questions were actively encouraged.

While many Catholic universities had, as a result of drift or conscious imitation of the mainstream, lost their distinctive mission, Notre Dame had not. Notre Dame defined its research foci in the light of its Catholicism, recognizing the formal advantage of having a distinct niche and the substantive advantage of underscoring thereby its Catholic mission. Its initial emphasis had been on philosophy, theology, and medieval studies. Other strengths then emerged around issues central to a Catholic university such as commitment to civil and human rights and programs of study on various geographic spheres where Catholicism is a dominant cultural marker, for example, Latin American studies and Irish studies. We developed expertise in an array of fields that make sense for a Catholic university: in the humanities, for example, religious and intellectual history, literature and religion, and sacred music; and in the social sciences, poverty, education, and development, as well as religion and politics and peace studies.

Where Ohio State had an identity crisis because of two visions or identities in conflict with each other, Notre Dame's identity was hampered by gaps between its complex normative understanding of itself, which was very appealing, and what it had achieved to date. As I pointed out in my address, gaps existed between aspiration and reality, and recognizing those gaps could foster improvement.

Beyond an overarching sense of vision, one needs to focus on specific goals, so early on as dean I articulated six goals, which remained vibrant for more than a decade. First, emphasize Notre Dame's triadic identity as a residential liberal arts college with a strong emphasis on student learning, a dynamic and increasingly ambitious research university, and a Catholic institution of international standing. Second, improve policies and procedures, to ensure greater accountability, more due process, and fuller faculty governance; and enhance resources through wiser and more efficient use of our own resources, increases in annual rate funding, and new initiatives in development. Third, become the best in the world in signature areas. Fourth, address the most significant moral issues of the coming century: new quandaries in ethics, challenges facing developing countries, and the ecological crisis. Fifth, foster those programs that have exhibited strength and are poised for excellence, including a selection of large and high-impact departments. Sixth, address previously neglected areas, above all the arts, economics, the foreign languages and literatures, and diversity. Two additional goals, identified only after I had been in office for a year, were improve our capacity to tell the story of the college and develop future faculty leaders.

At the end of my time as dean, I returned to all eight goals and gave the following accounts: first orally, to the faculty; then to the advisory council, the group of donors with whom I had worked most closely; and later to the board of trustees. Eventually, I composed a more formal account in writing, delineating what we had done well and what was still unsolved (*Dean's Report*). These, I believe, are the requisite steps for advancing a vision: (1) articulate an appealing and distinctive vision; (2) identify the gaps between that normative vision and one's current situation, developing strategies to help bridge that gap; and (3) give an account of progress and continuing challenges along the way.

Vision and Diversity

A university can articulate its vision in any number of ways. A Catholic university differs from a secular university, and a liberal arts college from a research university. A university that enrolls the best prospective students has a different mission than one that educates a wide range of academically prepared students. But these are still relatively formal and generic distinctions. One could imagine a university that has as its signature structure not departments but interdisciplinary initiatives; one that focuses on the challenges of developing countries or on the ecological crisis; one that orients the undergraduate years around discussions of great books; one that places a recurring emphasis on community-based research; one that offers bilingual instruction; or one that emphasizes the increasing prominence of Asia. Abundant other possibilities exist, as do combinations of the above.

In contrast to many other countries, where one model of the university predominates, the United States has a tremendous variety of colleges and universities: private and public, large and small, national and regional. The United States has institutions with fewer than five hundred students and others with more than fifty-five thousand; universities with tuition less than $1,500 per year and others that cost more than $60,000 per year. It has institutions where virtually everyone graduates in four years and others where a majority of the students work or online learning is the dominant model and graduation takes much longer and is less likely.

Historically, the country's vast size has played a role in fostering diversity, as has competition among the colonies and then the states, religious differences, and the boldness of both university founders and early investors. This range of institutions means that every student interested in an education has one avenue or another. No single model can address society's diverse needs. Countries that have traditionally lacked such variety have suffered.

One consequence of diversity is a tremendous range in quality and type of university, including the emergence of for-profit institutions, which exhibit no faculty or student interest in research and focus entirely on skills acquisition. Positive elements such as convenient locations, staggered start times for classes, and evening classes have unfortunately been offset by low standards (Angulo); low graduation rates (*Chronicle of Higher Educ., Almanac 2011–12*, 44); soaring student debt (*Almanac 2011–12*, 45) and high student default rates (Anderson; Angulo); as well as allegations of various kinds of fraud, often the result of the desire to meet the bottom line or enhance marketing (Angulo; Field). While only 11 percent of students attend for-profit colleges, they account for 44 percent of the student loan defaults (Angulo x). On average, the thirty leading for-profit colleges spend 17 percent of their budgets on instruction and 42 percent on getting students to enroll and paying off investors (139). Strayer Education, whose CEO earned $42 million in 2009, that year spent $1,329 per student on instruction and allocated $6,968 per student to marketing and profits (145).

Another result of American diversity and innovation involves massive open online courses (MOOCs). That such an innovation would emerge on American soil or that in today's age such courses would quickly become global is not surprising. Some MOOCs are for profit, whereas others are nonprofit enterprises. In many cases the faculty are among the best in the world. Advantages of MOOCs and of the broader integration of online learning include access for persons around the globe, independent of income; the diversity of learners and thus of contributors to discussion groups; the learning advantage of being able to rewind a lecture multiple times; the ability to analyze where students engaged in exercises encounter difficulties; opportunities for learning and enrichment beyond regular credit hours; the capability to pool faculty resources in selected areas across universities; the potential integration of individual lectures into student learning at one's own and at other universities, including less well-funded institutions, which also leverages class time for discussion and problem solving instead of lectures; and less inhibiting environments that may encourage shy students to contribute to discussions. Although critics tend to view MOOCs as completely incompatible with liberal learning, they can in fact make aspects of liberal learning available to larger segments of society as well as foster peer learning beyond the academy (Roth 11–18). Challenges of MOOCs involve the false perception that such courses could replace engaged seminar learning; the tendency to substitute more nuanced assessment measures with multiple-choice exams; the financial risk and potential loss of focus for the universities; the outsourcing of academic vision and priorities to corporations; the opportunity cost for faculty members as universities embark on such initiatives; the high dropout rates among those who are using online learning not as a diversion but as a primary path to education; and the complexities involved in ensuring and documenting student success.

Identifying a vision has an obvious normative moment. What has such intrinsic value or value for society that we should make it our obligation?

A vision should be noble and inspiring; it should stretch the institution, but it must also take into account facticity. What kind of university do we want to become, given who we are now? Realistically, what is our greatest potential? What would we do if money were no object, but also, what steps can we take to define ourselves and improve ourselves in the absence of new resources? Another lens that a university can adopt to help imagine a vision is to reflect on the weaknesses of the higher education landscape, as I did at the close of chapter 1, and then determine which of those weaknesses it can address and overcome so as to gain distinction and a competitive advantage. Yet another lens, one adopted to some degree by Jacobs University Bremen, is to look at the strengths of another system, in this case the American, and ask which of those strengths can we realize here, in this case in Germany, thereby becoming distinctive.

Jacobs University was founded and chartered in 1999 and enrolled its first class of students in 2001. The university has interwoven three elements to form a distinctive identity. First, Jacobs has sought to become like a private American university. Its campus culture fosters community through residential halls and extracurricular activities, such as a choir, a student newspaper, and sports teams. It stresses administrative flexibility. For the German university landscape, its small size, fewer than fifteen hundred students, is unique. A career center helps students move on to the next level, be it further study, volunteer work, or employment. In addition, the university has ladder professors (assistant, associate, and full), with tenure review; powerful deans; a fund-raising office; an admissions office to select and recruit students; and high tuition combined with need-based and merit-based scholarships. The student–faculty ratio, currently 11–1, is much like that of an excellent American university. Second, the university made a decision to become truly international, drawing students from all continents and employing English as the language of instruction. Its students come from more than a hundred countries, with students from Germany representing 25–30 percent. Diversity and learning from one's peers are principles of good learning from which Jacobs University benefits. On average, graduates speak three or more languages. Third, the university chose to become distinctively interdisciplinary. Programs exist in integrated social sciences, integrated cultural studies, and integrated environmental studies.

At Jacobs, the incentive structures, diversity, and campus orientation are all countercultural. It is helpful for identity to offer something distinctive. Thus far, the Jacobs University experiment has been successful in terms of student qualifications, graduation rates, and rankings. Its greatest challenge, as acute now as it has been at any time, involves resources.

With respect to students and their parents, mission is an advantage. Faculty members can also be attracted to distinction. In many cases, they will leave higher-ranking departments or universities to help create or advance a distinctive university. I have seen that firsthand in our hiring at Notre Dame. One must be prepared to counter the argument that hiring for mission is too burdensome—that hiring for quality and diversity is difficult enough without adding mission to the mix. Doing so will reduce the number of eligible applicants and lower the quality. That bias is simply not true. After my first seven years as dean, I reviewed the more than 150 tenure-track and tenured faculty members hired into the college. I sought to identify what most people would agree were the top one-third of these hires: those who had previously earned tenure at higher-ranked institutions, such as Harvard or Stanford; those who had received multiple offers of employment, including offers from higher-ranked departments; and those whose records had simply been stunning, for example, at the time of promotion and tenure. For each faculty member, I sought to identify the most significant factor or, if there were more than one, the multiple factors that led these faculty members to choose Notre Dame. The Catholic mission, broadly understood, was far and away the most significant, by a two-to-one margin, over the next highest factor. Distinction can be a great competitive advantage. The exercise was useful because mission hiring is often viewed by chairpersons as a third hurdle after quality and diversity. When one adds, for example, Catholicism to the mix, it may seem unduly complex and constraining, but one can take a different view and suggest that by stressing our Catholic mission, we could hire above our level.

Still, the concern on the part of faculty is not completely unwarranted, and it relates to the flip side of distinction. Our admissions office did a marketing study soon after I became dean and asked high school juniors to list up to three words they associated with seven different universities. Notre Dame was on the list along with six peer private universities. Students listed only two words for Notre Dame: "religion" and "sports." The students were then given brochures on the seven universities and time to review them. They were again asked to identify up to three terms for each university. Notre Dame was the only one of the seven for which students did not write the word "academics." They persisted with "religion" and "sports." If one or the other aspect of a complex identity becomes more recognizable than others, one needs to shift priorities on campus, adjust marketing materials, or both. Still, it is a manageable problem, and it is better to be distinctive than unrecognized. As multiple presidents and former presidents have noted on their visits to Notre Dame, most universities would love to have the trademark recognition that a university such as Notre Dame enjoys.

Despite the diversity of American higher education, one could argue that even more diversity would be welcome, for example, more associate degree programs for less academically minded students who are seeking a combination of basic liberal arts skills and technical training in practical fields, ideally combined with work experience. Germany, with its dual system of vocational education and apprenticeships, is far superior in training persons to become masters of a technical trade. Research makes evident that the German school-to-work system is better at ensuring employment for young persons and serving the needs of employers and society (Rosenbaum). It is also one of the factors in the enviable success of Germany's Mittelstand, its midsized manufacturers. In offering this option, Germany is more diverse, and in this diversity is better.

The greatest challenge to diversity may well involve the following paradox: Universities often feel a compulsion to become diverse internally, which is a value, but if, in the name of internal diversity, a university were to lose its distinction against the competition, then the diversity of American higher education would be reduced on a broader, national scale. The greatest brake on such homogenizing tendencies is a clearly expressed vision and effective socialization of faculty members.

The success of the American university has created new complexities relating to institutional diversity, because institutions often shift their missions and seek to race after the most prestigious colleges and universities, which have powerful allure. When institutional missions differ, some of the problems noted in the first chapter can be addressed by the variety of American colleges and universities, yet the tendency exists simply to imitate those that garner the highest rankings. The result is often less diversity in goals and greater diversity in quality. Despite their formal skills, career academic administrators who move from one institution to another may be less attuned to local history and distinction. As academic leadership positions become more complex and fraught with nonacademic demands on one's time, many faculty members shy away from pursuing leadership positions at their own universities. Some who do take on such positions are not prepared to deal with the onslaught of nonacademic issues before them or are disturbed by the rapid-fire pace that allows precious little time for contemplation. More and more leadership positions are taken by persons who have never been faculty members and who think more of branding than of having a distinctive mission, more of the financial bottom line than of academic quality.

The complexity of the leadership challenge is especially great at religious colleges and universities (Heft). Leaders of such universities must not only fulfill the generic expectations of academic leadership, they must have a special sensibility for the distinctive religious mission; that narrows the pool of candidates still further. Presidents of Catholic universities are more often than not laypersons and not priests, brothers, or sisters of the founding religious order (Morey and Holtschneider 3; Greene 125). On average these leaders have less knowledge of the Catholic tradition—intellectual, moral, and social—than their religious predecessors and tend to be less prepared for the challenges of engaging students not simply in their academic and intellectual development but also in their religious and personal formation (Morey and Holtschneider 14–15; Morey and Piderit). If the academic leaders of Catholic colleges and universities, especially the presidents, are not prepared, they will struggle, not least of all in having to deal with a range of complex matters: for example, wrestling with the role of mission in faculty hiring and articulating the role of mission within the academic life of the university, justifying to parents and students an unusual set of core requirements, guiding and overseeing distinctive extracurricular programs, handling criticisms from the different and often polarizing strands within Catholicism, and ensuring that new board members and advisory council members are appropriately educated into the distinctive mission along with its opportunities and challenges.

Two Sample Visions

What might a sample vision look like? Let's look briefly at two counter-cultural examples, a vision for a Catholic university in a predominantly secular academy and a vision for the liberal arts within a broader culture that tends to reduce education to job preparation.

A Vision for a Catholic University

Notre Dame has a storied past. In the 1920s, when Catholic immigrants were mainly poor, and anti-Catholicism was widespread, the remarkable success of the football team gave Catholics a rallying cry and an elevated sense of collective identity (Sperber). In those days college football games were among the nation's biggest sporting events, and Notre Dame won often and against the best teams. Notre Dame's games were broadcast across the nation by radio during the age of the radio, and they filled the largest stadiums in New York City and Chicago, with the team playing before more than 120,000 fans (Thelin 128). "The Notre Dame Victory March" became, and remains, one of the nation's best known songs (Sperber 24). The legendary coach Knute Rockne became so famous that a successful Hollywood movie of his life was made in 1940. After Notre Dame's initial success and acclaim in football, the university began to acquire a national academic reputation, an effort led most formidably across a stretch of thirty-five postwar years by its president, Rev. Theodore M. Hesburgh, an advisor to many presidents as well as popes.

When articulating my vision as dean, I felt the need to address the specifically Catholic dimension of Notre Dame. Why? I noticed when I arrived that most of the faculty were uneasy speaking about Notre Dame's Catholic character. They wanted to hide it or downplay it. First, they recognized that a Catholic university was an aberration among leading research universities. In a university climate where religion is associated with what is less than fully intellectual and academic, the concern arose that a Catholic university is an oddity. Faculty coming from secular universities, even Catholic faculty, had no sensibility for what might distinguish a Catholic university. Second, our faculty were not blind to the darker moments of the Catholic tradition. The Catholic Church has not been without corruption and authoritarianism. It has occasionally undermined the concept of individual responsibility, acted irrationally in the face of the advances of science, failed to rise to the challenges of the modern world, and fallen short of its moral ideals. Church doctrine has not always been in harmony with reason, and although Christianity helped awaken the concept of universal human rights, the Catholic Church has not always acted in accordance with those ideals. Many persons, even today, have suffered from these retrograde moments, and the Church has often been its own worst enemy, even if, as a result of Vatican II, the Church has made an effort to acknowledge and learn from its shortcomings and mistakes. Third, a few years before my arrival, there had been heated debates about Notre Dame's Catholic identity, which included some voices arguing that we needed a quota of Catholic faculty members. This, of course, made faculty who were of other faiths or nonreligious uncomfortable, not to mention Catholics who justly did not want to compromise on quality. As a result, many lost confidence in speaking about our distinctive identity.

A broader reason for our local crisis and embarrassment was that an easily identifiable vision for a Catholic university no longer existed. What makes a Catholic university distinctive? Two previous definitions were outdated. Initially, the presence of the animating religious order, in the case of Notre Dame, the Congregation of Holy Cross, made the Catholic presence manifest, but for decades dwindling numbers meant the founding religious order was no longer the driving force of distinctive identity. Another antiquated vision was Thomism, which, however, lacked the capacity to integrate new developments in the sciences and the subtlety for contemporary questions. Thomism had been abandoned as too dry and technical, too remote from the present, mere memory work (Gleason 297–304). Three other models were subsequently proposed, but they too were insufficiently compelling: they were too narrow. A vibrant residential life, with liturgies in the dorms and retreats, enhances formation and collective religious experience; however, residential life by itself is not intellectual enough and not necessarily holistic. Similar issues accompanied the assignment of Catholic identity to community service. Outreach programs to the disadvantaged are important, but these are not uniquely Catholic and not always linked to academic concerns. In addition, service is only one aspect of Catholicism. Finally, some universities invested in their theology departments or in Catholic studies programs, but these foci can also redirect the Catholic mission to a single unit and take other departments off the hook, when the ultimate task of theology is to integrate advances in the individual disciplines and encourage those disciplines to ask deeper, even ultimate questions. In short, the crisis of confidence was the crisis of an animating vision.

A further factor for my wanting to address the idea of a Catholic university was that for most of my tenure as dean, I interviewed every finalist for jobs in the arts, humanities, and social sciences. With more than forty searches per year and, on average, three finalists per search, that involved about 120 interviews per year over a few concentrated months—more than 1,000 interviews over time. Those interviews covered the candidate's scholarship, teaching, and potential fit for the university. One question we called the mission question: How might candidates contribute to Notre Dame's Catholic mission, broadly understood? Or put another way, what about Notre Dame's distinctive identity attracts them? The goal was to ask an open-ended question that allowed for an almost inexhaustible number of possible responses, but an inability to engage the question in any meaningful way was a sobering sign. We had been hoping to uncover faculty who would contribute to one or more of the distinctive aspects of a Catholic university—for example, by engaging students in spiritual questions, helping them develop as persons, focusing on social justice challenges, or exploring larger questions of ultimate meaning. What I discovered again and again was that the candidates simply knew too little about the idea of a Catholic university or about Notre Dame's distinction. I ended up offering some perspectives on the idea of a Catholic university, and I realized that the vision I was developing appealed to candidates almost independently of their religious backgrounds.

Notre Dame could best compete with the top secular universities, I argued, not by imitating them but by drawing attention to our uniqueness as a strength. A university that is academically eminent and also distinctively Catholic is not common, and contributing to that sense of distinctive mission can be a powerful motivator for every member of the community.

During the summer after my second year as dean, the president, provost, and deans had a retreat to discuss our distinctive mission. I outlined the few key points I had been sharing with faculty candidates and was encouraged to develop them into a short essay. The purpose was to communicate our vision and help increase recognition that our Catholic mission, far from being a disadvantage, not only had intrinsic value but was our enduring competitive advantage. When I had written a draft and wanted some feedback from the faculty, my administrative assistant sent out an e-mail announcing the availability of the paper and a workshop. Literally in a matter of minutes, the workshop, set for some thirty-five faculty members, was filled. There was a hunger to gain clarity on these questions, so essential to our mission. My reflections resulted in a short book entitled *The Intellectual Appeal of Catholicism and the Idea of a Catholic University*.

After making reference to some of the problems in the Catholic tradition that have given rise to modern suspicions, I addressed four principles that, I believe, should animate a Catholic university. I focused on those dimensions that, while true to the Catholic tradition, might also appeal to secular scholars and scholars from other religious traditions: first, Catholicism's universalism and intentionalism; second, its sacramental vision, that is, the idea that the divine is present in this world; third, Catholicism's elevation of tradition and reason; and finally, its emphasis on the unity of knowledge. I will not repeat that vision here but will instead simply note that it helped guide my work as dean. It has since been used to help prospective faculty members enter the conversation of what a Catholic university can and might be.

Not only in general but very specifically, vision helped to guide me. In the book I identified three issues with profound implications for coming generations that deserve special consideration at a Catholic university, and I directed funding, incentives, and time toward those purposes. First, the general crisis of values and orientation, resulting from the partly legitimate abandonment of previous value traditions; from cultural changes; and from complex developments in science, technology, the global economy, and world politics. Second, the increasing gap between developed and developing countries, a topic of great concern to a universalist religion. Third, the ecological crisis, which can be addressed only by truly collaborative work and which is intimately connected to both the crisis of values and relations between developed and developing countries.

When articulating the ideal of a Catholic university, one needs to find language that, on the one hand, appeals to persons of diverse backgrounds and faiths and, on the other hand, ensures that distinctively Catholic dimensions are fully integrated. Too much Catholic rhetoric can alienate faculty members of another or no faith tradition. To say too little is to lose the distinction. It is not simply a matter of rhetoric; the challenge is to articulate a conceptual ideal that is intellectually compelling and attractive to persons who are not Catholic and, at the same time, is deeply Catholic. That such a vision will not appeal to everyone is, however, a given and simply the necessary consequence of distinction.

A Vision for the Liberal Arts

A vision may arise from a new and dynamic direction, but just as frequently it emerges out of necessity and a sense of crisis. Already Plato recognized that calls for legitimacy tend to surface only after a framework has begun to crumble or at least become vulnerable. In the early decades of the twentieth century, about 70 percent of US undergraduates majored in the liberal arts; today the figure is more in the range of 36 to 44 percent, depending on which disciplines one includes (Brint et al. 155–56; Natl. Center for Educ. Statistics, *Digest*, table 322.10). Beyond the premier liberal arts colleges, which are likely to thrive indefinitely, liberal arts colleges that are less selective and much more dependent on tuition dollars have required a compelling vision.

My own reflections on the liberal arts, published in a book called *Why Choose the Liberal Arts?*, resulted from a concern about three factors that seemed to threaten the liberal arts. First, when I became dean, Notre Dame had a high number of business majors. With my colleagues I introduced a series of initiatives to reduce the number, and we succeeded, lowering business majors for ten straight semesters. This book developed out of the story I was telling parents when they asked, "What can my child do with a major in philosophy?" I wanted to make the case to both parents and students that a liberal arts education could meet their practical concerns about employment, that it is superb preparation for a career in any number of fields, including business.

Second, although I could recognize this practical value, I was disturbed by the ways in which so many Americans were reducing the purpose of higher education to merely practical ends. The national debate on undergraduate education had been—and continues to be—overwhelmingly about job preparation. I wanted to make the case that an arts and sciences education can be defended first and foremost as an end in itself; that is, it is of value for its own sake independently of its preparation of students for eventual employment and citizenship.

Third was my sense that the idea of moral formation was disappearing from the landscape of American higher education. College catalogues tend to mention the concept still, but faculty are less supportive. Their main focus is disciplinary learning and critical thinking. Understandable reasons exist for this bracketing of character and virtue, but even more compelling counterarguments are available. I wanted to argue that not only should a liberal arts education help students develop virtues of character and a sense of higher purpose, we as faculty members were in many ways already invested in this mission even as we denied it.

In *Why Choose the Liberal Arts?*, I consider three partly overlapping grounds for a liberal arts education: first, its intrinsic value, or the distinction of learning for its own sake, the sheer joy associated with exploring the life of the mind and asking the great questions that give meaning to life; second, the cultivation of those intellectual virtues that are requisite for success beyond the academy, a liberal arts education as preparation for a career; and third, character formation and the development of a sense of vocation, the connection to a higher purpose or calling. Exploration of these three values—the intrinsic, the practical, and the idealistic—constitute the core of the vision, which was a guiding force as I sought ways to improve learning at Notre Dame.

Parameters of Change

Change can come in varying levels of intensity. Cosmetic change involves surface alterations, for example, renaming a position or process, that do not address underlying structures, including inefficiencies and external constraints. Normally, such activity consists of busywork. Cosmetic change tends to be a subterfuge that avoids fundamental issues and so simply cultivates business as usual.

Incremental change involves modest adjustments over a long period. It allows a university to become better slowly, but in the meantime other universities are improving as well, some quite aggressively and quickly. So from a competitive standpoint, one does not move ahead but at best stays in place or, more likely, falls behind.

Transformative change—confronting challenges directly, making significant changes, and seeking major advances—is the most radical form of change and is necessary for any university that wants to compete. It alone demands a compelling vision.

Transformative change is not only the most desirable but also the most difficult. To be successful, it must satisfy at least four conditions. First, a clear and compelling vision must be a guiding constant amid rapid change. A lack of vision is problematic insofar as change without a telos is threatening. Indeed, rapid change without a guiding vision may well be worse than no change at all. Change and innovation cost time, so without a persuasive rationale, one can expect resistance from faculty, who legitimately desire to focus on teaching and research and not to lose time and energy on unimportant structural and administrative issues. Second, one needs courage to introduce and bring forward transformative change that addresses the big and potentially contentious issues that most would prefer to avoid. Third, one needs a certain level of support from the faculty, the core of the university. Fourth, one needs to ensure that the changes reinforce one another and integrate well to serve the larger vision or goal.

As one introduces change, one must ask two distinct questions: First, what is the highest priority? Second, what is most realizable? By sifting those two dimensions together, one can advance the most important changes that can indeed be realized. Essentially, this involves combining a sense of vision and priorities with knowledge of the lay of the land, that is, the normative and descriptive spheres. Still, if something is a major priority and support is mixed, one must have the courage to lead and move ahead despite resistance. In such cases, one must listen carefully to counterobjections. Greater support can come after disagreement as long as one has listened well and either adjusted the policy in the light of valid objections or made clear the rationale for one's final choice.

PART II

Embodying and Funding the Vision

Essential to a university's excellence are its ideas and its people, which together bring to the university the third presupposition of excellence, resources. The most important idea on any campus is the distinctive vision. To ensure that people connect with the animating ideas and ethos of the institution, one needs to hire the right people and mentor them toward the vision through a socialization process that will help them flourish and ensure that their good ideas are integrated into the dynamic articulation of the university's mission. One also needs to find strategies and incentives to realize the vision. None of this is easy, and any dean is likely to encounter competing interests and conflicts along the way. Further, one needs to find avenues to fund those priorities and incentives.

Although what I address in this part of the book involves distinction, to the extent that all universities are at some level distinct, linking vision, personnel, and resources with one another and ensuring that each advances the other are common and central tasks of any college or university. My recurring example of distinction, as I note above, is Notre Dame, a Catholic university. The content of other colleges' visions will differ from the one I describe. But the benefits of distinction, including the fact that distinction can help a university garner resources, strike me as universal. Further, the various ways in which distinction can be embodied or fail to be embodied will apply broadly across campuses.

CHAPTER THREE

Embodiment, or
Why Not All Meetings Are Dull

The legitimacy of a vision derives not only from the question of whether it is compelling and distinctive. Other puzzles remain. Does it draw on tradition, has it been conceived in conversation with faculty, and is it open to further development and refinement? Is it effectively communicated through language, symbols, support structures, incentives, and priorities, from budget to fund raising? Has it been linked to specific goals? Are the leadership and the campus community connected by a common sense of the vision's intrinsic value, which is reinforced by social and emotional dimensions?

These are all essential questions for any enterprise but especially for a university, where shared governance is the norm and faculty support is voluntary. The complexity of the challenge is partly captured by Woodrow Wilson, who served as president of Princeton before becoming president of the United States. Wilson said that he learned politics in the first half of his professional life as a member of the Princeton faculty and then practiced it for the second half in Washington: "As compared with the college politician, the real article seems like an amateur" (Baker 266).

Communication

Communication is central in one respect after another. I once spoke with a professor who lamented that at his university there was no recognition, not even a thank you letter, for extraordinary success in grantsmanship, and that sending the central administration concrete ideas and recommendations on ways the university might improve received no response whatsoever. One study notes, "Viewed from a management perspective, the greatest flaw in the operation of a college or university is, invariably, poor communication" (Tucker and Bryan 84). This is a matter not simply of rhetoric but of recognition. Intrinsic motivation comes not only from vision but also from a sense of belonging, of being valued as a participant in a common enterprise.

The questions one asks of job candidates when assessing their potential contributions to the university's distinctive identity can lead to a give-and-take that opens up new insights into the mission. One must welcome new faculty candidates into the vision, inviting them to offer ways to help shape it anew beginning at the job interview. Not to do so is to perpetuate a generic university, which only rarely has the capacity to develop a deep emotional attachment among its constituents; it is also to miss an opportunity for regeneration.

Ideally, vision infuses discussions and informs decisions about everything, even space. Notre Dame's performing arts center includes an organ chorale hall that provides performance space for our programs in sacred music, as is fitting for a religious university. When the board of trustees, concerned about costs, pushed me on the need for this space, I recall there being immediate agreement with my argument that such a space was indeed essential for our vision as a Catholic university. To be more precise, when they called me in to defend the organ chorale hall, I argued, drawing on mission, aspiration, and need, for two such halls, and they quickly shepherded me out the door.

Communication occurs at every opportunity: when one advertises positions, interviews candidates, and orients new faculty members. Job candidates remember the institutions that treated them well and respond favorably in future years when the department comes calling again or when faculty members are counseling prospective graduate students or evaluating departments or universities. Solicitation and acknowledgment letters offer opportunities to articulate the department's and the institution's strengths and distinctive features. Giving candidates sample syllabi sends a message about the importance of teaching and the willingness to mentor teaching. Questions during the interview articulate priorities indirectly. One aspect I sought to emphasize at Notre Dame is that we value *both* teaching and research. A very good interview question in this context is, "How will your research help you as a teacher?"

Indicating one's willingness to read future manuscripts also sends a message, as does search committee members' demonstrating, through their questions, that they have carefully studied the candidate's application materials and read their writing samples. The participation of colleagues from other departments conveys a broad sense of intellectual community. Welcoming gestures like having everyone involved in the search contact the candidate once the offer has been extended, encouraging him or her to accept the position and offering to be a resource, can make a tremendous difference.

Good communication leads of course to new ideas. I asked one of my associate deans to organize focus groups for women faculty members to explore best practices and practical suggestions that would help us enhance the college's supportive environment and sense of community, particularly with an eye to recruitment and retention. We then formed a task force on women to implement the parts of the report that had not already been advanced. One of the most significant was a web page devoted to "Women in Arts and Letters" that included a range of materials, from faculty profiles to policies and procedures, resources, and tips on both academic and nonacademic issues.

Good communication also involves ensuring—through informal conversations, group meetings, and wider fora—that one has aired an idea before it becomes reality and communicated the conditions motivating the change. Not doing so is a mistake that may be more frequently made by the support side, which does not regularly encounter the faculty governance model. For example, in 2014 Notre Dame revised its faculty savings options for retirement. The goals seemed sensible and involved simplification of options, improved performance of funds, and better reporting. The changes, however, were not sufficiently aired with the full faculty in advance, the rationale was never communicated with clarity or force, and anticipated objections and questions, such as why the old options were not being grandfathered in for those nearing retirement or why social choice options were being eliminated, were not proleptically addressed. Only in private conversation did I learn that the entire initiative was the result of a federal regulation requiring that the university itself stand behind the viability of its fund choices, that finding a social choice fund that met stringent criteria was difficult, and that the nonprofit company that was a faculty favorite had itself decided not to participate under the new conditions. Despite there being various glossy brochures about the changes, none of those more meaningful messages made it to the faculty as a whole. Making a sensible decision is only half the job; communicating its rationale and giving faculty time to comment are no less important.

One amusing incident underscored to me early on the value of listening first and speaking second. In my first year as dean, one department was split on a prospective faculty appointment. I had read the file and brought the promotion-and-tenure committee before me. I spelled out the issues I thought were at play and asked if the analysis was basically correct. Both sides disagreed immediately with my analysis. At the next meeting and every subsequent one, my modus operandi was different. I opened the meeting by saying that the file was complex and asked every person to tell me the strengths and weaknesses of the case and the rationale for his or her vote. We would go around the room, ending with the chairperson. I took assiduous notes as each person spoke. I then asked a number of questions, some prepared in advance and some developed in the course of my listening. My job at that stage was simply to listen in order to understand every facet of the case. Here communication meant listening.

One of the best ways for an administrator to communicate is to meet with groups of faculty, above all, departments. Otherwise, information is channeled to faculty through administrative lines, and that can lead to miscommunication, often inadvertent, but not always, especially if the chairperson disagrees with a given policy. I did not immediately grasp this lesson. Interacting with groups of faculty is not only an efficient use of face time but also a great way to convey information, knowledge, and interest while enjoying a frank and meaningful exchange.

Targeted fora, for example, to communicate promotion-and-tenure standards and share suggestions and strategies, can serve similar purposes as well as reduce uncertainty. Mission can be productively addressed in open fora. At Notre Dame a panel of internal and external speakers addressed three questions: What are the most important ways in which we should resemble the best secular universities, and what are the most important ways in which we should differ from them? How should we educate our undergraduates so that twenty years after graduation they are likely to be the kind of people we want them to be? What qualities should mark the teacher-scholars whom we recruit, so that we can advance both our academic reputation and our distinctive mission?

Meetings are ideally interactive and discussion oriented. As the saying goes, not all meetings are dull; some are cancelled. Little is more valuable on a campus than faculty time; few administrative actions are more egregious than wasting faculty time in needless or inefficient meetings.

A wise colleague once told me that the worst thing he could imagine was a meeting with two associate deans. While the joke hints at faculty unease with administration (two deans is worse than one dean), its deeper point is that time is hugely valuable. Only those whose presence is necessary should be summoned to a meeting, and no unnecessary meetings should be held. Meetings should have an agenda and move toward action items. Still, they can be necessary to form common visions, to thank colleagues publicly for their contributions, to trade best practices, to reflect on common challenges, to do some initial brainstorming, to solicit input before making decisions, to hear what is not going well, and to make sure that everyone is on the same page.

One of the meetings I most enjoyed was a weekly executive committee meeting I initiated with the associate deans, senior staff, and faculty fellows. The meeting served two purposes: first, to keep everyone in the loop on important issues in areas beyond their purview, which was accomplished relatively quickly; and then to think out loud about puzzles and priorities. The back and forth was rapid and intense, and anyone who veered off topic or became repetitious was cut off.

Communication is also conveyed nonverbally. An academic leader wants to embody the goals and values of the institution. When academic administrators serve as effective role models, they garner more authority and are better able to motivate others. Teaching; continuing to publish; playing an occasional role in national media; manifesting a strong work ethic; and being continuously optimistic, available, and visible can all be part of this broader sense of indirect communication. Administrators should, where possible, seek to model mission, for example, by offering courses in mission areas or by reflecting publicly on mission-related puzzles. It was helpful to me, in a strategic sense, although that was not my original aim, when I offered a course called "Faith, Doubt, and Reason."

At times a university can be seduced by its public relations successes, in such a way that instead of vision driving public relations, public relations drives vision. We had, as I noted, a university-level puzzle during my tenure as dean: enrollments in the business college had grown too large for the size of the business faculty, conflicting with their desire for community, and the idea of a Catholic liberal arts university. Having a high number of students in an applied undergraduate major was not compatible with our emphasis, as a Catholic university, on the value of learning for its own sake, the Catholic intellectual tradition, or our identity as a leading arts and sciences university. The College of Arts and Letters adopted informal strategies to encourage majors in the liberal arts, and we succeeded. When I stepped down in 2008, the numbers in business again skyrocketed: the Great Recession led students to seek out seemingly more practical majors, and from 2010 to 2014, Notre Dame's business college received a number one ranking from *Business Week*.

Instead of continuing to work on reductions in business enrollments, through indirect strategies, such as addressing incoming parents and students, requiring business students to take more advanced courses in economics, or adding the kinds of core requirements, such as competency in a foreign language, that existed for the arts and sciences, the business college and the university regularly trumpeted the number one ranking. Unaware that in many other rankings, our business college was not at the top, that many premier colleges don't even offer an undergraduate business major, and that arts and sciences colleges are not ranked in the same way as business schools, students were drawn to business in many cases because of the ranking ("How can I turn down a number one ranking?"). The hunger for publicity triumphed over mission. As a result, what we had successfully avoided years earlier, a gate or quota for business majors, had to be introduced.

Communication is not only about lofty matters such as vision. For an administrator, it also involves the rather mundane process of answering each day what can easily be several hundred e-mails or letters. I once wrote an op-ed for *The New York Times* on a controversial topic and received some national press, invitations for radio and television interviews, and more than a thousand e-mails and letters. I responded to every one, even the letter from an alumnus that began, "Dear Asshole." It took some time, of course, and many responses included some basic language I had formulated for certain types of letters, but still, I thought it important because of my office to respond to all of them.

Not only salutations but also closings can be colorful. Sometimes instead of the basic "Yours," one receives a note signed "Cheers." I tended to sign mine "Thanks." My favorite closing came from a faculty member who was frustrated with changes in our economics department; he signed his note, "Fed up."

There are occasions, both private and public, when a dean will be attacked with a rhetorical vehemence that can border on rudeness or inappropriateness; the only way to respond is to listen with an open mind, focusing on the issue, not matters of style, and to speak with fairness, clarity, and composure. One odd circumstance helped me to ensure I would be diplomatic in e-mail. Because I lived in the country, during my entire eleven years as dean I had only a slow dial-up modem connection. When I arrived home in the early evening, I downloaded all my messages. After dinner I started answering them. When I was done for the night, I sent all the messages. In the meantime, I had queued each one, which meant that I could conveniently read them a second time before hitting send. It worked so well, I configured my office computer the same way. I read every message a second time before releasing it.

The op-ed I wrote was on the 2004 presidential election, specifically the puzzle of how a Catholic should vote, given that neither party platform lined up perfectly with Catholic views. Because the op-ed ultimately favored Senator John Kerry over President George W. Bush, I received a call that day from the Kerry campaign and was asked a number of questions. The conversation ended with an open invitation to come back to them with any advice. My op-ed had emerged rather unexpectedly at the same time I was planning to teach a class session on religion and politics, and I did not expect to have any new perspectives. A week or so later, as I was driving from the Minneapolis airport to give a talk at one of the liberal arts colleges nearby, I was listening to the final Kerry-Bush debate. Kerry briefly mentioned that he had been an altar boy. That gave me an idea. I sketched out a little address. The idea was to have Kerry speak more fully about his faith. People responded favorably to his reflections on faith during the debate, both his upbringing and his ideas, and the Catholic vote was crucial, especially in the larger swing states. Such a talk would likely receive more press than the standard, slightly repetitive sound bites that are also a necessary component of a campaign's final stage. The timing would be good, I suggested, insofar as people might be looking for more reflections after what was said in the debate.

The speech was to have four parts. In the first, Kerry would articulate more fully his faith upbringing. He could open, I proposed, by expanding on the personal reflections he offered during the debate. He might talk more about his service as an altar boy. He might speak about other aspects of his faith journey as a boy and a young man. Was grace always said at the dinner table? In what ways did he identify with his parish community? What symbols and rituals and moments inspired his belief in, and thinking about, God? What readings from the Gospel were inspiring to him? Who were his mentors in faith? What faith lessons did he teach his children? This section would help reinforce his personal connection with other believers. It would ensure that others see the depth of his religious persona, which had for the most part been missing from his self-presentation. Kerry would hardly risk alienating secular thinkers, who were already strongly for him.

In the second part, Kerry would reaffirm the Kennedy principle—that he does not want to impose his faith on America. He could place himself within a venerable tradition. He had already done this well and could pull from other documents. It would reinforce the consistency of his position.

In the third part, Kerry would state that faith often overlaps with reason and the societal consensus, providing an additional rationale for good works. This, I said, could be the Kerry principle. It could build on Kerry's comments during the third debate—that the emphasis on loving one's neighbor and fostering good works has religious roots. Kerry would suggest that while the Kennedy principle fits some issues, other topics exist on which faith is in harmony with reason and society's needs. In short, he could say that he endorses a set of issues on the basis of both reason and faith. Here he could use religious rhetoric in a way that his opponent had already done when appealing to the culture of life. Kerry might turn to corresponding language on social justice: for example, the dignity of every person before God; the value of the common good; and our moral obligations to address poverty and human needs, especially the needs of children. In terms of specifics, Kerry could draw, I suggested, on social justice rhetoric to explain that both faith and reason offer support for an expansion of health care options, the reintroduction of more equitable taxes, an increase in the minimum wage, the creation of jobs with dignity, and the support of integral human development. He could also suggest that we have moral obligations to future generations exemplified in his concern about the debt and the environment, which could also draw on papal documents. I suggested that there would be lots of options in this section, and the senator would want to pick and choose, but the bottom line would be that, when both faith and reason are in harmony, religion can reinforce motivation, rhetoric, and policy.

In the final section, Kerry would argue, I proposed, that although abortion falls in his eyes under the Kennedy principle, he was also committed to creating conditions that would reduce the number of persons choosing abortion out of desperation. Kerry could say that on the issue of abortion, there is no compelling rational answer and no clear societal consensus in favor of the faith tradition of which he is a part. (Some Catholics, I noted, including myself, would disagree with the view that there are no rationally compelling arguments against abortion, but that would not be relevant in this context.) He could then return to the Kennedy principle. However, he could say, more clearly than he had, that while he would protect the constitutional right of choice, he was eager to create the conditions under which fewer abortions would take place. He could speak of supporting women and addressing poverty. He could also cite statistics showing that under the Democrats fewer abortions had taken place. I suggested that he would hardly lose the support of pro-choice women with this argument, but he might well gain the support of some persons who were pro-life and unhappy with President Bush for other reasons.

The talk could be fairly brief, I suggested, a side bar to the necessary repetition of his major points on the economy and so forth, but it would get coverage as a different kind of address. It would certainly receive abundant press in religious circles, where there were many swing voters. He might deliver it, I suggested, in a church courtyard after Mass or on a religious campus in one of the swing states.

What happened to the suggestion? Well, Kerry did give a version of the address in Fort Lauderdale a week or so later, ten days before the election, after Mass on Sunday, but without the first part (the personal dimension) and the fourth part (his personal position on abortion and desire to reduce abortions). The second point, the Kennedy principle, was not new, but the third, faith motivating politics, was to some degree new and in any case had been further elaborated; the story led the evening news, but it was not enough to win over a requisite number of pro-life voters in the swing states. I ended up developing versions of the third and fourth points myself in a postelection op-ed for *The Chicago Tribune*.

Two things strike me about this story. First, a dean likes to name a complex problem head-on and seek multiple strategies to solve it. In an academic climate, that is a good plan. By leaving out the fourth element, Kerry ignored an important option. After the election I received a follow-up call from the campaign, which was doing a postelection analysis. They confessed that Kerry was so disturbed by the volatile nature of the abortion issue, including the threat that he might be denied communion, that he simply wanted to steer clear of it, giving it as little attention as possible. Unlike a dean, who wants to address issues, he, as someone seeking election, sought to avoid controversy. Second, what I was essentially suggesting to Kerry was what I had slowly learned from my own mistakes as dean. Having ideas and formal skills is not enough; one also needs to connect as a person. By not exploring his own religious upbringing or stating his own personal (as opposed to political) views on abortion, he came across as less warm than his opponent.

Vision, to draw this section to a close, must be communicated also beyond the campus, above all to alumni and supporters. Beyond the kind of outreach to alumni and donors in which every university is engaged, Notre Dame has had a long tradition of appealing practices, triggered by the enthusiasm of its alumni. The university regularly offers informal faculty lectures to alumni clubs. A brochure of topics, ranging from cultural and spiritual themes to history and current events, is made available each year to regional alumni groups, which can sponsor, often in collaboration with a local college, an informal lecture and discussion. Faculty members who give the lectures receive travel expenses as well as modest honoraria from an endowed fund. Universal Notre Dame nights occur annually at most clubs as well. For these an administrator or faculty member speaks about recent events on campus, for which purpose a speaker's handbook is prepared and an information session offered, although faculty can also talk from their own experiences. The handbook includes talking points on academic advances, building projects, controversies, and recent events, along with data about admissions, financial aid, academics, athletics, and alumni clubs. I offered these for over a decade and then rotated out of the cycle, so that others could take a turn. Often they were not far away, in Michigan or Ohio, for example, but I also gave them, in the context of other travel, either individually or jointly with the president, in Beijing, Hong Kong, Shanghai, and Seoul.

Important for the reception of our academic priorities was a program for alumni and supporters. On six or seven Saturdays each fall, nearly a hundred thousand people come to the Notre Dame campus to watch a football game; millions of others watch on television. Alumni tend to focus their activities on attending the football game, renewing friendships, participating in one of the masses, and enjoying the beauty of the campus. The core of the university, academics, is thereby underplayed. Partly to help address this gap, we introduced the Saturday Scholar Series, which became a great success. Several hours before the start of each home football game, one of the college's scholars presents an accessible lecture on an engaging topic, followed by a question-and-answer period. Regularly well attended, the Saturday Scholar Series has become an institution at Notre Dame. It has since been imitated by other colleges and centers on campus.

Faculty Orientation and Development

Ideally, a university offers an extended orientation for new faculty members, perhaps a short retreat before classes start and then a monthly event throughout the year, to introduce them to the institution's fabric, history, student life, and aspirations. A detailed campus tour, including a visit to a residence hall, as well as unusual information on the local area, can add to the appeal. The orientation, at which mission should be a guiding principle, can also address practical issues, such as faculty governance and tenure expectations, and include helpful tips and advice. Other activities might involve a discussion of the mission statement or current strategic plan, an informational session on the athletics program, and a meeting with the director of admissions, including a presentation of data. If a good local university history exists, a discussion of such a work or a selected chapter would make eminent sense. One session might involve a document by the president and a discussion with him or her. Continuing events across the year allow faculty to renew their relationships across disciplines. Besides ensuring that faculty meet colleagues from other disciplines and become familiar with appropriate resource persons as future questions arise, such an orientation fosters loyalty and community. It ensures that new faculty understand how the missions of their new and former universities differ.

Although I prominently addressed mission in interviews and at public meetings, I did not recognize early enough the advantages of an extended orientation. The insight in fact came to me for the first time early in my tenure, when I was being interviewed for a book on religious colleges and was asked how Notre Dame socializes faculty into our distinctive mission (Benne). As faculty members enter the university, they need to be integrated into the continuing conversation about how to understand mission, and the institution needs to allow the mission to be enriched by their voices. Identity and voice are connected.

Chairpersons should also provide new departmental colleagues with a tailored orientation. In addition to introducing mission at the departmental level, this session might include a description of the undergraduate and graduate curricula, with sample syllabi; strategies for the evaluation of teaching and learning; information concerning support for research and an offer to assist with grant applications; introductions to colleagues in other departments with related interests; an open discussion about short- and long-term research goals that includes the tenure process and expectations; descriptions of the various duties of the office staff and other support persons; and an offer to facilitate access to non-academic resources such as child care, medical care, or housing. One wants new faculty members to feel welcomed. For a long time it festered in my mind as an assistant professor that my chairperson delayed for many months arranging to have the tape of my dissertation placed on the mainframe computer at Ohio State, so that I could get back to work on revising and expanding the material: he was hoping to use my request for space to garner extra computer resources for the department. But when one enters a community, one wants above all to be supported, not used in a strategic game.

Orientation need not end upon arrival. Programs can also be created for newly tenured faculty, who are at a crucial juncture and eager to learn more about their institution, to help them become more fully part of the community. I myself had never been as curious about the profession as during the summer immediately after receiving tenure. Most of my book purchases at the time were targeted toward teaching and research, but that year I bought myself as a tenure gift Henry Rosovsky's *University: An Owner's Manual*, which had recently appeared and was for me at the time eye-opening reading. I also naturally grew more curious about Ohio State.

Faculty seminars can offer a kind of continuing orientation. At Notre Dame we sponsored for some years an annual university-wide, year-long seminar on a topic involving Catholicism, such as the Catholic intellectual tradition, the Catholic social tradition, the Catholic idea of liberal learning, and theology and science. Recognizing that many faculty members could not give that much time to such a demanding initiative, we also sponsored each semester single-afternoon workshops. These offered an introduction to Catholicism, explored a classic work in the Catholic tradition, or engaged a topic involving Catholicism and contemporary society. In this way virtually all faculty could find something of interest. One could imagine equivalent activities at any kind of university, for example, seminars on the university's history or prominent figures from its past. We also offered course releases for study of the Catholic intellectual tradition. Faculty members from outside theology and philosophy could enter a competition to receive a one-course release from teaching in order to take a course or independent study in philosophy, theology, or another discipline on aspects of the Catholic intellectual tradition; these experiences were designed to enrich the faculty member's teaching, scholarship, and connection to the university. In this case, as elsewhere, support structures convey messages about institutional priorities.

Why are such orientations important? For the simple reason that faculty, as was evident already in the 1960s, tend to identify more with their disciplines than their institutions (Jencks and Riesman), and one must work as a campus leader to shift some of that allegiance. Further, a faculty member at any institution with a distinctive identity—and that includes, among others, community colleges, liberal arts colleges, and religious universities, almost none of which will be similar to the new faculty member's doctoral-granting university—must learn to grasp what makes the new institution distinctive and not, either immediately or over time, seek to remake it into a mirror of his or her previous institution. Without such an effort, mission creep is inevitable.

Chairpersons and Mission

Chairpersons are central in ensuring that mission becomes reality. Identifying both with faculty and the administration, they have a complex mediating role. Chairpersons at religious universities encounter an even greater complexity. Whereas faculty tend to be attuned almost exclusively to disciplinary standards, chairpersons are asked to support a distinctive vision as well. Faculty may be uninterested in mission and may not have the categories for any goal beyond generic excellence. This lack of categories can surface also with religious faculty members who come to a religious college but whose careers have been at nonreligious institutions.

Ideally, at their orientation, chairpersons receive information not only about finances, policies, and processes but also about mission. The best chairpersons are both *cosmopolitans*, that is, scholars who regularly influence thinking on a national and international level within their disciplines, and *locals*, that is, scholar-teachers who foster the community of learning at their current institution, thereby also contributing to its flourishing (Gouldner). Only a small number of faculty members at any institution excel at both. They need to be recognized, rewarded, and supported, receiving the kind of compensation that ensures they will not be tempted to apply for positions elsewhere in order to feel appreciated.

Moreover, such faculty need periodic breaks from service and leadership, so that they can preserve their emotional, intellectual, and psychological energy over the years, as well as retain their standing as cosmopolitans. As an administrator, you become so absorbed in the job that you are always thinking about puzzles and opportunities; rest and renewal are not easy. One year I decided to take a week's vacation and free myself completely from administrative work. My wife and I rented a cottage on the New England coast, and well in advance I notified all of the chairpersons and others that I would be away, advising them to take care of all pressing business before I left. I did not yet have a smart phone and had just bought a cell phone, but the number was unknown to anyone but a few people in the dean's office. The day of my arrival, I received a call from one of the associate deans about a complicated hiring package. After that I had no contact for over a week. When I returned and turned on my home computer, I could not remember the password. I tried all kinds of strategies, from thinking through what I could possibly have chosen to physical memory. It took some forty-five minutes before I finally broke through, but there was submerged joy in my puzzle, for my failure to remember the password gave ample indication of a genuine vacation. Vacations and appropriate leaves are essential.

Some faculty members, as I have said, worry that mission can create a sense of exclusion or even embarrassment. One needs, therefore, to articulate why one should elevate rather than hide a distinct identity, what its advantages are for faculty members, how it can give an institution focus and foster community, and how it can be used to attract faculty. I discovered in my first weeks, from feedback from new hires, including those who were not Catholic, that we did not always draw sufficiently on our Catholicism as an advantage in hiring. A distinctive university should look for colleagues who can actively contribute to the university's broader mission, and we needed, I suggested, to highlight our distinction, not downplay it. I proposed that we suggest to prospective colleagues—with confidence and excitement—that Notre Dame is an international institution with a strong sense of community; that many of our disciplines study social justice issues and our students are unusually committed to service and the welfare of others; that the university places great emphasis on philosophy, theology, and the humanities; that our students have an existential interest in the spiritual implications of their studies and see learning as related to the development of character; that we seek to offer students an integrative experience; and that we value teaching and research equally. Such a description, I argued, should attract and energize Catholics, as well as persons of another or no faith tradition. If one cannot articulate the distinctive mission without embarrassment, one should probably drop it.

Before a search begins, chairpersons might initiate departmental discussions about desirable qualities, including how the faculty member would contribute to the distinctive mission and how the department might most effectively win over the best candidates. What is distinctive and attractive about the department and the university? Otherwise, departments search for generic candidates and forward generic recommendations to the administration. If the faculty members take the lead in such discussions, they will be more likely to commit to the institution's ideals.

When our departments identified Notre Dame as a Catholic university in job ads, they discovered that more candidates self-identified as Catholic or gave reasons why they wanted to work at a distinctive university. We therefore moved from recommending to requiring such inclusion. We also insisted that convention interviews include some questions on mission. This allowed us to sift early on and became an advantage in helping candidates prepare for the more demanding questions that arise in a visit with the dean.

Of course the puzzle can be quite complex. I once called a chairperson after interviewing a faculty candidate to say that he had done very poorly on the mission question, and I could not imagine hiring him. The chairperson said, "But he is Catholic!" Being Catholic and being good on mission were not always one and the same. Although I already kept track each year of the percentage of hires who were Catholic, I started also keeping track of what I called "mission hires," persons who, irrespective of faith, worked on topics that were a superb fit for a Catholic university or who exhibited a deep understanding of our distinctive mission and a desire to contribute to it. To me mission hires were more important.

Helping chairpersons in generic ways also serves mission, for it makes them more effective in all areas, including mission. One can support workshops on chairing or visits to departments that a chairperson knows have developed in exemplary ways. Regular panels on generic issues, from saving time to mentoring faculty, are useful. Helpful were the monthly sessions at Notre Dame, during which chairpersons spoke about exemplary innovations or strategies: letters to prospective majors, that is, to students who were performing well in lower-level classes, to encourage them to consider the major; presentations to majors by career center specialists; targeted events for parents and students on special weekends; innovative graduate seminars specifically designed to help students develop publishable essays; various forms of feedback for assistant professors and graduate students; strategies and incentives for allocating travel and research support; postcards advertising new websites; and a host of other issues.

Mentoring chairpersons presupposes identifying weaknesses. In faculty evaluations of chairpersons, the most common weakness I saw was by far in the area of communication. This partly involves communication to the department; faculty always like to be consulted and never like to be left in the dark, even if they hate meetings and often scorn administration as an activity. Laments about poor communication also involve one-on-one communication. It is sometimes amazing to hear a chairperson say that she or he has been fully supportive of a faculty member and then later to hear that faculty member indicate that the chairperson was not at all supportive. Faculty members cannot hear often enough how well they are doing or how meaningful a particular action was. It is important to stress as well that communication must be substantial. True recognition requires knowledge. One cannot create an academically superior and a friendly, communicative environment without substantive, knowledgeable praise (and truly informative constructive suggestions).

Another expectation of being chairperson is generosity. One of the jobs of a chairperson is to nominate colleagues for awards, both internal and external, and that is not easy for someone who has little sense of initiative or suffers from envy or jealousy. Selfless generosity, rare though it may be, is essential to fulfilling one's role as a steward of the larger collective.

Arguably the two most important factors that hold a dean back from allocating resources to departments that might otherwise merit them are lack of vision and lack of leadership. One wants to invest in departments or programs that have ambitious and meaningful goals and the leadership to realize them. Because languages and literatures were a priority for me as dean, early in my tenure, I set aside $100,000 in annual-rate dollars, the equivalent of $2.5 million in endowment, for a yet-to-be defined initiative in foreign languages and literatures. In my early years I had other, more pressing priorities and so banked the money, using it for onetime initiatives elsewhere, and waited to see what good ideas might surface from the ranks. I also indicated to the director of the foreign language center that I would be supportive of ambitious proposals. Nothing compelling emerged. I then appointed a committee, which filed its report after two years; it was both slow in arriving and unpersuasive. I held on to the resources. Some years later, I charged another committee with the following question: How can we best improve advanced language learning and the flourishing of the foreign language and culture majors? The committee came back with little intellectual or academic substance, no answer to my question, and an unconvincing recommendation that, since a few peer and aspirational peer universities had superb language centers, we needed one too. I told them to come back with an answer or set of answers to my question. They finally did, and we put together a memorandum of understanding. The departments would do a number of things—such as enhancing recruitment efforts, increasing contact hours in beginning courses, offering extracurricular conversational opportunities, expanding curricula, introducing pre– and post–study abroad activities, and developing assessment strategies–and I would invest in peer tutors as well as a language center. It is now a flourishing entity. A dean who did not see the overriding importance of languages and cultures would have said after the first failed report, I will simply invest elsewhere, and that would have been a rational decision.

Without the right leadership, any program, however compelling its idea, will suffer. I saw that firsthand with a program I myself helped introduce. When mission is involved, the risks associated with poor leadership are even greater. Not only excellence is at play but distinction. If a new or not yet fully formed program has as its director someone who is clueless on mission or inattentive to distinction, the situation may not be recoverable, for the general tendency is toward generic disciplinary identity.

A veteran observer has suggested that presidents and deans are less important at the very top of the academic ladder (Lombardi 196–97). The idea, which makes intuitive sense to me, applies, I should think, also to chairpersons. When an already strong department has an array of senior colleagues who understand academic quality and know what constitutes a great department, that surrounding leadership can partially offset the effects of a weaker chairperson. The corollary to this is that, in any department that is not already superior, having what I call a maintenance chairperson, someone who can keep the department running but who has few aspirations on its behalf and little skill in administrative leadership and team building, will rather quickly weaken a department. That description applies to all but a very small number of chairperson slots across the United States.

Still, it is not always easy to find strong chairpersons, as I suggest below. One puzzle is that one can sometimes find such persons, but they are at the associate rank. Since it was important to me to let such persons develop, I can recall several occasions when I appointed a less qualified chairperson, knowing that in a few years an associate would be promoted and the college would then have a better solution for the long term. In several cases I found it useful to bring in as chairpersons seasoned leaders from other departments to address a leadership gap at full professor or to help alleviate the tensions that often arise in weaker departments without strong internal leadership. In one department we had two external chairpersons across almost a decade, but in the end, the department transformed itself. Looking toward the long term is always a wise policy.

Positive Reinforcement

In the realm of mission, as in other areas, positive reinforcement is important. When in an annual evaluation or in thank you letters, chairpersons note meaningful activities with regard to mission, they communicate its importance. If distinction is valued, it must pervade every aspect of the institution. Awards not only for excellence in teaching and research but also for fostering distinctive mission may be appropriate at some colleges. Faculty members recognize that publications at the departmental, collegiate, and university levels indicate the institution's priorities. Each year, I released a *Dean's Report* that had the following four sections: Undergraduate Studies and Learning, Graduate Studies and Scholarship, Catholic Identity and Mission, and Diversity and Internationalism. Distinctive contributions in those areas were recognized.

Although communicating aspirational standards is important, early on as dean I challenged faculty members a bit too much, focusing more on the gaps between where we should have been and where we were. Though challenging faculty was necessary, as we were hardly reaching our full potential, there is a fine line, depending on the level of change and improvement needed, that must be kept in mind. Looking back at my leadership time, I realize that, although I did thank persons in my annual addresses—indeed I began and ended each speech that way—I did not express sufficient gratitude for the important work of my predecessors or thank the college enough for what it had done to date. It is natural to see oneself bringing forward something new, but anything new is more likely to be accepted if it is seen as building on the past. I asked too often, "What would you change about Notre Dame?" I needed also to be asking, "What do you like most about Notre Dame?" "What are you most proud of when it comes to Notre Dame?" "Tell me a story that exemplifies what is best about Notre Dame."

Over time, I made better use of affirmation and praise: congratulations letters, thank you letters, personal notes of various kinds, impromptu visits to faculty offices, receptions, and dinners of recognition. A phone call or letter or e-mail in response to a major distinction is another strategy. Publicly acknowledging persons is another. One can never give sufficient thanks and recognition, and there is no substitute for thoughtful and well-expressed gratitude from a person in a leadership position. Over time I realized this was no less important than reading documents, studying data, or developing initiatives and policies and was in some respects even more meaningful. Helping people to feel good about their contributions encourages further accomplishments. What motivates many academics more than monetary or other incentives is recognition for the work they have already done and continue to do. People buy into a vision partly by being affirmed for their contributions to that vision. Greatness increases with praise and recognition.

As chairperson at Ohio State, I along with virtually all of my colleagues had problems dealing with one faculty member, who for various reasons seemed unwilling to cooperate in virtually any positive enterprise. Three strategies helped to mitigate the divide. First, our code of conduct became an ideal norm to which one could appeal and which one could use to point out deviations from our agreed-upon norms. Second, I sought to find areas of common interest, for example, the support and common mentoring of a student we shared—in other words, progress through vision and intrinsic motivation. Third, I bent over backward to praise the faculty member's positive achievements publicly. Such praise and gratitude cost nothing and indeed reinforced high standards and fairness.

One way to underline an appealing vision is to develop a success narrative, that is, to draw attention to efforts and achievements that are helping to realize the vision. One must be able to craft such a story for both internal motivation and external marketing, even if the vision needs to retain elements of intrinsic value, independent of its marketability. One hopes that through the acquisition of new resources and consistent devotion to the vision, success will occur, making the narrative ever-more appealing. One wants to see that one's actions are helping to move an institution forward. At Notre Dame, for example, it made a difference that we were able to add, over ten years in the college, more than seventy-five new faculty positions; that annual research funding in the arts, humanities, and social sciences rose tenfold; or that graduating seniors devoted their class gift to undergraduate research. A success narrative lifts morale and contributes to a sense of belonging. Essential is not only that a story be told but that it be meaningfully explained; one goal of such a narrative is to encourage replication and enhancement, and for that one needs not simply a story but reflection on the worthiness of the goal (to reinforce motivation) and successful strategies that have been undertaken (so that paths to replication are evident).

As dean, I saw that it was imperative that we invest in publicizing our academic advances both within and beyond the academy. Whether one looked at teaching innovations, external research dollars, national fellowships, faculty appointments, or virtually any other dimension of our scholarly life, we had a compelling story to tell. Although we still needed to improve in many ways, and although I am cautious about the overly common claim that "we are better than our reputation," there did seem to be some evidence that our reputation did not match the extent of our success. To some degree this was because Notre Dame is not part of an academic consortium and so does not find itself in as many natural venues for sharing advances with others as do our peers. Another challenge, not easy to quantify, was the university's association with athletics and religion, both of which are seen by some as in conflict with academics. Faculty were on board with the idea of investing in public relations because they sensed the gap between our activities and our recognition, and they understood that better recognition meant more qualified students, better colleagues, more resources.

In order to tell our story better, we reallocated funding to invest in web support and college and departmental publications. We hired an outside firm to do a major overhaul of the website, which eventually received several national distinctions. It was fascinating that the consulting firm began with questions about our distinctive vision. Everything else, from audience to design, was to follow from the vision, not the other way around. I was at first surprised, and then impressed, that during the consultants' initial two-day visit, they did not say a word about technology or presentation: all they cared about was understanding the vision we had for the college. Everything else would flow from that.

What I learned over time was the extent to which one needs to identify a target audience, usually one discrete slice of our collective constituency, and to craft a targeted publication. What we had been producing both in the past and during my early years were general publications, which were simply too long. Such publications are rarely read and can border on the unintentionally comic. They invariably end up in the circular file. It was not by chance that our web consultants asked as their second priority question: How would you quantify the ranking and importance of different audiences for your website? Because higher education rankings are not of arts and sciences colleges but of universities overall and departments in particular, we increased the number of departmental newsletters and sought to improve existing ones. We also created DVDs for students and prospective students—on the value of a Notre Dame liberal arts education, undergraduate research opportunities, honors opportunities in the arts and sciences, and opportunities for Asian Americans and students from Asia. We introduced a variety of informational brochures, including a view book on the college for prospective and first-year students. A quarterly e-newsletter sought to reach alumni. We also worked to increase the placement of faculty op-eds in national newspapers and saw modest success in boosting the number of radio and television appearances as well. But it was just a start.

Weaknesses

At the same time that communication is designed to lift spirits and motivate others, one cannot ignore gaps. One of my goals as dean was to address four weaknesses in the college that I had publicly identified—in foreign languages and literatures, the arts, economics, and diversity. Acknowledging weaknesses allows an institution to shape its focus so that it can truly improve; lifts the spirits of those in underdeveloped areas since it indicates an interest in seeing them get better while also putting them on watch by recognizing that as they are now is not good enough; and, perhaps most importantly, allows one to gain credibility with donors and others.

One cannot focus enough, at least in one's own thinking, on what needs to be improved, even if it is in an area that is excellent but could be better still. When I met with students, I always asked them, "If you were in my shoes, what would you change about Notre Dame?" After I gave a lecture in Germany on differences between German and American universities, I was reminded during the discussion by a German professor in the audience that, when he was concluding a visiting semester, I invited him to lunch on one of his final days, took out a pad of paper and a pen, and said, "Now, tell me everything that did not go well during your visit." One becomes better not by glancing past but by understanding one's weaknesses. When I had informal lunches with groups of faculty, I said that I wanted above all to hear what was not going well so that we could work on it. Here, too, I had my pad of paper. I found it advantageous to learn from informal conversations with a range of people. I loved to find out how we could become better and what we should change to ensure that Notre Dame would improve and come closer to realizing its vision.

Much of the Notre Dame culture when I first arrived involved celebrating ourselves as being the best of our kind. We were proud of our distinction, and it was not immediately apparent which universities were in our peer group, which made self-congratulations easier. I adopted a different lens and focused, perhaps too much, on our gaps. The library holdings were too modest, faculty mentoring was haphazard, the standards for promotion and tenure were too low, and some departments were clearly very weak. My desire to name our weaknesses caused much consternation and alienated some faculty members. However, it endeared me with donors, who wanted to see how the institution was wrestling with its challenges. During my initial years, we were so weak in economics that I said I did not want any gifts for that area, as the money would not be well placed. That gave me the credibility to push successfully for gifts to economics some years later once we had established a new trajectory for the department. Afterward, my successor had even greater impact in raising funds for economics.

One strategy is to link investment in, and enthusiasm for, a weak area with vision or other goals. Recognizing the connections between Catholicism and the arts, an area in which we needed to stretch, was not difficult. The history of art is inextricably linked with Catholicism. Further, a defining principle of Catholicism is the belief that the transcendent reveals itself in finite reality; the arts are privileged in this context insofar as they bridge the spiritual and sensuous worlds. Art contributes to the collective identity of a culture, and our reception of earlier artworks links us to previous generations, fostering a community across time, a tradition. Finally, the creation of art builds community: productions and performances in a variety of artistic fields combine creativity with disciplined collaboration and self-transcendence; the various ways in which the arts function as ritual reinforce this sense of community.

One initiative was to announce the Decade of the Arts. The university was planning to open the 150,000-square-foot Marie P. DeBartolo Center for the Performing Arts, home to five cutting-edge performance venues, in the fall of 2004. A development campaign begins with a so-called silent phase; during this period, funds are raised, so that when the campaign is announced, the university can say that it is already so far along. Drawing on this idea, I announced the Decade of the Arts a few years before the facility opened, which gave us more than a decade to focus on advancing the arts. We received a number of gifts: endowments for performance scholarships and student productions, a competitive fund for faculty projects, and endowed chairs (we moved from zero to six chairs in the arts). An initiative in sacred music led to our being able to hire endowed chairs away from Princeton and Yale. One of our film scholars now offers a seminar every summer on teaching film to faculty colleagues outside of film studies, and a new graduate interdisciplinary minor in film studies was introduced. Students responded to our efforts. The number of majors in the arts rose from just over three hundred in 2000 to more than five hundred seven years later. The arts were also invited to play an integrative role, bringing faculty members from a variety of disciplines together for a biennial theater production and conference, with the drama having been read in classes across the university.

Another story woven together with the realization of vision involved our foreign language and literature departments. Given the global dimensions of Catholicism, I was modestly surprised when I arrived to find that the foreign language and literature departments were to some degree service oriented and for the most part lacked the scholarly depth found in other humanities departments. In the next decade the departments transformed themselves. Some of the best faculty hires and strongest promotion-and-tenure cases were in the languages and literatures. We added faculty members in Arabic, Chinese, Irish, Italian, Japanese, Latin, Russian, and Spanish. We began teaching Quechua to advance our study of Latin America, a distinctive strength at Notre Dame. We also saw the introduction and flourishing of Portuguese, which enhanced our connections to Brazil. We began teaching Korean language and culture, partly supported by grants from Korea. Language enrollments grew ahead of the national average, climbing in the final seven years from under four thousand to well over five thousand. Although enrollments rose dramatically in Arabic and Chinese, the overall growth was across languages. Foreign language and literature majors increased from just over three hundred in 2000 to more than six hundred in 2009. We far exceeded national averages in the percentage of students who were enrolled beyond the minimum language requirement. We located funding to send students abroad during the summers for language study, research, internships, and service projects, funding that increased dramatically under my successor. One of the innovations of our newly inaugurated Center for the Study of Languages and Cultures was a peer-tutoring program, which gives beginning and intermediate students a greater opportunity to hear and speak the language and allows advanced students to gain pedagogical experience in helping other students develop their language skills. A new initiative supported faculty in developing their own foreign language competencies for purposes of teaching or scholarship, partly so that they could model the practice for students.

Because Notre Dame had historically privileged the hiring of Catholics, the faculty, overwhelmingly white and male at the senior ranks, was less diverse than its peers. We realized that we could add diversity in personnel and curricula and give minority students faculty role models partly by hiring more internationally. Because Catholics are far more diverse elsewhere, our identity, which had triggered a gap, gave us new opportunities. In placing greater emphasis on diversity, we improved; yet with some groups, such as Africans and African Americans, progress was modest.

In no category were the numbers as high as would have been ideal, but a few factors helped. These included publicly articulating college goals in both female and diversity hiring and reporting on those figures (both for the past year and cumulatively) at the annual spring faculty meeting; ensuring that departments had written policies that outlined strategies and goals with respect to diversity; writing letters to chairpersons in advance of searches about their longer and more recent track records in female and diversity hiring; ensuring that on each search committee, at least one person had the partial task of attending to diversity issues (this was not meant to free others from thinking about the issue but to guarantee that at least one member of the search committee was especially attentive to diversity); encouraging departments not to reduce diversity to a difference maker in otherwise equal cases, but to weigh the positive rationale for diversity (above all the link between diversity and better learning and the value of giving our female and minority students more models in the faculty ranks); requiring a justification whenever a finalist set of candidates did not include a women and a minority (basically explaining why the best candidate in a given category did not make the final cut); offering various hiring incentives that I articulate in greater detail below; introducing a postdoctoral program for African American scholars, some of whom became faculty candidates and faculty members; and discussing and sharing best practices, including being more proactive, at meetings of chairpersons, so that departments searched for applicants and did not simply sift them. We collaborated with admissions on strategies to recruit minority first-year students, as expansion in minority student population helps an institution attract minority faculty members. We also introduced third-party interviews with every faculty member who departed voluntarily, initiated focus groups, and developed a set of action items to enhance the community for women. All of this helped but did not suffice. One of the most sobering experiences for any long-serving dean is to see faculty members one worked hard to recruit and support leave for another university, so everyone has to start all over again. When the departing colleagues are also women or minorities, the frustration is exacerbated. This is one reason why resilience is a sine qua non for a dean. Although female and diversity hiring increased, the issue was not solved in eleven years. Even many years on, an emphasis on hiring African Americans, after tremendous recent success in hiring Latinos, has become central to the current narrative. Challenges that can be solved only over a longer period reinforce the sense that an administrator is simply a brief link in a longer institutional narrative. Of course, such insights can also be helpful for putting oneself in one's place.

The flip side of identifying gaps of one kind or another is articulating high standards, which can be inspiring. One can identify any number of impressive statistics if one has been successful as a dean, but probably the most significant advance one wants to see is not captured by numbers but involves instead widespread recognition of what it takes for a college or university to be great when measured against others of its kind. There is no number that can capture the practice of departments making tough decisions themselves after previously making mistakes or pushing troubled cases along to the dean for a negative vote. We saw a greater willingness on the part of departments to close a faculty search and open it again the next year if an outstanding candidate could not be hired. I suggested colleagues eliminate from their vocabulary the phrase "failed search"; that would apply only if we hired the wrong person, not if we closed a search because we wanted to continue looking for the right person. A recognition and a self-confidence emerged in the college that we were indeed competing for faculty hires and graduate student recruits with the country's best universities, and when one of our colleagues turned down offers from Harvard or Johns Hopkins or the University of Chicago, faculty were eventually no longer surprised—pleased, but not surprised.

Support Structures

Appropriate support structures and incentives help universities to realize a vision. Ideally, vision drives the budget. Support is a kind of communication, a test of the legitimacy of a vision, if you will; support structures and incentives ensure continuity between aspirations and what is necessary to meet those aspirations. Notre Dame moved very quickly from an undergraduate college to an ambitious research university and needed to fill tremendous infrastructure gaps involving the library, sabbaticals, course load, internal research funding, space, computer support, lab technicians, graduate student stipends, and start-up funding. All of those not only enable better work, they make a statement about what the institution values. We had been moving as an institution so quickly that the year before I became dean, some tenure-track faculty were still sharing offices. Also, nonsalary support for research and travel was so sparse as to be laughable. That, too, changed quickly, as supporting the research vision became a priority, and funds must go to priorities. We developed pilot funds for social science faculty to work with students in developing track records that would increase their likelihood of obtaining external funding. When such support is provided, one can expect more.

Fully supporting current faculty may mean fewer new positions, a shift that takes some effort to defend to faculty, who think of positions, what one can count, as a first priority. Such investment includes basic research support for all, additional support for the strongest, and strategies to help those who have fallen behind but are still capable of doing good work. We designed one innovative program, Career Enhancement Grants for Tenured Faculty, to support professional development, so that faculty members who had fallen behind might have a greater chance of getting back on track with their research.

Incentives are a form of communication, which must be complemented by corresponding support structures. A university that wants to see its faculty obtain more grants should have a support office that serves as a clearinghouse for information. Staff members can organize grant writing workshops, determine the range of funding sources, share copies of successful proposals, review drafts, and assist in the preparation of proposal budgets. Our college's office has two purposes: it offers internal seed money in order to help faculty with their research and teaching, and it provides assistance to faculty seeking external funding. Many of the internal grants require that faculty then submit external applications.

If hiring more women is a priority, then a special lecture fund can be designed for women who are early in their careers, thus encouraging departments to nominate pretenure women from other universities to give addresses on campus. Our Rising Scholar Series encouraged departments to nominate pretenure women as well as minorities and Catholics to deliver addresses at Notre Dame.

To send a message about Notre Dame's support for recruiting Catholic faculty members, we created an office to identify the greatest possible number of Catholic scholars of high quality at all ranks and in all disciplines, as well as excellent scholars of the Catholic tradition. The goal was not to load the burden of mission onto another office but to have resources available to help departments. The database, which was eventually expanded university-wide, greatly increased our capacity to identify potential Catholic candidates from around the world.

Support is ideally placed in the hands of chairpersons. One wants to give them options to be creative. One chairperson I reappointed had gaps in two areas: fostering dialogue and supporting mission. I gave the chairperson a significant one-time allocation of cash to focus on improvements in those two areas.

The value of service and leadership can be conveyed through informal and formal support structures. Initiatives in mentoring, including special workshops that introduce a select group of midcareer faculty members to hidden aspects of the institution and various dimensions of leadership, including best practices, are essential in developing future faculty leaders. An enhanced mentoring environment for faculty helps meet a secondary goal of retention.

After a few years, we created a rotating position for an executive fellow, who served for a year as an apprentice in the dean's office. The apprenticeship gave interested tenured professors an opportunity to develop their leadership skills and contribute in diverse ways to the life of the college. The program was designed to mentor future leaders, especially women and minorities, so that there would be a larger pool of qualified candidates to assume leadership positions in the coming years. In addition, we thought it wise to give them opportunities to develop skills and knowledge in advance of assuming formal leadership roles. It has been said that the first few months of an administrative position are a bit like learning to ice skate in full view of one's colleagues. Moreover, we wanted to have as many faculty members as possible, whatever their future administrative trajectories, gain a fuller sense of the ways in which the dean's office operates in seeking to assist departments and faculty members. We also benefited from the perspectives of the fellows as they were integrated into our ongoing work. Finally, if one is confident about the way one's office works, one wants to be transparent and have people in the faculty ranks who can convey to others some sense of the spirit of such an enterprise and its ambitions on behalf of the college's faculty and students.

Courage

Courage is a neglected virtue among academic administrators. Bowen and McPherson note the tendency among academic leaders to be "overly risk-averse" (62). One could, if one wanted to use ideal types, identify three kinds of administrators. First are the many who seek to return as seamlessly as possible to being full-time faculty and therefore avoid alienating their colleagues. They want to be liked. As a result, they may do little to help advance the institution's mission, especially if it involves making potentially unpopular decisions.

Second are those who strive to move onward and upward and thus need to avoid controversy. For this type, a reform that is modest and innocuous so that it will not upset too many persons is preferable to radical change. Such persons do not develop deep attachments to their current institutions. Their formal skills and efficiency tend to operate at a higher level than their interest in, and capability for, articulating vision, not least of all because they often move from institution to institution.

Third are the individuals who serve in administration to make a significant difference and are willing thereby to sacrifice in order to move forward on bold goals. This kind of administrator would not be unhappy to be fired and then return to the faculty ranks. Because leadership is an opportunity to improve a community of learning, such administrators are willing to make difficult decisions, even when situations are complex and there are costs. These scholar-administrators should be particularly fostered. The most likely source of courage in the face of conflict and risk and in the absence of external incentives is deep identification with vision and priorities. Courage is not unrelated to wisdom, for wisdom means having a sense for the whole; when a local weakness is addressed for the sake of a larger community, a difficult individual decision becomes easier. External approbation for administrators tends to be rare, and change may mean long drawn-out encounters. The goal of such an administrator is to embed new policies in the work of the university, so the need for further conflict is diminished. Such change makes the sacrifice worthwhile and means that, once a certain level of work has been accomplished, one can indeed return to the faculty ranks.

Taking lines away from departments, closing programs, splitting mediocre departments, ensuring differential raises, overturning recommendations for insufficiently strong hires and weaker promotion-and-tenure cases, and introducing strategies of accountability such as enrollment management are all examples of decisions that can create vehement resistance but can also help to change a culture.

An example of a difficult decision I found myself embroiled in came in the process of reforming our economics department, which meant confronting decades of entrenched mediocrity. For a number of years, I encouraged change but made little progress. I found myself vetoing prospective hires. The department had by far the lowest ranking among arts and letters departments and had been strongly criticized in three previous external reviews across decades, but nothing had happened. Why? The department had successfully deflected attempts to make it adjust by alluding to its close link with our Catholic mission: mainstream economics, the department argued, was not compatible with Catholic social teaching, so faculty had moved to heterodox economics. I was not moved by the argument for two reasons: first, the Catholic rhetoric had in many ways become a shield to hide mediocre publishing or complete inactivity among a large number of faculty members; second, my own explorations made clear that the leading journals in economics did in fact publish abundantly on social justice issues, but the journals demanded the integration of sophisticated methods. When I was eventually ready to place the department in receivership, essentially taking away, temporarily, its right to govern itself, the provost wanted to protect me from the expected political fallout and proposed instead a blue ribbon committee to assess the situation.

The committee recommended splitting the department in two. Although initially cool on the idea, I was persuaded that this was the best way for a new department to advance unfettered and for different standards to exist within the original cohort, which focused more on political economy. I took the issue to the College Council for an informal advisory vote, which I lost. If we were also to lose the more important university-level vote at the Academic Council, I knew the administration might not push forward with the reform. In advance of that more important vote, I wrote a twenty-page, single-spaced memorandum outlining why we needed to advance in this way. When spelled out in detail and to an audience that was further removed from the local politics, the issues no longer seemed so difficult. The Academic Council voted overwhelmingly in favor of a split. The conflict had seemed intractable, and the number of hours invested in the reform were incalculable. In addition, there were human costs for the persons left behind. I understood why others had not wrestled with the status quo. The situation was so uncommon that at different stages it received not only local but also national press. Two business professors, one in the United States and one in France, alerted to the story through the media, have done research on the puzzles involved, partly on the extent to which distinctive institutions wrestle with external developments and standards (Bouchikhi and Kimberly, "Micro Processes") and partly on the ways in which academic leaders seek to effect change and deal with resistance (Bouchikhi and Kimberly, "Subversion from the Top").

The transformation was significant and included radically improved faculty hires; more rigorous curricula; far higher student numbers; and, in the wake of reforms, tremendous support from donors and the central university, which targeted the department for selective excellence funding. The department's 2014 external review opened with these lines: "What has happened to Economics at Notre Dame since the current department was created in 2003 is a minor miracle . . . The trajectory of growth and improvement exceeds even the most optimistic forecasts from the early 2000s. The complete rebuild of an Economics Department, essentially from scratch, in one decade is virtually unprecedented in the profession—and doing this with a plan so coherent with the University's mission makes the accomplishment all the more spectacular" (Abowd, Hotz, and Ramey 1). The department has been able to integrate sophisticated theoretical and econometric techniques with a principled focus on social justice issues. Today economics is the largest major and arguably Notre Dame's greatest overall success story in recent decades.

In order to be willing to take hits, including being willing to be sacked, a senior administrator seeking significant change needs a continuing profile as a scholar-teacher. The faculty activity ensures that one can act in a principled way and not make decisions with thoughts about preserving one's administrative tenure or enhancing one's administrative options. One must be willing to make the right decisions, even if they exhaust political capital or have other troublesome consequences.

Effective leadership depends also on timing. On the one hand, one may or may not be the right person for the time. One might be lucky. On the other hand, timing is a deeper puzzle that is not unrelated to courage as well as discernment: one must know when one has enough political capital to move ahead, even against resistance, and when to wait for another opportunity, an insight that reaches back to Plato's *Laches*. A related piece of advice I received from an associate dean when I had just become chairperson was never to take an important vote when the outcome was not already certain. I did not always follow the advice, but it underscores the value of knowledge and of timing. In David Lynch's *The Elephant Man*, as the governing board of the London Hospital is about to vote on whether or not to continue to offer John Merrick, who had incurable severe deformities, a home (a proposal to which there is unambiguous opposition), Alexandria, the Princess of Wales, arrives and reads a communication from Queen Victoria commending the hospital for its charitable face, thanking its leaders for their kindness in providing Merrick a home, and counting on them to continue to do "the Christian thing." The board then votes in the presence of the princess, winning a positive vote even from the board member who had just previously expressed his "unshakable" opposition.

Social and Emotional Elements

The intrinsic motivation associated with a compelling vision should be reinforced by social and emotional dimensions, including a strong sense of community. Working at a university is not only an intellectual matter. Ideas are embodied. We are social beings. Personal relationships play a role in any sense of collective identity and in any complex organization where any one person is dependent on others for success.

The best way to undertake change is to emphasize the extent to which it is already embedded within the (best of the) culture and history of the institution. I realized this only after stepping on many toes. I had radically underappreciated the importance of the social and emotional elements of change. I was considered an outsider, having been at the university only one semester before becoming dean, with lots of new ideas, some of them more common at public universities, such as differential salary adjustments and greater accountability. That was an unwelcome combination. The larger a university's ambitions and the deeper the sense of tradition and stability, the greater the importance of the social fabric, since change threatens the stability of what is and has been. Because intrinsic motivation comes not only from vision but also from a sense of community and belonging and from being able to contribute to the whole, one needs to think of strategies to embed change within continuity and collegiality. In the end, this contributes to the efficacy of intrinsic motivation.

Meals and receptions with faculty members and donors occupy a remarkable percentage of an administrator's time, not the ideal outlet for faculty, who prefer more than distraction and chitchat. At a breakfast session for new faculty, my predecessor as dean introduced his leadership team. He spoke of the "working deans," the associate deans responsible for budget, advising, and research. He said that the term had been introduced to him when he arrived. Since they were the working deans, he wondered what kind of dean he might be. He looked down at his belly and said that over time, after attending all of these receptions and meals, he had realized he was the "eating dean."

In my introduction I shared the story of the occasional brief birthday celebrations in the dean's office. These were initiated by a senior staff member, who was kind enough to bake delicious cakes for each event. When she left the university, I told our senior staff person that we should probably eliminate these ten-to-fifteen-minute celebrations instead of buying cakes. I was always looking for ways to gain time, it wasn't exactly healthy for me to eat cake at midmorning or midafternoon, and, unlike one of the associate deans who always set her cake aside for later, I had no power to resist. There was a polite revolt after I had made my decision, which I then reversed: these were the only times, the staff told me, when we were all together, and being with me and the others meant something to them! When I told my successor this story, so that he would not make the same mistake, he laughed and told me that if I had been more conversant with popular culture, I would have known this was a bad idea. *The Office*, he said, had an episode on just this topic; you don't eliminate birthday celebrations!

A leader can help ensure a meaningful social and emotional fabric by being cheerful and resilient and conveying a sense of optimism, as the tone of the college often comes from the infectious attitudes of its leader; ideally this involves enthusiasm and good cheer. Over time

I unconsciously developed a recurring response whenever someone, in greeting me, asked how I was. The response was "Great!" I somehow intuitively sensed the need to convey and embody enthusiasm, and that automatic response has tended to stay with me even today. When one has an administrative role, one encounters an insider's perspective on problems that could in principle elicit cynicism, and this temptation needs to be avoided. Good cheer and laughter are essential. One of our best chairpersons survived only a few years, partly because he could not gain distance from his work; the job, which he did well, bothered and consumed him. Laughter allows an administrator not only to process the absurdities one sometimes encounters but also to foster community and emotional bonds.

I engaged the communal and social dimension also through open faculty meetings, special events, receptions, regular lunches, meetings with departments, and talking with colleagues about teaching or research. Getting out of the office, so as to have casual human contact, to listen and be informed, was important. Contact in the field also helps to bridge difficult situations and conflicts. One cannot solve problems as a stranger; one must build relationships first. Even brief conversations can help to build bonds.

What emerges and becomes prominent in such an environment is trust. Trust begins with respect, recognizing the valuable gifts and contributions of everyone. Trust is strengthened if one knows where people stand and if communication is effective. If faculty members know what the priorities are, whether they meet them or not, they are more likely to trust administrators (because of transparency and grounded decisions). Without truth you can't have trust. There is thus both an intrinsic and an extrinsic reason to communicate and to communicate well. It is good for morale, which itself is both an end and a means (to fostering better work down the road). One can take it further. Failed university presidencies are often the result of a president's introducing change and reform without also creating trust through one strategy or another, be it exhibiting respect for the distinctive nature of the institution, building relationships with faculty members and students, or articulating a clear and compelling vision along with corresponding goals and expectations.

When I asked one of my media-savvy colleagues how to prepare for a *Nightline* television interview on a moral and political topic that was complex and nuanced, he said, decide what message you want to convey, condense it to two or three sentences, ignore the questions, and simply repeat that message again and again. I had developed a reputation for listening carefully to every question and expressing detailed interest in the full range of activities in the college and the varied and nuanced concerns of faculty members, even when I disagreed with them, in short, for speaking honestly and with knowledgeable detail. I was simply incapable of changing my ways and adopting the recommendation, so I struggled greatly with the television interview, but I was reminded of the value of my modus operandi for the different setting of faculty administrator.

Trust is especially needed whenever there is change and unease. It can come from many sources beyond vision and relationships. Just as a well-grounded narrative of success inspires trust and confidence, so too does increased decentralization, matched of course with an appropriate level of accountability, and having as leaders academics who understand the university's higher purpose. Trust is further nurtured by fairness. Being sufficiently visible is also important; people trust those they see and communicate with more frequently. The blossom of common purpose and trust is friendship, which may begin in an atmosphere of mutual utility and cooperation but can be reinforced by common purpose and values.

Although I struggled early on, partly by being extremely ambitious for the institution, which triggered some resistance, and partly by underestimating the social dimension, when I stepped down there was a truly joyful reception—as much like a wedding reception as a retirement party. It may be self-deception, but my sense was that there was more gratitude for what had been accomplished than for my leaving office. How is it that things seemed to turn so remarkably? First, we developed together a success narrative, certainly helped by the vision and by good decisions; things were better in almost every respect. Second, over time people saw that my tough decisions were not about me but about wanting to see the institution reach its highest potential. Third, I became better at communicating and at the social dimensions of leadership, including listening and thanking. Fourth, I was stepping down, which meant to some that I was no longer on the dark side and to others that my motivation had indeed been genuine: I had assumed a role that needed to be done and then instead of looking for more power was moving back to the teaching and research that I had partially relinquished as dean.

That week there was a reception not only with faculty but also with about sixty donors, who traveled from across the country to participate. The morning of the first reception, I asked my wife at breakfast, "In your wildest dreams did you ever imagine that I would be dean for over a decade and that there would be celebrations of this kind for my contributions to Notre Dame?" She looked up from her coffee and said, "Mark, you're not even in my wildest dreams." Among the roles one's family plays is keeping one grounded.

It is of course essential not to stay in office too long, independently of one's success. One must know when to step down. There is the story of the new dean who bids farewell to his predecessor. The new dean asks if the outgoing dean has any advice to offer. The outgoing dean says, "Yes, I have prepared two envelopes and left them for you in the desk drawer. You will see that they are numbered 1 and 2. Do not open them until you find yourself in a real crisis for which there is no good solution. When that happens, and it will, open the first envelope and do what it says." "Thanks," the new dean replied, "but what about the second envelope?" "Follow the same pattern there," he says. "Wait until your second impossible crisis, then open it, and follow the instructions inside it." The new dean found the two envelopes and kept them carefully sealed until the day he found himself in an impossible situation. Remembering his predecessor's instructions, he opened the first envelope. Written on a small sheet of paper were the words, "Blame me." The new dean did as he was directed, was excused for the mess he had gotten himself into, and went about the business of the college. Then some years later, he again encountered an insoluble problem and finally, hoping against hope, opened the second envelope. On the enclosed sheet were three words: "Prepare two envelopes."

CHAPTER FOUR

Resources, or What a University Needs Besides People and Ideas

It is said that the core of a university is its faculty. While that is at some level true, one could also advance the argument that the core of a university is its students. Why? Faculty usually choose to teach at the university with the best students, and it is above all the former students, the alumni, who, on the basis of their positive experiences, give resources back to the university, which allows it to hire the best faculty, who in turn attract the best students. If universities in other countries want to cultivate the kinds of resources associated with American universities, they will need to create a university culture and ethos whereby students and alumni identify with their institutions and seek to enhance them as communities of learning. Emotional identification with the institution becomes important in this context.

The distinction of the American system is the combination of federal aid (for research and tuition), tuition (which, though widespread in other countries, is hardly universal), and fund raising. Although many would justly argue that education is a public good, that it should be available to all and benefits all, the private benefits are also apparent, and individuals should be asked to help subsidize the costs. There is a clear tendency internationally toward tuition and higher fees (Johnstone and Marcucci 102–28). In countries without tuition, some redistribution of money is made from the poorer classes, who take less advantage of the university, to the wealthier classes, who partake more readily of university education and also benefit in terms of higher income, social prestige, and lower chances of unemployment. With state support ubiquitous and tuition widespread, development is now the most distinctively American piece of the funding puzzle. A recent survey indicates that "increased fund raising" is far and away the most widely undertaken action to reduce costs to students (*Chronicle of Higher Educ.*, "What Presidents Think" 25). Presidents are engaged more with fund raising on a daily basis than any other activity (22).

Arguably the greatest challenge to universities across the globe is inadequate funding, which has a trigger effect in multiple areas, including student–faculty ratios and their resulting effect on quality of learning. Funds affect everything from hiring the best faculty to ensuring access for underprivileged students. The most important factor in ensuring that students complete their doctoral studies, more important even than mentoring and advising, is financial support (Council of Graduate Schools, *Ph.D. Completion* 14–15). Although the United States and a few other countries stand well above others in average funding per student, the situation in the United States is various. Funding universities through a variety of sources instead of through the state alone, as many other countries do, results in individual universities having extremely diverse resources. The Council for Aid to Education has noted that 28.7 percent of the funds raised for higher education in 2015 went to just twenty institutions. Many colleges struggle greatly, not least of all in providing adequate support to poorly prepared students (Bok, *Higher Education* 405). Moreover, despite the American advantage in resources overall and the remarkable advantages enjoyed by some, there is scarcely an institution where administrators and faculty do not lament inadequate funds.

Development

In order to compete, a university needs resources, above all donations. To be in a position to raise funds, a university must do the following. First, it must have a compelling story and the leadership and strategies to tell that story. It must not only have a distinctive vision, it must communicate the vision and story well, through various media as well as through the efforts of academic leaders and development personnel. "Individuals do not give to needs. They give to dreams and dazzling visions" (Panas 172). Indeed, surveys show that "belief in the mission of the institution" is far and away the most compelling reason for a gift, a statement that holds true for both average and higher givers (231).

Part of having a story to tell donors is knowing the institution's distinctive vision and priorities and then engaging donors with those priorities, which means being able to explicate those priorities, that is, describe how the gift will make a difference—in the lives of students, the discovery of knowledge, addressing important problems, the advancement of mission, and so forth—and how the effects of that gift will be measured, that is, how we will know whether and how well we are succeeding. Development personnel are not always the best people to make the detailed and passionate case for priorities; for that one needs academic leaders and faculty members, though not all faculty members know how to speak effectively to donors.

One could say that one should try to "guide" donors to priorities, but the verb is not quite correct in two ways: for one thing, the priorities should already be visible to donors, so that one doesn't need so much to guide them as to draw attention to what is already consistently front and center; and for another, one wants to reach a place where, after explaining various aspects of the university's aspirations, one hears the donor say, "I would like to fund that." Instead of suggesting a project to the donor, the donor sees it as his or her own idea. In other words, there must be reciprocity, subtlety, and a strong desire to have the donor take ownership of the gift, to make the project his or her own but still to have it reflect a university priority. Challenges arise when donors want to make restricted gifts in areas outside the university's highest priorities, though a collaboration of university vision and donor interest can also lead to appealing advances and is likely to engage donors even more. Still, it is absolutely essential that mission drive gifts and not vice versa.

Second, the university must develop and cultivate friends, contacts who are potential donors: "friend raising comes before fund raising" is a common saying. One cannot stress enough how important relationships are to fund raising, which is why fund raising is so time consuming, partly for staff but also for academic leaders, since donors want to be in touch with the leaders. As with great teaching, there is no substitute for one-on-one relationships. Basically, fund raising boils down to vision, relationships, and some commonsense attention to details. The core of any donor base consists of those graduates who have an affective relationship to the college, who experienced a student-centered environment while they were students. Others include parents of prospective, current, or former students; persons in the area who want to see the local university flourish; and persons or foundations interested in the distinctive features of the university or specific kinds of projects.

Because developing relationships before an actual request for resources is made is essential, patience is demanded. The quality of the undergraduate experience is the first trigger to cultivating a gift some thirty to fifty years later. Donors are commonly developed over years, with an ambitious request emerging only after long periods of contact and multiple smaller gifts, although all kinds of slow and rapid developments occur. I once received a short e-mail from an alumnus who had never contacted me before but offered to contribute $100,000 to a project that he had read about in a university publication and which resonated deeply with him.

Third, one must have a professional development staff who can cultivate relations and address the full range of tasks involved in fund raising. One needs to do research on the funding capacities of donors, develop relations with them, and then be willing to ask for a gift, something that not all persons, and certainly not all academics, are capable of doing or doing well. Also, one needs to steward donors by showing them the ways in which their giving has made a difference and will continue to make a difference. Stewardship, or thanking and staying in touch with donors, is not only the right thing to do, it cultivates future giving.

A challenge in fund raising is the mobility of the workforce, as both administrators and development officers change institutions more quickly than donors or alumni shift their loyalties. Thus, it is important to have enough distinction and financial support at one's institution to cultivate loyalty and longevity. A successful strategy for Notre Dame has been to hire its own loyal graduates for many, if not a majority, of its development positions. One looks in any case for persons who are both entrepreneurs and team players, as both qualities are essential and not always found together.

Finally, one needs a high number of volunteers who are willing to assist by organizing or hosting events, providing contacts or access to other donors, soliciting gifts together with the academic leadership and the development team, and of course giving leadership gifts themselves.

There are essentially two models for organizing a development effort: a centralized option, with development staff in a central university office, or a decentralized option, with development staff working directly for each dean. The decentralized model encourages entrepreneurship and has built-in incentives—you keep the money that you are able to raise. However, it means that deans are busy not only closing the deal with donors but also finding and courting them, which curtails their focus on academic matters and can make this administrative position less appealing to faculty members. Advantages of the centralized model include its being more efficient for academic leaders, its avoidance of any fragmentation of vision, and its being able to avoid duplication. You don't want a donor to receive in the same week solicitations from four different parts of the university, as once happened to an Ohio State donor, the director of a major bank, who told me the story over lunch one day. He packed them up in one large envelope, wrote a brisk note, "Set your own priorities!" and sent the package off to the president. Centralization also allows the university to set priorities at a higher level, and it encourages cooperative training. Advantages of the two can be realized by a hybrid model, that is, having a primarily centralized office but with development staff who are also embedded in the colleges and have direct access to the faculty and the deans and deeper insight into academic priorities and successes.

Innovative at Notre Dame was the creation of a central office for principal gifts, staffed by a small number of persons who seek gifts of $5 million or more. Although having a wide base is important, a few very large gifts can make all the difference, especially when some needs, such as capital projects, are extremely expensive. Although education, including all levels, receives only 14 percent of giving in the United States, larger gifts go disproportionately to higher education (Center on Philanthropy 6, 58). Even without huge gifts, one can reach one's goals much faster with gifts of $5–10 million or above. In its campaign that concluded in 2001,

Notre Dame had five gifts of $10 million or more; in its most recent campaign, which concluded in 2011, it had thirty-seven such gifts. This was partly the result of renewed energy being placed on principal gifts.

An appealing event that regularly occurs at Notre Dame is the so-called Fly-In Weekend, attended by six to nine couples who have giving potential of at least $1 million or more, likely at the level of a principal gift, but who have yet to develop a significant relationship with the university. They spend intensive time with the president, provost, executive vice president, director of development, and selected others. Afterward they know they will receive a visit from someone in development asking them if they would like to make a significant contribution. This is a great way to jump-start a relationship with a potential major donor.

Several persons in development devote their time to honoring previous donors with annual reports, which contain both financial and academic information, and with appropriate celebrations or ceremonies, such as when an endowed chair is named. Donor services also involve responding to a wide array of donor requests, from having a faculty member meet with a prospective student the donor knows well to obtaining tickets for athletic events. Stewardship is also the engine that helps to facilitate thank you notes from scholarship students to their donors; that personal touch makes all the difference. When I stepped down as dean, a group of donors established an endowment in my name that supports undergraduate research, which was my top priority at the time; we had moved from having less than $5,000 for undergraduate research in my first year to over $200,000 in each of my final two years. Faculty members also established an endowment in my name, to support undergraduate study abroad, which recognized both a priority of mine as dean and my status as a returning faculty member in German. The total of the two endowments is over $1 million, and each year I receive letters from students explaining what they are doing and how the support has advanced their intellectual development. Such notes motivate further giving. Stewardship works closely with marketing in preparing occasional booklets, for example, of endowed chairs, which highlight both the donor and the chair holder.

Deans tend to be very active in development. At many universities, an appointed group of donors—at Notre Dame these are called advisory councils—come to campus once or twice a year to meet with the deans.

These weekends provide a welcome venue for donors to find a window onto the university, hear from its leaders, and meet students and faculty. At Notre Dame over six hundred people are on advisory councils for the various colleges and institutes. They stay connected with the university through their visits and other communications. Advisory council members are chosen on the basis of their competence and willingness to serve as mentors to members of the administration, faculty, and students; their expertise in vital areas, such as international affairs or media; their ability to serve as representatives of the university in their communities; their capability to help members of the university develop connections and access; and above all their financial support. Most individuals are invited to join a council after they have already demonstrated a significant commitment to the university through their contributions.

Part of the agenda at meetings is social and part is informative, but since the donors are all successful persons, I made an effort to move away from a dog-and-pony show to engage them on substantive issues. I tried always to have discussion groups to consider various issues, such as addressing challenges in faculty retention, motivating midcareer faculty members, locating summer internships, ensuring jobs for graduating seniors, marketing the college, reducing majors in business, expanding international opportunities for students, increasing student participation in arts events, evaluating teaching effectiveness, and developing a strategic plan. Some of their suggestions were quite good. Some were less productive, for example, the suggestion that a less productive faculty member might spend a day watching what a more productive faculty member does.

We always tried to bring donors into contact with students. When I was jokingly accused of preselecting the brightest and best students, I specifically asked my associate dean to gather a random sampling. The advisory council met with students in focus groups to discuss what was and was not working well in teaching, mentoring, and learning. One student said that he was planning to transfer, which at first sounded worse than it actually was: He wanted to go to Columbia to be in New York City. But the accusation of preselecting was never made again. I also had the council spend time with a cross section of faculty members. In one case two faculty members went at each other quite vociferously. In another, a faculty member handed all council members his solicitation for funding to support his area of research. They gained a modest window onto my daily routine.

At Notre Dame, the advisory councils usually come to campus for a home football game, which makes the visit attractive to them for an additional reason. When I hosted Notre Dame's Advisory Council for the Performing Arts in advance of our hiring an inaugural director, I had the advisory council members meet on campus in the winter and spring when major performances were taking place. After I passed the baton, I discovered, partly to my surprise, partly not to my surprise, that members had asked to meet instead over a fall football weekend.

The campus visits are an effective way to develop relations with key donors. The terms are renewable, in most cases on the basis of giving, although some persons might be there for their breadth of knowledge, their special contacts, or their diversity. Since it is awkward to retire someone whose current giving is modest but whose planned giving could be significant, the best strategy is to have term limits, so that one must sit out for a year, after which an invitation for another term might be extended. Being removed based on statute is better than by decision.

As a result of occasional drops in endowment, many American universities have had to endure cuts. Notre Dame has been unusual in being exempt from such cuts; when other universities were desperately cutting in the wake of the Great Recession of 2008, we received budgetary increases. How could that be? Beyond having had a superb investment track record, Notre Dame has traditionally had a very low endowment payout, much closer to 4 percent than 6 percent. When the endowment grew very rapidly, the endowment payout was for a brief time below even 3 percent (in order not to increase the payout too dramatically from one year to the next, since unexpected rapid increases did not always harmonize with good long-range planning). The modest payout was of course not publicized, but I discovered it when I was surprised how little payout I was receiving from new endowed chairs. Although I complained at the time about how much of the college's annual rate funding I had to invest to compensate for the modest payout, the prudent policy turned out to be fortunate. Also, as I looked more closely at the dynamics of fund raising and the endowment, I grasped with some initial surprise that a superb investment office, with a good base, can make more money in a year than even a successful development staff; investment is at least as important as fund raising.

Funded and Unfunded Priorities

Fund raising is a continuous activity. Still, every seven to ten years a university embarks on a campaign, with a specific fund-raising goal and usually a number of priorities or set targets such as x amount for financial aid, y amount for new endowed chairs, z amount for new buildings, and so on. The campaign is an intensive effort to raise extraordinary gifts during a defined period for specific needs central to the mission. In advance of the campaign, the campus community discusses and establishes priorities in light of its overarching mission and goals and undertakes a feasibility study, the latter designed to determine the institution's overall potential for raising funds; the viability of specific projects; and the internal costs, in both time and money, of mounting the campaign. One needs to set a goal that will make a difference but is also doable. A reasonable initial estimate for a seven-year campaign is a figure that is at least ten times what annual giving has been in the past. If one does not meet the goal, as happened at the University of Virginia (which at the end of 2011 fell short of its $3 billion goal), one can extend the deadline until the goal is reached. However, one wants to pick a realistic goal. By its initial deadline, Virginia had raised $2.6 billion, a truly remarkable amount that will make a huge difference in the life of the university, now and for generations to come, but at the time of the announcement, the media wanted to talk only about how the university had failed to reach its goal.

For a campaign to be successful, one needs to ensure superb teamwork among the president and other academic leaders, the development professionals, and volunteers. Further, one needs excellent research, including identifying potential nonalumni donors; superb record keeping; mass mailings, increasingly in the form of e-mails, with web links; personal visits with key potential donors; and regional alumni events. As soon as the goals and priorities are set, one begins raising funds from key donors during the campaign's silent phase. Then with great fanfare and orchestrated events at multiple locations, the university announces the campaign, both a target figure, with broad categories, and an end date.

Simultaneously, one announces that one has already raised a certain percentage of the funding. To give the campaign a focus in the minds of its supporters, it usually has a name. Recent Notre Dame campaigns were called "Generations," so as to stress continuity, tradition, and intergenerational support, and "The Spirit of Notre Dame," which took advantage of the dual meaning of spirit as intellectual and spiritual, captured the distinctive campus ethos, and evoked connotations of the enthusiasm vibrant in the athletic culture, where one also speaks of the spirit of Notre Dame.

One wants to have three results, beginning with widespread participation. A high percentage of alumni donating reinforces the strong sense of community and teamwork and signals widespread approval of the educational experience. Giving each year, even in smaller amounts, is a great way to develop a habit of giving that could turn into larger gifts over time. A sign of future substantial giving at the level of principal gifts, for example, is the number of $1 million gifts given by persons under a certain age.

Second, one wants to bring in significant resources, which usually means a certain number of very large gifts. Previously, development personnel used to speak of an 80/20 rule, that is, about 80 percent of the resources would come from 20 percent of the contributors. In recent decades, one tends to speak of a 90/10 rule, with 90 percent of the resources coming from 10 percent of the contributors (Worth 12). Even that figure can underestimate the power of a smaller number of significant gifts. Frank Rhodes and Inge Reichenbach tell the story that in one campaign at Cornell University, fewer than 0.5 percent of the donors gave 60 percent of the funds, fewer than 2 percent gave 83 percent, and fewer than 3.8 percent gave 90 percent or $1.356 billion of the total amount raised (7). Thus one understands the rationale behind an office dedicated to principal gifts. The Cornell situation is not unique. In Notre Dame's last campaign, advisory council members, some 600 of them, gave 32 percent of the dollars. The board of trustees, some 60 members, gave 16 percent of the funding. Thus 48 percent or nearly half of the campaign, almost $1 billion, was raised by these 660 people. In the seven years of the campaign, there were approximately 130,000 donors. Of these, 1.6 percent gave 84 percent of the total. To be included in that 1.6 percent group of 2,000, one had to give $100,000 or more. A university with many

$100 million gifts along with additional very large gifts might easily discover that less than 1 percent of the donor base has given 90 percent or more of the gifts.

Third, one wants to find a match between the funding given and the goals articulated. Reports should be prepared on the extent to which the funding matches the priorities, assuming they are still relevant years later. Donors sometimes want to give to their preferences instead of to the university's priorities, and there should be an incentive to move donors to university goals, so that these are not left unfunded. The impetus for oversight must come from the academic core, for the development staff tends to evaluate itself on numbers alone and not on its ability to match donors with priorities.

The strategic plan, though it is often preparatory to it, is not one and the same as the campaign. These are linked insofar as the strategic plan often identifies priorities that are to be funded by the campaign; so the campaign has not simply a dollar figure but specific goals, some of which should be undesignated to allow flexibility for future priorities. The two are different insofar as much of what happens as a result of a strategic plan can and should occur without additional funding.

I can recall advancing a priority at Ohio State without additional funding and without reallocating dollars. We wanted to address a gap between our vision of preparing excellent teachers and the reality of their gaining pedagogical experience only in beginning and intermediate language classes. In our new graduate teaching apprenticeship program, graduate students worked with a faculty member in an advanced undergraduate language, literature, or culture class, studying the material as well as the pedagogical principles employed and taking over at least one class session in the course of the quarter. Students arranged to work with material in which they were becoming experts or with material that was not frequently offered at the graduate level but was of interest to them. The apprenticeship program fostered close interaction between faculty members and graduate students even during terms when faculty members were not directly involved in the teaching of graduate courses, and it helped break down a common schism between research mentors and teaching mentors. The apprenticeship did not require extra funding, for it represented course work that was independent of the student's assignment as a teaching or research associate.

To develop a strategic plan, four sets of questions are essential. First, what do we want to become? What is our ideal vision of ourselves? Second, where are we now? What are our current strengths and weaknesses? What are our current challenges and opportunities? Third, what strategies can help bridge the gap? Fourth, how will we measure success? Although traditionally a strategic plan was written once per decade, the pace of competition and change has created a culture where strategic planning is virtually constant.

Vision is renewed whenever a strategic plan is formulated. Such planning begins with a robust discussion of ambitions and aspirations, followed by difficult decisions about which aspirations are to become priorities, translating those aspirations into measurable goals, and developing initiatives to achieve them, including recognizing and working through barriers to the aspirations. Such a process ideally involves the full community in conversations of one kind or another, even if the university's leadership will need to set the final priorities.

In developing such a plan, one seeks to identify several (ideally interconnected) areas of academic focus. Criteria can be established for these foci. For example, they should allow a university to address a significant and objective problem, as some topics are simply more important than others; should resonate well with the university's distinctive mission and reinforce it; and, related to the first two, should build on existing strengths, thereby allowing a university to leverage what it already does well.

Strategic planning needs to be dynamic to be able to adjust to unexpected circumstances and changes among key personnel. At the same time, goals should not be relinquished simply for lack of attention to fund-raising success. Accountability in fund raising is necessary but not always practiced. Because development offices like to create success narratives and compete with one another as well as with their own previous track records, they tend to focus on participation rates and total dollars. The university needs, however, to be honest with itself. If a campaign reaches its overarching dollar figure but not the specific goals that determined the figure, then it needs to ask whether the goals have changed (presumably yes to some degree) or whether some pressing goals have not yet been met (also likely). If a specific campaign goal has not been met, but a total dollar figure has been, then it makes sense to reaffirm that specific goal to current donors. Rhetoric that simply implies the goals have been met gives evidence of insufficient accountability.

Working with Donors

Donors, who for the most part are alumni or parents, are especially eager to support scholarships. That is wonderful for many reasons. Still, the challenge exists to get them excited about other needs, but that can be done. For example, donors at Notre Dame have been very enthusiastic about undergraduate research funds, especially when the donors hear directly from students about their experiences. Undergraduate research creates a nice bridge between the undergraduate college and the research university.

Notre Dame has an office that provides infrastructure support for faculty applying for competitive external grants. Donors, who are often in business, understand the value of ensuring advantageous proposals that will be sifted in competition with the best in the country or the world. As a result, when it was initially proposed, this office not surprisingly received significant funding from donors.

Research on donor potential is part science and part art. The following two stories indicate that one can shoot both too low and too high. At Notre Dame, a donor funded some activities in a particular area with one-time money. A graduate of the university, he had potential to give considerably more. One of the top development people went to his home to ask if he could stretch from his one-time donation of around $50,000 to a gift of $1 million. The donor said, no, he would not give $1 million, but he would give $5 million. Another donor might have given the lesser amount, and the university may never have known about the lost opportunity. Over time, as the relationship continued, the donor gave more than $50 million. In another case, I was involved with development in approaching a donor for a gift of $3 million. The donor was a bit taken aback. Clearly, it was beyond his intentions. He ended up giving $500,000 for a different purpose. To ask for too little is to lose out on opportunities. To ask for too much, without a back-up proposal for a lesser amount, which, however, one does not want to introduce too quickly, is to risk straining relations with the donor. A nice metaphor for the prelude to an "ask" is an accordion, which one can stretch wider or contract, depending on what develops in a conversation or a series of conversations. Donor giving is complex because it is a function of multiple variables: What is the donor's level of wealth or capacity? What is the donor's level of generosity in general? What other nonprofit entities have a claim on this donor? What is the donor's (and the donor's family's) emotional connection to the institution and to the particular project or set of projects placed before the donor? What does the donor currently think of the university's leadership and trajectory? It is not always clear that the donor has, in advance of an ask, clear answers in his or her mind. One wise donor would listen each fall to what I said was my highest priority; then within a week a substantial check of $100,000 to $300,000 would arrive. He was always ahead of the ask and able to give at the level that was most comfortable to him.

Some donors want to fund a building with his or her name or the name of a loved one or favorite teacher or administrator on it. One donor, who was weighing whether to support a building or a major academic program, suggested that after several centuries a building might need to be replaced, but if one endows a program, it lasts in perpetuity. After making his gift, he stated, "I wanted to be able to do something that would allow students to take a piece of it away with them. Buildings you leave behind. But the idea of a program that could grow, evolve, and have an impact on the lives of students appealed to me."

When one seeks funds for endowed chairs, which are a priority for any university, a few points are easily made. Academic excellence comes primarily through chairs. Chairs also reduce the student–faculty ratio; students learn more in a student-centered environment, that is, in small discussion classes (for which one needs a larger faculty size) and through independent research projects (with eminent professors). Chairs can be in areas of particular interest to the institution or the donor. Chair endowments provide not only salary but also extra support, so that chairpersons can pursue their work more effectively. At Notre Dame we were able to state that all endowed chairs teach not only graduate students but also undergraduates and that student evaluations of teaching rose in tandem with increased research activity. Hiring stronger researchers did not result in lower student evaluations; on the contrary. Also, some chairs have gone on to become program builders and chairpersons. When I arrived as dean, the most common rank among department chairpersons was associate professor. Toward the end of my term, the most common rank was endowed chair.

Offices of development find that mission constitutes more of an opportunity than a challenge, as donors are generally attracted to a distinctive identity. Indeed, many donors want to give specifically to a university's distinction, so, for example, at Notre Dame we have had donors give endowed chairs for faculty members who are Catholic or for faculty members of another or no faith who work in fields, such as religious history, sacred music, the sociology of religion, or religion and literature, that are central to our mission.

Telling stories of current endowed chairs helps. Especially appealing at Notre Dame were stories of hiring faculty, especially mission faculty, from higher-ranking universities, which reinforced the idea that distinction indirectly strengthens academic quality. I mentioned earlier that donors want to hear an honest assessment of weaknesses. They want candor, and they want to know that a plan for improvement is in place, but that is a double-edged sword. Donors also want to be part of a success narrative, so such stories, especially when told in the faculty member's own words, can be hugely compelling.

The pricing of a chair is an interesting puzzle. If the endowment payout for a chair were to fund the position fully, the endowment would need to be in the range of $5 million or more: at a 4 percent payout, that would cover a salary of $150,000, with benefits at 25 percent or $37,500, plus a discretionary account of $10,000 to $15,000 to support research, travel, and so forth. However, $5 million is a significant gift, and not all donors can reach that high. Thus one must become creative. Here are four options we pursued:

- Fund a chair at $3 million but recognize that the dean needs to harness other funds from the reallocation of the college budget that is undertaken every year to advance priorities. If, for example, the dean were to replace a departing or retiring senior person with a junior person, then money would become available and one could accept a chair without full funding.
- Offer a rotating junior chair, that is, a named position for an assistant professor. Advantages include the unusual nature of such a chair and the prestige thus accorded a junior appointment, which makes the

university more competitive in hiring; having the freedom to rotate the chair every three years to another new hire or someone the university is trying to support or retain; and the ability of many more donors to give smaller amounts. At Notre Dame, I could offer to fund junior chairs at $1.5 million. This was partly because salaries are lower in the arts, humanities, and social sciences than in other fields and partly because the large size of the College of Arts and Letters, which accounts for half of the university's faculty positions, permitted me to do more with internal reallocation than my five counterparts, who collectively had about as many faculty positions as I did. As a result, we had much more success establishing new endowed chairs than the other colleges.

- Locate two donors and give the chair a hyphenated name. Over time the chair will outstrip inflation and become large enough to be split, thus creating two chairs, each with its own name. Obviously one doesn't raise the possibility of a split with a donor who can fund the whole cost!

- Fund a chair with a combination of expendable resources and endowment. For example, a donor was able to give a $1.5 million chair but needed ten years to do so. The plan was for him to give us $150,000 a year for ten years. I suggested that if he could give an additional $60,000 per year in expendable dollars (the equivalent of a 4 percent payout on $1.5 million), I could hire someone immediately, thus allowing him to enjoy having realized a chair right away. There is of course the risk that such donors will not pay the full amount, but that is unlikely if one has done the research and keeps the donors enthusiastic and they do not run into unexpected financial difficulties. If they do, then one turns to internal reallocation the following year. Also, the university must reserve the right, if funding is not completed, to remove the name. To that end, gift agreements are essential.

A final selling point for chairs, then, is that the university often contributes to the endowed chair. Take a $1.5 million chair and assume a $60,000 payout. The starting salary for a junior person would likely be well above $60,000. In some fields, such as economics, it could easily be more than double that. The university has to add 25 percent for benefits and then some support for research and other infrastructure needs, so there is a subsidy even for a beginning faculty member. The subsidy is greater still at the senior level. A $3 million chair spins out funding for benefits, a substantial teaching-and-research account, and about $70–$80,000 in salary. That's often less than half of what it costs to hire an endowed chair, so the university match is basically one to one.

During my eleven years as dean, new endowments and internal re-allocations drove the addition of more than eighty funded faculty positions, including well over fifty endowed chairs and directorships, not counting pledges for an additional ten more chairs. That represented growth of more than seven positions per year. Tuition dollars do not allow for such growth.

Whereas one can sometimes be flexible in accepting less than one needs to fund a chair, one must be careful about doing so in the case of a center. Once a center is named, funding options in the future become more difficult. It is a complicated puzzle, as one does not like to turn down gifts, and because gifts have traditionally grown dramatically, over time the gift might indeed fund a center. But I can recall a center at Notre Dame that was funded before my time for $1 million. The gift was simply too modest for the ambitions of the center, and since the center had already been named, it was difficult to solicit another large gift. We were forced to try to solicit gifts to name smaller entities, such as fellowships, lecture series, or what we called endowments for excellence.

An important principle for fund raising is that development staff should not determine the goals but should instead be guided by priorities set by the academic leadership; ensuring that this guidance exists is the responsibility of the academic leadership. The last thing any development office wants is freelance academics knocking on their doors and spelling out their own priorities. Without priorities, confusion results. Steering potential donors to campaign priorities is one of the most challenging aspects of fund raising. One Notre Dame donor had been supporting intramural sports. By speaking with him about other projects, we were able to move his support to an academic priority. Another redirected gift was from a businessperson, who was interested in leadership. He first met with the business college and was tossed the idea of business ethics, which, he told me, was either an oxymoron or common sense, he wasn't yet sure. After a brainstorming discussion with our College Council, at which I realized that we didn't want to invest directly in a chair or a program in leadership studies, I proposed that the donor support our College Seminar, which places tremendous emphasis on great questions and oral skills, two important ingredients of future leadership. We had a match and a gift.

The university once discussed with a donor the possibility of Notre Dame winning more Rhodes Scholarships; a decision was reached on a trial basis to give a scholarship to the best applicant each year, but that was not a great predictor of success. It was also difficult to award because the most outstanding students would also be accepted at other premier colleges and thus might or might not enroll. The funding was then redirected instead to an innovative project that brings more than a hundred of the top admitted students to campus each year, so that they can get to know one another, meet with faculty members, and see the campus before deciding whether to choose Notre Dame or another college. The acceptance rate for such students, who are being recruited by the top universities in the country, has been over 50 percent. While Notre Dame's general yield tends to be close to 60 percent, its win–loss ratio with Ivy League universities had tended to be closer to 30 percent; this was tremendous bang for the buck.

Another donor wanted to fund either a residence hall or an academic project. Because the donor was deeply interested in our academic ambitions, we did not want to have him fund a residence hall, for which finding a donation is easier than for an academic priority. The donor's main academic interest was in recruiting the best students to Notre Dame. He had been enamored of a program at another university that supports strong students with scholarships and special academic opportunities. One option would have been to ask him to support merit scholarships, but the university had traditionally prioritized need-based aid over merit aid. Instead, we brought forward the idea of endowing our arts and sciences honors program, which now gives more than a hundred students in each class a common social and intellectual environment; a higher number of small seminars with premier scholar-teachers; and summer funding for research projects, language study, and other academic opportunities. The donor was happy, as this involved enlarging and enhancing the program, thereby increasing our yield of these top students, who could have gone to Harvard or Stanford, Williams or Amherst. It also resonated with his own insights and priorities. The funding helped us attract and recruit a larger pool of superb students and allowed us to offer them a peerless undergraduate experience. The funding also paid for some of the program's indirect costs, including staffing small classes, by allowing us to add new faculty members. In addition, the gift ensured program funds and supported a student-led conference and visits to performances and museums in Chicago and beyond. Such a program combines the benefits of a leading research university and an elite liberal arts college by offering a small group of the university's most promising undergraduates a wide range of rich academic opportunities, as well as individualized mentoring and a student-centered experience enriched by an abundance of small discussion classes and independent research projects.

One must also be willing to turn down gifts that do not match mission, as I did once for a possible gift in support of an academic program in athletics, leadership, and ethics. One first tries to redirect the donor toward a campaign priority. The performing arts, for example, is one area where disciplined collaboration, creative innovation, and teamwork, in the spirit of competence and leadership, are fostered, so I initially hoped a gift in the direction of student productions in the arts would be a possibility. But if the proposed gift in the end does not match priorities, and if one does not see an academic rationale for moving into that area, then one simply passes, staying in touch with both development and the donor in the hope that something else might catch his or her interest in the future.

Following is a fascinating example of a way to show donors the importance of priorities. Funding had been secured for a first-class football office and practice facility, the kind of facility that helps attract the best high school recruits. The funding was fully in place to move ahead. Notre Dame's executive vice president, who oversaw building projects, made a bold decision. He told the donor and other supporters of athletics that moving ahead with this building was not nearly as high a priority as securing full funding for a new science building, for which the university had yet to reach the threshold of $70 million. The executive vice president told the donor and anyone else who would listen that ground would be broken for the football facility only after the science building had reached full funding. The incentive worked. Athletic supporters found themselves giving to the science building and convincing others to do so. When the threshold was reached, the university broke ground on both buildings.

PART III

Structures, Strategies, Struggles

What besides vision, personnel, and resources are necessary to advance a university? What structures and strategies have helped animate the rise of the American university? Which are likely to be privileged as universities elsewhere seek to match or exceed the success of American universities? Which were significant for my work as dean?

I would name above all five structures or strategies. First, flexibility, which makes possible autonomous and quick decisions and so renders positions of responsibility more meaningful. Second, the strong competition among (and partially within) universities that has fueled an ethos of improvement. Third, incentives, which play an important role when motivating others to advance an institution's goals. Fourth, accountability, which ensures that universities have clear ambitions and that progress toward goals is measured. Fifth, the sense of community that nurtures collective identity, helps faculty reach their potential, supports students in their academic challenges, and in the long run helps bring resources back to the university.

This part of the book, although in some ways more generic, is closely related to vision and distinction, for all of the structures and strategies are empty unless they serve what is ultimately a normative vision of what a university can and should be; distinction, moreover, is realized only on the basis of structures and strategies that can motivate and foster advancement.

In many ways the structures and strategies are interwoven. The stakes at play in competition among universities force each one to change more rapidly than it would otherwise. In this sense competition fosters flexibility. Competition functions only when there are incentives, both within and across universities. Although in the United States the federal government does not control universities, it does have influence through incentives on faculty research. The immense amount of federal funding makes individual faculty members and teams of faculty members into entrepreneurs, who become flexible in seeking available funding; incentives and competition thus work together to encourage flexibility and initiative. Some of the initiatives I describe below interweave not only competition but also incentives and accountability. Finally, competition and accountability are easier to accept when a campus is enriched by a sense of community and common purpose.

Even as these categories are the motors for effective advance, problems and challenges can arise with each of them. And while I can recognize them as the source of various successes, they were equally present in my struggles and stumbles.

CHAPTER FIVE

Flexibility, or How to
Juggle Just about Anything

Student flexibility in America is greater than in countries where students must chose a single and binding course of study before they enroll. Today, about half of Notre Dame first-year students change their intended majors between the start of classes and the spring of their first years. Many colleges offer a self-designed major, so that a student may design a curriculum that integrates multiple disciplines, have it approved by a faculty committee, and major in that field. Moreover, an undergraduate who majors in mathematics can pursue a doctorate in economics; an undergraduate who studies art history can choose to do a graduate degree in law; an undergraduate who majors in anthropology can go on to medical school; and an undergraduate who majors in history can do a graduate degree in French literature. This flexibility is important to the full development of talent and to the breadth of interests one finds among engaged students. Not surprisingly, America has many second-chance college graduates, students who initially failed at college but then returned some years later. The flexibility of the American student is mirrored across the university landscape.

Limited Regulation

In comparison with many other countries, American universities are relatively autonomous in their freedom from federal and state regulations and are far more flexible in their capability to act. Federal regulations primarily involve eligibility for financial aid; accounting for research dollars; and reports on policies, procedures, and activities in such areas as animal and human subjects. The government wants to know under what conditions its resources are being used. Much of this makes eminent sense, and the requests tend not to affect the everyday work of most members of the university community.

But there are two caveats. First, oversight is increasing, creating regulatory burden (Dunham), with the rise coming partly because Congress is eager to show voters that it is introducing accountability together with its funding allocations, even if what it controls is only data collection (Jones). Whenever the government offers funding, it has the right to collect information, and such requirements have been increasing. This results in more staff devoted to regulation and more faculty time lost in keeping records and filling out forms. Second, the laws are complicated and not always easy to decipher; one hears stories of energetic government bureaucrats implementing policies in burdensome, rigid, and not always productive ways. The tendency to elevate detailed legality over prudential judgment has been lamented as a general trend in America, culminating in "the death of common sense" (Howard). When I asked the provost of a major research university what his greatest challenge was, he said it was compliance. That is unfortunate for many reasons, not least of all because so much of compliance is intellectually uninteresting.

Most public universities are part of a state system, and generally a state board of overseers sets policy for the state institutions, in such a way that a community college cannot suddenly redefine itself as a research university or so that universities are held accountable for their graduation rates. Here a link exists between funding and regulation. For fiscal year 2015, only 4.9 percent of the operating revenue for the University of Michigan came from state appropriations (Regents 9); in return, the university has had the autonomy to raise funds aggressively and admit more out-of-state students, who pay higher tuition. Already in 1997, Michigan had completed the first $1 billion campaign of any public university in the country.

The relatively limited set of regulations leaves considerable room for innovation, which is deeply linked to flexibility, competition, and incentives, as these tend to set a context for creative ideas. With independence come dynamism and quick action. Contrast this flexibility with Germany, where academic freedom is part of the constitution; 2012 salaries of some professors were deemed inadequate by the Federal Constitutional Court; state regulations determine even the selection process for a dean; and, contrary to the older German tradition, such fine questions as whether attendance is obligatory for classes or whether grades are to be awarded on the basis of exams or papers, can be and in some cases are decided by the state ministry of education. The average American administrator or professor does not suffer from such constraints. As a result we are able to adapt, evolve, and change as needed. There is no command system from above, but a great sense of independence and vitality.

Tuition increases and payout rates for the endowment are set by the universities, with the exception of some state universities, whose tuition increases are managed centrally and at times capped, a major obstacle to flexibility. States that are pressed for funding know that public universities can raise their own funds, so they cut higher education instead of areas that have no such potential and then cap tuition increases. At the University of Arizona the state appropriation dropped from $440 million in 2008 to $340 million in 2011; at the same time the state capped tuition increases to ensure access (Ashburn).[1]

That the most successful public universities tend to suffer less central control is interesting. The University of California, Berkeley, which has for decades had one of the nation's strongest research reputations, has

---

1. In the past five years Arizona's state funding for public colleges and universities has been reduced further, but the cap on tuition has been abandoned. Though flexibility has been reintroduced, the burden of reduced state appropriations has simply shifted from the universities to students and their families: state spending per college student in Arizona has fallen 55.6 percent from 2008 to 2016, while tuition at Arizona public colleges and universities has increased 87.8 percent (Mitchell, Leachman, and Masterson 5, 12).

considerable constitutional autonomy. That applies as well to the University of California, San Diego, which was not founded until 1960 but ranks fourteenth in the *Academic Ranking of World Universities 2015*. Much more constrained, for example, are the University of Colorado and Ohio State, which have had greater difficulties reaching the top echelon. The more rigid the regulations, the more creativity, innovation, and risk are stifled. There is good reason for public universities to be concerned about politicians who want to engage in unproductive meddling that goes beyond basic accountability.

From the perspective of flexibility, private universities have an advantage. Bureaucracy, regulations, and oversight are more cumbersome at public universities. When a faculty member wanted to propose a new course at Ohio State, four different committees in succession had to give approval. Eventually, our department invented variable topics courses, that is, broadly configured courses with rotating topics into which we could plug whatever courses we wanted. But at most private universities, no such hoops are necessary.

Often a university will legislate some things but also allow considerable choice. For example, we stipulated that job advertisements should include a reference to Notre Dame as a Catholic university, but we offered a half dozen model phrases, depending on discipline or other issues, and would have allowed even more hybrids, if requested.

Flexibility and Initiative

Provosts are free to guide overarching academic advances. Deans have remarkable autonomy over budget, appointments, and curriculum; in many cases they have their own development staff. Chairpersons also have autonomy in distributing resources within their departments and making recommendations for salary adjustments. By granting so much power to the local level, the university can move rapidly in terms of appointments, differential adjustments, and the like. As a result of this power and flexibility, administrative positions become reasonably attractive. Eighty-nine percent of American provosts strongly agree or agree that they are glad they pursued administrative work (Jaschik and Lederman, *2015 Inside Higher Ed Survey* 27). Though the positions consume great amounts of time, provosts, deans, and chairpersons can make a tremendous difference in the life of a university. Naturally, if such persons have resources and power, they need to be accountable and show that they are indeed making progress toward their announced goals. And if there are radically insufficient resources, these can become nightmare positions. Annette Kolodny, for example, tells the sobering tale of her work as dean of a public university under fiscally strapped and stressful conditions.

By extension, just as chairpersons have power, so do departments. Because we were concerned that faculty might be inclined to prioritize numbers of publications, which can result in work of lower quality, my colleagues and I at Ohio State changed our promotion-and-tenure documents in the early 1990s in such a way that, at each promotion review, the faculty member identified his or her five most important publications. That addressed a local concern or, more precisely, allowed a local unit to address a national problem in its own way. The result was fewer but more thoughtful publications and less repetition. It sent the signal to faculty members that what counts is quality, not quantity.

For the most part power resides in the departments and the so-called (reporting) line positions above the departments—dean, provost, and president—all of whom have independent resources at their disposal. Importantly, the line positions control the budget. The faculty senate tends to restrict itself to rules and regulations and sets guidelines that in fact delegate tremendous power to the line positions. Deans have had powerful roles since at least the end of the nineteenth century (Veysey 312), even if shortly thereafter the departments and with them the legitimacy of disciplinary judgment had likewise become influential (Geiger, *To Advance* 37). A deliberative faculty that represents diverse disciplines and is highly cooperative, democratic, and risk averse, like the traditionally strong faculty senate in Germany, is not likely to make the kind of differential allocations that a president, provost, or dean will make and is, as a result, less poised to position a university competitively.

Sometimes in searches, flexibility plays a role. An important innovation immediately in my tenure was to say that once a position is released to a department, it cannot be taken back. That was an incentive for departments to keep looking for superb quality hires instead of simply filling the position in order to retain it. I myself benefited from a long courtship at Notre Dame, one that stretched over a good two years. The university's willingness to be patient and persistent, to invest for the long term, made a great impression on me.

At least until recently, at most American universities senior chair holders have been or are overwhelmingly male. One way we recognized more women was to create three-year, rotating chair appointments at the junior level, that is, for assistant or associate professors. We used those prestigious and well-supported chairs to recognize excellence but focused overwhelmingly on women. The flexibility to name them at the junior level enhanced our support for women.

Flexibility can be an advantage with retiring faculty members as well. I received a visit once from a senior faculty member. He told me that he had been diagnosed with cancer. It was under control, but he realized that he was slowing down and still had much he wanted to write. Could I imagine a scenario where he could have more time off, perhaps for less pay? We developed an agreement whereby for the next five years, he would teach one semester each year, after which he would retire. During that time, the university would pay him 50 percent of his salary. His name would continue to be associated with Notre Dame, his research would accelerate, and I could hire someone at less than half his salary. In this way, I would save some money right away (and more later), and in the interim, we would have six courses to offer (four from the new person and two from my retiring colleague) instead of four. That was in my eyes an obvious win-win situation. In a more bureaucratically controlled environment, a creative arrangement like that would be unthinkable.

The Academic Entrepreneur

Whereas the board of trustees governs, it does not manage and certainly does not micromanage. Its job instead is to ensure that the university is well administered in accordance with its vision. The faculty and administrators lead and manage the university. Just as boards represent a distinguishing feature of American colleges and universities, so, too, does the tradition of strong presidents. The president must be able to articulate a compelling vision, communicate goals, locate the resources to realize the goals, and hire the right people to support their implementation. The president is expected to be an entrepreneur. Indeed from the very start the American college president "had to be an entrepreneur in the broadest and best sense of the word" (Thelin 34). After surveying examples of strong and entrepreneurial leaders, W. H. Cowley wrote, "Name a great American college or university, and you will find in its history a commanding leader or leaders who held its presidency" (70).

The president increasingly devotes her time to fund raising, and her energies are distributed across the university in areas that transcend academics, from student services, alumni relations, and athletics to budget, buildings and grounds, and public relations. Provosts thus have strong control over the academic mission, but at most universities they are not directly involved with the departments, tend to be further from the action, and are dependent on deans. At many universities, even provosts spend increasing amounts of time on fund raising and community relations. In a 2014 survey, 92 percent agreed or strongly agreed that the provost's role has evolved beyond its traditional focus on academic affairs (Jaschik and Lederman, *2014 Inside Higher Ed Survey* 33).

In terms of academic advance, deans could be said to occupy an axial position. As a recent article in the *Chronicle of Higher Education* suggested, "Deans have their hands on more levers than almost anyone else on campus" (June A21). At universities that do not separate out a dean of undergraduate studies and a dean of the faculty, the college deans are responsible for the entire academic arena, from faculty personnel and student learning to resources and policies; unlike higher-level administrators, they tend to know all the faculty for whom they are responsible, and they have tremendous opportunities to be entrepreneurial and creative, independently of the provost and president. Autonomy from federal and state regulations, a spirit of competition that motivates departments, and a role for academic administrators—presidents, provosts, and deans—to articulate a vision, introduce incentives, ensure accountability, and foster a spirit of community have contributed greatly to the ascendance of the American university.

The president, provost, and deans are not elected by the faculty but are instead appointed, usually after a national search. Such searches sometimes arise even for chairpersons. At most universities, the chairperson is appointed, not elected. Before an internal person is to be named, the dean consults with the faculty, asking their views in writing or in person about potential candidates, after which the dean selects a chairperson. Elected administrators are not likely to have taken strong stands and be prepared to upset the status quo; appointed persons, in contrast, are more likely to be agents of change. The authority of administrators is not always exerted, and when it is, it is sometimes thwarted, but the exercise of that leadership is essential to a great university. In reflecting on the ingredients of an excellent university, Jonathan Cole rightly states, "Bold, decisive, entrepreneurial, and indefatigable leadership is an essential ingredient for a preeminent university" (*Great* 115).

Faculty governance is the principle for virtually all academic decisions—development of the curriculum, the formulation of degree programs, the hiring of faculty, promotion-and-tenure recommendations, and so forth—even if ultimate authority in these cases lies with the dean, provost, or president. An administrator must have a very compelling rationale to overturn a faculty recommendation, and each time such action is taken, political capital is relinquished. Mutual trust is essential. So, too, is knowledge of the local culture. Presidents who assume a second presidency learn more aggressively and systematically about the culture and subtleties of their new institutions than they did as inexperienced presidents (Amer. Assn. for Higher Educ. 2–3).

Flexibility within Universities

The quality of faculty is partly enhanced by the university's flexibility. For example, a dean can take a vacant faculty position at the senior level and split it into two junior lines if the quality of candidates is stronger at the junior level or if the department has a need for a larger number of faculty members. At the same time, the dean can take two junior positions and create one senior line in order to attract a particularly eminent faculty member.

Because in any one year, some departments may have frozen lines, others may be required to stagger their searches, and a few searches will not result in a hire, the dean may have the temporary resources to make prehires. Drawing on the importance of incentive structures, the dean can invite departments to nominate outstanding candidates for faculty positions, and the dean can hire in advance of retirements and anticipated departures. In short, if a department can bring forward a superb applicant, it may temporarily receive an additional line. In this way the department is also guaranteed a replacement position for a future departure.

Internal Reallocation

Internal reallocation of budget is one of the most powerful tools of flexibility enjoyed by a dean and one of the most important and effective for the establishment and implementation of priorities. Each year my greatest budgetary exercise, outside of salary adjustments, involved the systematic consideration of what I called internal reallocation. All faculty positions, with the exception of negative tenure decisions (excluded so as to avoid inflated recommendations from the department simply to keep a line), came back to the dean for possible reallocation, a decision that would be based on a number of factors, ranging from enrollment pressures to gaps in coverage, new areas of study, and departmental quality.

Because these lines and their funding return to the dean, each year I could decide what funding should go where. That involved serious reflection on priorities. Each year I created an Excel chart numbering several hundred lines, with pluses for money becoming available because of departures, retirements, internal cuts, new gifts, increases in the base allocation, or endowment enhancements and minuses representing commitments to faculty lines, nonsalary support, and new initiatives. It was an important and enjoyable exercise to see a vision become realized through those adjustments. Once the decisions were made and the budget for the new year was frozen, I passed it on for implementation to my staff and began thinking about the next year's reallocation.

What does a dean adjust? Certainly faculty positions from one department or area to another. Over the course of eleven years, nearly half of the departments lost a line, some temporarily and a few permanently. Many managed to net pluses as a result of reallocation, competitive searches across departments, or new endowments.

Internal reallocation also involved movement between junior and senior lines. Several departments were authorized to search at the junior level, with the understanding that if an extraordinary candidate were to emerge, we would consider a senior hire; in a given year, easily half a dozen departments would be engaged in such searches.

Another option, when, for example, a senior person was retiring and significant funds were being released, was to convert the departing senior line to a junior hire and redirect some of the savings to upgrade a departing non-tenure-track line to a tenure-track line, thus serving the priority of linking teaching and research. Also, as dean, I was free to move funds within various nonsalary, as well as between salary and non-salary, categories. I liked to say that I did not have lines, I had money, which gave me even greater freedom to think outside the box. If nonsalary support was the highest priority, then I could move funding from faculty or staff positions and use it to support travel, lectures, and the like. I had complete freedom to advance priorities as long as I stayed within my budget.

Funding was released whenever a center or graduate program was eliminated, and we closed three centers as well as three graduate programs, including one in my own department. In some cases, one can close centers that are inadequate while holding on to the resources for reinvestment in the same area but with different concepts.

Early in my first year as dean, I had lunch with our new graduate dean, who told me that he had just awarded two new graduate stipends to one of my departments. I told him that we needed to communicate better: the department was so dysfunctional that I had frozen three faculty positions and appointed an outside chairperson; I later closed the graduate program. Some years after I was dean, I chaired a university committee to review graduate studies. A primary recommendation was to move the graduate stipends, with the exception of premier stipends, for which an annual competition is healthy, to the colleges. This permitted the college deans, who have greater knowledge of departmental quality, to do more long-range planning and have greater flexibility to move graduate funding from one department to another or from one field to another within a department, on the basis of performance.

One of my first priorities as dean was to ensure that every line was budgeted, not only lines that were filled. This innovation ensured two things: First, it enhanced my flexibility for the future; second, it increased my amount of uncommitted dollars for any given year, that is, one-time funding or soft funding, what I called "cash," which I kept track of through internal reallocation. Beside each minus category indicating a new or revised commitment of funds, another column listed committed funding that would not be spent in the following year, say, because certain faculty positions were temporarily vacant or because funding was being set aside for a future project. That cash became, along with expendable giving and grants that were not tied to specific purposes, my annual allocation of one-time funding. Some of the funding supported visitors and adjunct professors to fill gaps in coverage that could not be handled by departmental recovery money, but that allocation was modest because I had moved all visitor and adjunct funding to zero-based budgeting, that is, the previous year's allocation was irrelevant to future allocations. Instead, we required annual requests outlining the specific courses needed, projected enrollments, and proposed instructors, and the allocations differed annually. The cash mainly funded one-time special projects, often initiatives involving incentives or experimental programs for which I was seeking to create an initial track record that might help us garner more permanent external funding. The cash could in principle also have been turned into endowments or saved for future initiatives or emergencies, and I made sure to leave my successor some uncommitted annual-rate dollars and some cash, which gave him flexibility from day one.

Because I had moved to zero-based budgeting for nonsalary support, we also had an opportunity to reshape nonsalary support each year. I uncovered historical inequities, created by any number of contingent but not rational factors. For categories that should be symmetrical across departments, funding for phone lines, for example, we moved to a per-faculty-member formula. We allocated the most important items on the basis of quality. For example, while travel funding was allocated to departments on the basis of a figure per faculty member, the formula differed considerably. The strongest departments had 2.5 times the funding per faculty member of a department with modest research productivity.

One tries to avoid giving any funds in perpetuity, which works against the principle of flexibility. This applies also to centers and institutes attached to individual professors. If donors sign agreements that permit flexibility in the future use of resources, even if a clear preference exists to stay within the same broad area, a future dean can shift the focus, on the basis of new priorities and the kinds of professors the university can attract. Many universities have endowments that are too restrictive to be used on a regular basis, for example, a scholarship for a band member from Iowa, who wants to study medicine; administrators want to avoid such restrictions.

Variable Assignments

Flexibility also means that faculty members can be asked to undertake different assignments. When I was a chairperson at Ohio State in the early 1990s, we introduced a document, unanimously approved by the department's more than twenty faculty, on variable teaching assignments. It ensured that faculty who did more and better research would correspondingly have fewer demands in teaching. At a university, an adjustment in teaching is normally made as partial compensation for extraordinary service obligations. Because research is central to a university's mission and because more balanced assignments nurture more and better research, compensation, we argued, should also be given for outstanding research. Increased research opportunities also help a university keep and attract the best scholars. Placing research time in the hands of faculty with the best track records increases in turn the university's collective research endeavors. Faculty who do less research but are exemplary teachers and citizens should be given the chance to excel and be rewarded with assignments and recognition in those areas where their expertise and interests lie. The document described the expectations for teaching three courses per year, including the quality of and productivity in research; external recognition and impact; and extensive advising of graduate students. Descriptions were also given for four, five, six, and seven courses annually. Our goal was not to hire pure researchers or pure teachers, but if, after tenure, faculty stood out as researchers or fell behind in the area of research, then it made sense to balance the loads more appropriately.

At Notre Dame I had to wait longer for the culture to accept such a change. When, in my first semester, I told chairpersons that I wanted to move to a variable system, I had the support of one chairperson out of twenty, not enough to introduce the change without destroying morale. But I did make the change in my final year, a gift in a sense to my successor, since I realized that the culture was finally ready for it and its introduction under my watch would place the political costs on me. As at Ohio State, so at Notre Dame, though at a very different pace, we found the variable system to be a more equitable way to share faculty obligations, reward individuals whose contributions lie more in one area than another, and enhance faculty research productivity.

For approximately fifteen years, Notre Dame's College of Arts and Letters had a research university course load of six credit hours per week, essentially two classes per semester, for all faculty members. However, about 10 percent of the faculty members, spread across almost every department, had not developed a research profile that came close to meeting expectations. Those faculty members were to provide compensatory contributions in teaching or service. The goal was not to create or foster a two-tier system but to recognize what we had and to work with it; indeed, the conscious recognition only reaffirmed the importance of developing tenure standards that would help prevent a two-tier system in the future. The policy also sent a message to the next generation of persons receiving tenure that they would be expected in the coming years to be active in research; at a research university, faculty must continue to publish and have an impact. Such a university awards tenure as much for future trajectory as for work already accomplished, but if the promise is not fulfilled, there must be consequences; otherwise, resources will be poorly utilized.

Faculty who taught extra courses were rewarded for their additional contributions. We thought it the best strategy to improve the institution overall and recognize faculty members for the excellence that they were able to contribute. To help with acceptance, we introduced the program with a phase-in period of one year. That is, when we announced the program, faculty still had one year to change their records.

Some chairpersons raised concerns about the morale of those who were to teach more, but I was more concerned about the spirit of faculty members who pulled their weight in all areas and observed colleagues who were not contributing as much. Those are the faculty members about whom an academic leader should have the greatest concern. Moreover, to have people contribute in the ways they can may even aid morale.

Another concern expressed was that we should not assign so much teaching to persons who were on the cusp of breakthroughs in research. Unfortunately, such breakthroughs are rare. Whereas I had seen many faculty members over time go from accomplishing modest to very strong research, seeing someone go from five to ten years of no research to truly active research is much rarer. Variable teaching assignments were made on the basis of proven effectiveness and accomplishment, not promise and intentions, which are notoriously difficult to weigh. Nonetheless, we wanted to offer faculty members every reasonable opportunity, and we recognized that it would be unfortunate if a higher teaching load (or simply the lack of a reduction) were to keep significant research projects from being realized. Therefore, we introduced at Notre Dame a concept like the one at Ohio State, which we called "course borrowing": depending on scheduling considerations, a faculty member might receive fewer courses than would otherwise be allotted for a set number of semesters in the form of borrowed courses. These assignments were to be made specifically on the basis of potential and promise and would be awarded to faculty members who, even though they had not met expectations in past years, could make the reasonable case that they were on the cusp of doing good research. The system was set up as follows: a short and simple memorandum of understanding was signed by the faculty member, the chairperson, and the associate dean of research. The memorandum indicated a temporary reduction in teaching and stipulated an ambitious research goal that was in some sense measurable. If the faculty member achieved the stated goal, the reduction was well calculated on both ends; the contract was fulfilled. That would also usually translate into a lessening of the extra teaching going forward. If the faculty member failed to achieve the goal, the faculty member paid back the reductions—in full or in part, as determined by the associate dean, with advice from the chairperson—in subsequent semesters.

Another concern was raised about faculty members who were not strong in teaching. Fortunately, this was a tiny minority, even among those faculty members who were not meeting research expectations. But for those who were not meeting teaching expectations, we worked with the teaching center to develop a rigorous set of activities that faculty members were required to work through during the academic year in order to improve. In the first year they taught their normal course loads, and they went through the workshop. We set up the system at Notre Dame so that they also received the maximum allowable pay reduction, which was 2 percent, as determined by the Academic Articles, since they were not able to contribute what we expected in either teaching or research. The next year they would teach their obligatory overload, and if they kept struggling, in such a way that they were a liability in the classroom, then they would continue to receive cuts in pay and be required to take more workshops. A grievance appeal could be filed and sent to a faculty review committee, but faculty members in such situations normally do not want to expose their inferior records in both areas to peers.

Problems and Challenges with Flexibility

Problems arising from flexibility and autonomy include inconsistency of policy, with resulting unfairness. Excessive autonomy without oversight or attention to precedent can be disadvantageous. For example, if a chairperson were to free a faculty member from teaching a full course load for no compelling reason, flexibility would be a problem. To avoid such cases, flexibility needs to be coupled with appropriate and clear guidelines, including documented procedures for exceptions and modest decanal oversight.

Unintended consequences can be another challenge. An example would be allowing a dean to create faculty positions without paying a tax to the central administration for the indirect costs—space, utilities, and the like—that might be borne by another part of the university. In such cases, one needs to ensure that there are no externalized costs.

In addition, once one permits autonomy, reining it in is tough, so one needs to think twice before introducing it. An example was the decision made before I arrived at Notre Dame to reduce the teaching load from the previous three-three to a research university load of two-two, as the university became more research focused. As I noted above, there were no allowances made for faculty who never got their research on track or who fell out of a research mold. For years, they continued to teach a two-two load, whether they did research or not. As the culture slowly evolved, we were able to change the policy, but even that was difficult. In the annual budget meetings devoted to salary recommendations, I spoke individually with each chairperson. One chairperson was uncertain about the proposal, three were opposed but then realized the counterarguments were stronger, and seventeen were supportive. When I announced at a collective meeting of chairs that I had polled them all and we were moving ahead, the person who had been uncertain criticized the decision, and some of the others followed suit. We were able to move ahead nonetheless, but it was not easy. The imperative for administrators not to make mistakes that will burden their successors down the road is especially important during transition periods; introducing the earlier change in policy not carte blanche but with expectations and accountability would have been preferable.

The stronger a faculty is, the easier it is to decentralize, but if quality is uneven, keeping some control in a more central area, such as with the dean, is better. One cannot increase flexibility without either great confidence in future decisions or strategies of accountability, and yet without flexibility one cannot really innovate. Whenever possible, that is, wherever trust and confidence exist, decisions should move to the most local level possible. During a transition period, a central office can provide incentive funding to help initiate the kind of differential decisions for which as yet no track record exists.

The greater the decentralization, the more one needs capable administrators. With flexibility and power, chairpersons and deans must be good leaders; someone who simply sits in the office will not do. The most visible and pronounced challenge with flexibility is that finding people who are strong in research and teaching, and thus likely to be good judges of other persons' contributions, and also interested in and suited for administration is not always possible. Occasionally no candidate for chairperson embodies even the minimal traits. In a recent survey, provosts identified the difficulty of cultivating leadership in others as their second greatest challenge after never having enough money (Eckel, Cook, and King 12).

When helping faculty members assess whether they want to take a turn in administration, I've found the most interesting question to be, Is there a match between your interests and capacities, and what is currently needed in an administrative position? In other words, can you personally make a difference? Do you have something special to offer, or could others do the job equally well? One of my colleagues at Ohio State put an interesting spin on the matter. When as an assistant professor, I asked him if he were interested in becoming chairperson, he responded that it depended on who else wanted the job. He elaborated that he did not want to do it and would not be a candidate if someone good wanted it, but if the only one who wanted the position was not in the least desirable, he would rather do it than be led by such a person. He had invested his career in the institution and was willing to take a turn but only if needed.

Less common, but unusually valuable, is the colleague who is both a strong scholar-teacher and more than willing to take a leadership turn.

The demands on administrators are considerable. The positions are challenging not only because of the long hours and many events but also because faculty are so autonomous. Governing, let alone leading, is difficult enough. The dean, it has been said, is the conductor of an orchestra made up entirely of composers. The demands on administrators are so great that chairpersons usually do not remain fully active in scholarship; for a dean, provost, or president to teach or do any research and to return to the faculty ranks as an active scholar is even rarer. This exacerbates already existing tensions between faculty and administrators. At some universities, the complexity of administration results in ever-more full-time professionals, even in leadership roles (Ginsberg). The tremendous burdens on administrators are understandable, perhaps even inevitable, as knowledge of legal precedents, marketing, management, information systems, federal regulations, administration of grants and contracts, fund raising, and various other forms of increasingly specialized knowledge and practices occupy one's time, and as the demands of the various constituencies are endless. When faculty members take on these roles, they are invariably surprised at the heavy workload and extraordinary pace.

To make leadership positions appealing, one must give administrators flexibility, authority, and resources. One must also compensate them with temporary funding (permanent salary adjustments create the wrong incentive, as there is no financial incentive to stay in the role). The incentive to stay in administration becomes the temporary add-on funding, and the incentive to perform well involves the potential for higher merit increases. Some universities pay a standard two-ninths of the academic year salary, but differential amounts tied to position (some departments are larger and more complex than others) and performance are wiser. A bizarre incentive arises whenever a weak department has only one potentially good leader; in principle, the weaker the department and its candidates, the better able the person is to negotiate. The best strategy is to rule out negotiation in principle, and to make adjustments a matter of performance. Otherwise, negotiating power increases, the worse the department is in terms of having developed potential leaders.

To ensure that administrators remain active as faculty members (and one wants active faculty members making academic decisions), one also needs to give them course releases. The administrative demands were considered so great at Ohio State that the normal teaching load of five courses per year was reduced for chairpersons to one course per year. Notre Dame has had a 50 percent reduction, with chairpersons teaching two courses per year and associate deans and higher-level administrators not teaching at all unless they make a special request to teach. Notre Dame's not uncommon if still modestly generous policy of postadministrative leave permits those who serve for three years to receive a one-semester administrative leave after their terms expire. They may instead take a full-year paid leave at the conclusion of two terms or six years. The appointment of a targeted research assistant or a postdoctoral scholar can help an administrator remain current in research. Also essential are top-flight staff persons, including, where appropriate, persons who can help with numbers. Not all faculty administrators are comfortable with numbers, and the more I dealt with numbers, the more I realized that there are three kinds of faculty members: those who can count and those who can't.

A final challenge is that while the academic positions of dean and provost can still be interesting, the presidency has become increasingly oriented toward nonacademic matters. As a result, recent surveys indicate that only 24–30 percent of provosts would like to become presidents (Hartley and Godin 32, 36). Among the reasons for not seeking a presidency, the unappealing nature of the work was named by 66 percent of provosts (Eckel, Cook, and King 20). A survey from 2011 revealed that presidents' three most prominent activities involve budget and financial management, fund raising, and community relations, not necessarily the most attractive activities for someone who has chosen the life of a scholar-teacher (American Council on Educ., *American College President* 34).

CHAPTER SIX

Competition, or How American Universities Have Always Embraced the Market

A distinctive dimension of the American academic landscape is the long tradition and immense culture of competition, which helps to counter complacency and inefficiency. Each university seeks to become outstanding by competing for research dollars and donations, hiring the most distinguished faculty, recruiting the best students, and having an impact in the public sphere. An institution that measures itself against others is naturally encouraged to absorb and integrate the best ideas and strategies of the competition. A friendly rivalry encourages an institution to bring to the fore the very best it has to offer, knowing that if it is deficient, others will supersede it. Competition encourages a university to reach its greatest potential and to learn from other models.

In an environment in which faculty want to teach the best students, faculty seek to hire colleagues who are better than they are themselves, that is, faculty who can attract even better students. Faculty members also seek to hire the best colleagues for engaging scholarly and intellectual discussions. I like the phrase once used by a colleague at Ohio State: "I want to hire a colleague from whom I can learn." What competition means in practice is not only that the best professors have opportunities at any number of the leading colleges but also that colleges and universities develop elaborate procedures to protect themselves against mediocrity and incompetence. From negative tenure decisions to zero percent raises, colleges and universities find strategies not only to reward those who contribute more to the common mission but also to delimit the influence of those who do not push the university forward.

To trumpet its vision, faculty, students, and campus facilities, universities market themselves. How does one market a university? Essentially, three questions are asked. First, what outstanding qualities does this university embody that are sought out by many kinds of students? The quality of the students and the faculty, class size, placement record, array of majors and courses, campus facilities, and so forth are all highlighted. Second, what makes this particular university distinctive? What sets it apart from others? The admissions brochure for the University of Notre Dame is entitled *Nowhere Else but Notre Dame*. Distinction may involve a unique vision, an unusual set of curricular programs, special study abroad opportunities, a remarkable setting, and so on. Third, in what ways and in what fora can the university tell its story? By marketing the university effectively, one gains more and better student applications, more recognition among peers, and of course more donors. Ideally, personnel in support of publicity are funded and report centrally but are housed in the different parts of the university. In this way the university's story is consistent but informed by the detailed knowledge of the activities and accomplishments of the various units.

Diversity and Competition

Diversity and competition are related: states that have been able to develop premier universities, such as the University of California, Berkeley, and the University of Michigan, have recognized the advantage of elevating one or two flagship campuses. These universities, which have historically had access to resources, are internationally competitive. At the same time other public colleges and universities exist in the respective states, which means that students who are not admitted have other options.

Already in the 1930s, California began developing a tripartite system of higher education. Essentially the University of California campuses have the most rigorous academic standards; among them Berkeley stands supreme. These campuses have professional and doctoral students; their mission is strongly driven by research and public service; and they have traditionally served the top echelon of California's students as well as qualified out-of-state students, who pay higher tuition. The California state campuses, the second group, are solid, but not at the same level of distinction; they are more accessible and cater more to regional needs; they primarily offer bachelor's and master's degrees, and their research and public service functions are relatively minor; their focus is on the transmission of knowledge. The community colleges, finally, have served as an extension of secondary education, offering vocational education as well as helping late bloomers succeed and make a transition to the other campuses. High school graduates who are not accepted at the higher tiers are welcome at the community colleges. The basic principle, consistent across time, has been to match students to institutions on the basis of talent and performance, which has required explicit diversification. Fascinating is that the state, as the central authority, took control away from the various local politicians and entrepreneurs, but in doing so, actually enhanced and rendered more logical the level of diversity while also avoiding duplication and ensuring efficient use of public funds.

Most universities desire to have a few areas of distinction and so develop appealing niches that resonate with mission. An often overlooked advantage of diversity is the possibility of convincing professors, students, supporters, and others that their own university is doing something different. One wants to contribute to something that is not easily interchangeable. Of course any university that is competitive must also be superb in areas of high impact, where other universities also compete aggressively. These include disciplines with large faculties at every leading university, such as biology, economics, and history.

Even when the desire to build on complementary strengths or address gaps on one's own campus leads to greater cooperation and collaboration across universities, either partnerships or clusters of universities, such collaborations can enhance competition. In 2009, for example, when Duke University and the University of North Carolina, Chapel Hill, created one German graduate program out of two departments at two universities, the attractiveness and competitiveness of the program internationally was quickly enhanced. Even cooperation can be a strategy that strengthens distinctiveness and competitiveness.

At least one aspect of competition is linked with accountability, the idea that universities are ranked. One element of competition is comparison. One needs to be able to compare before making an informed choice. In principle, rankings foster competition and accountability, but they can easily steer universities in wrong directions, and they tend to work against diversity insofar as the same factors apply to each institution.

America had already embarked on college rankings in the 1920s (Geiger, *History* 495). More than forty countries have since acquired our predilection for ranking universities (Wildavsky 10), and international rankings exist as well. Some of these are highly problematic. The *Academic Ranking of World Universities*, for example, ignores contributions in the arts and humanities and offers, as a result, a truncated understanding of a university. The *QS World University Rankings* is heavily based on reputation, with surveys of academic quality accounting for 40 percent; it is hardly likely that many voters have detailed knowledge of a high number of universities in other countries, which means that the ranking is based in large part on hearsay and anecdotes along with marketing and previous rankings.

U.S. News and World Report bases its well-known rankings on a set of purported indicators of academic excellence, to which it assigns percentage weights depending on their importance. The ranking has serious limitations. There have been published reports of submission of fudged data and strategic voting, that is, absurdly low peer assessments of the competition, so as to elevate one's own ranking. In addition, institutions have been known to distort their own activities to improve their rankings, which can lead to instrumentalizing others: for example, a college can lower the percentage of students it accepts by encouraging applications from persons who will never be admitted. An institution can accept students solely on the basis of test scores and class rank, whereas most admissions counselors rightly prefer a more holistic model. The incentive to keep or garner a high ranking encourages colleges to admit students with high test scores, a group that includes above all students from wealthier backgrounds, over students whose scores are lower and who are likely to come from lower socioeconomic backgrounds. To take the poorer student is to risk falling in the rankings. High retention rates can be the result of grade inflation instead of pushing students to meet expectations. Even if one were to endorse the areas tracked by the rankings, no defense of the weighting could be given that would justify a firm rank of any kind.

Many other rankings exist—and of various kinds. One ranking integrates social mobility (recruiting and graduating low-income students) and the engagement of students and graduates in public service, such as the Peace Corps (*Washington Monthly*). Another focuses on a combination of academic quality, on the one hand, and cost and financial aid, on the other hand, which is valuable in making clear to students and their parents that most of the premier colleges and universities offer generous financial aid packages (*Kiplinger*). The focus on common elements in these and other rankings, while supportive of benchmarking, hardly promotes another central principle, appropriateness to mission, which presupposes some level of differentiation in purpose and thus also in assessment. For that very reason the variety of rankings with different measures is an advantage. It sends the indirect signal that no one ranking can capture the distinctive characteristics of any university, so that readers must weigh their own priorities. Indeed, one of the most promising developments involves rankings (e.g., the one done by *The New York Times*) that chart universities according to the service they provide to low-income students; such rankings provide superb counterweights to the *U.S. News and World Report* ranking, which offers indirect incentives not to accept low-income students, who tend to have lower test scores (*New York Times*).

Competition for Faculty and Students

Competition for the best faculty, both junior and senior, and setting a high bar for tenure are arguably the greatest factors in determining a university's success. Berkeley made great academic strides when its longtime chancellor Clark Kerr raised the standards for tenure to such a high level that he refused some 20 percent of the positive recommendations that had passed all other hurdles (Geiger, *Research* 80). One wants to reserve positions for faculty who will raise the average quality of the department and the university. An indirect way to assess quality is to consider both the institutions that new faculty turn down to come to one's university and the ones faculty reject in order to stay.

Moving toward a holistic selection process for students and away from purely academic criteria was originally introduced at the Ivy League universities early in the twentieth century. This development was partly a strategy to unjustly restrict the percentage of Jewish students, especially immigrant Jewish populations from Eastern Europe, who were, because of their high grades and test scores, effectively reducing the traditionally high number of Christians, including persons from socially influential families (Karabel). Despite its sinister origins, the idea of using qualitative rather than merely quantitative measures to achieve meritocracy, with some accommodation to special groups (e.g., children of donors and alumni, minorities, and first-generation college students) has received widespread acceptance as a positive mode to ensure that an entering class of students has persons with wide-ranging capabilities, including character, leadership skills, and the potential to have a positive impact on society. Of course, debates continue about which and to what extent non-academic criteria should be applied, but the idea of looking beyond the pure numbers is widely supported. Until World War II, many of the less competitive colleges and universities admitted students on the basis of their high school records alone, but experience with war veterans convinced colleges that formal preparation mattered less than motivation and native intelligence (Jencks and Riesman 281); here the movement away from mere numbers was motivated by positive experience.

Universities track admissions competitions, both at the undergraduate and graduate levels. One interesting facet of yield is that high yield can derive from both academic quality and distinctive mission. *U.S. News and World Report* annually lists on its website the "most popular universities." Harvard, with a yield of 80.9 percent, ranked first for the fall 2014 entering class (Ross). Notre Dame, with its distinctive mission, has had a consistently higher yield, spanning multiple years, than comparable academic institutions, such as Duke, Northwestern, and Vanderbilt, and even unambiguously stronger research universities such as Johns Hopkins. More valuable than yield are market-based rankings that draw on the real-life decisions of admitted students, in other words, revealed student preferences. An economic study asked the question, if the student were admitted to Harvard, Princeton, Stanford, and Williams, for example, which college did he or she choose (Avery et al.). The top universities, not surprisingly, were Harvard, Yale, and Stanford. Four liberal arts colleges made the top twenty. The highest ranking public university was Virginia, at number twenty. Underscoring the idea that a distinctive mission can aid student recruitment, two Catholic universities landed in the top twenty, Notre Dame at 13 and Georgetown at 16.

In recruiting the very best students, including underrepresented minorities, a university will often pay for transportation, so that students can spend several days on campus visiting classes, meeting current students as well as other prospective students, hearing administrators talk of opportunities and the institution's distinctive mission, and listening to faculty speak of their teaching and scholarship. During such visits prospective undergraduates live in the residential halls with other students. This is a wise investment in resources that has a high payoff at minimal expense, and it is an area in which it is easy to find donor support, for donors tend to support students and whatever enhances competitiveness.

The Global Paradigm

Competition in today's world is not restricted to one nation. Every superb university hires faculty from abroad and attracts international students, whose numbers continue to increase dramatically. In 2000, there were just over 2 million college students studying outside their home countries; by 2012, the figure had reached more than 4.5 million (OECD, *Education at a Glance 2014*, chart C4.1). American universities will increasingly face new challenges from Asia, which is investing billions of dollars and which, in several cases, such as Hong Kong, Singapore, and Taiwan, has a much higher percentage of its student-age population enrolled in college than is the case in the United States. Although not nearly at this level today, China can be expected to make dramatic advances in coming years. It is not by chance that the *Academic Ranking of World Universities* was developed in China. China and India are expected to account for 40 percent of all young people with a college education in G20 and OECD countries by the year 2020, while the United States and EU countries will account for just over a quarter; that will be a major shift (OECD, "How Is"). China alone seeks to have 20 percent of its citizens—or 195 million people—receive higher education degrees by 2020, which would be roughly equal to the entire projected population aged 25–64 in the United States in that year (OECD, "How Is"). According to the National Science Board, the United States accounted for 19 percent of the world's total science and engineering articles in 2013, down from 26 percent in 2011 and 34 percent in 1995 (*Science and Engineering Indicators 2016*, ch. 5, p. 92; *Science and Engineering Indicators 2014*, ch. 5, p. 6; *Science and Engineering Indicators 2012*, ch. 5, p. 34). In 2007, China moved past the United Kingdom, Germany, and Japan to rank as the world's second-largest producer of articles in science and engineering, up from fifth place in 2005 and fourteenth place in 1995 (Natl. Science Board, *Science and Engineering Indicators 2012*, ch. 5, p. 34).

In some cases, to compete, one must cooperate. For example, one must adjust to international standards for what constitutes a degree in a specific discipline, so that students and graduates can be mobile. This recognition partly drove the Bologna Process, whose motivation built to some extent on the earlier European idea of students moving from one university to another. The Bologna reforms in Europe have ensured a certain compatibility of academic programs now exists in almost fifty countries. One must also set up consortia for exchange, so that in attending one university, students have the option to enrich their studies in other countries. Cooperation applies to faculty as well. Coauthored articles have been on the rise. In 2012, more than two-thirds of the world's total science and engineering articles were coauthored by scholars from different institutions or different countries, compared with just half fifteen years earlier, and articles listing authors from institutions in more than one country grew from 16 to 25 percent over the same period (Natl. Science Board, *Science and Engineering Indicators 2014*, ch. 5, p. 7). Not surprisingly, the nation that most often coauthors with the United States is China, a collaborator on almost 19 percent of US internationally coauthored articles in 2013 (Natl. Science Board, *Science and Engineering Indicators 2016*, ch. 5, p. 106). Collaboration across countries is increasingly becoming a common avenue to better competitiveness.

Internal Competition

Competition exists also internally. In the past few years, for example, Notre Dame awarded more than $80 million in internal competitions for strategic investments in research. These were focused on projects that would advance the university in research, potentially attract further funding, and contribute meaningfully to world challenges. In the first of two competitions, faculty submitted seventy-two proposals. The university invited eleven expanded proposals and after consultation with external reviewers awarded five grants, with the goal that all of the recipients would be in advantageous positions to compete for federal, foundation, or donor support. Although such an incentive system could foster mainstream work, the call for proposals specifically stated that the committee wanted to invest a certain percentage of the funding in high-risk projects. Not all incentives need succumb to the dictates of the market.

In the initial competition, the university awarded significant funding to create the Notre Dame Institute for Advanced Study. Annually, a dozen scholars pursue their research in residence. Though all disciplines are welcome, two interrelated emphases, both in accord with mission, shape the institute. The first is the incorporation of integrative and ultimate questions that often escape scholars enmeshed in everyday and sometimes narrow disciplinary practices. The institute encourages fellows to reflect on questions that probe the bases of their disciplines or extend beyond their disciplines to integrate the insights of other fields. The second is the relationship between the descriptive and the normative, between the world as it is and the world as it ought to be.

Another example of internally sponsored competition intended to enhance external competitiveness is a postdoctoral fellowship program we introduced, which was also related to our desire to be flexible in reallocating resources. Awarded on a competitive basis, twelve two-year named postdoctoral fellowships afforded selected graduates the opportunity to gain teaching experience and develop their research credentials. The result was they became more competitive and enjoyed the security of applying selectively for only the best jobs during their years of graduation and the first year of their fellowships; the purpose was to meet the goal of placing more graduates at premier colleges and universities. Notre Dame gained quality teachers and interlocutors in the short run and an improved record for placing graduate students in tenure-track positions at premier institutions in the long run. It was designed, then, to help us recruit incoming graduate students and to help them be better poised to compete for positions at the nation's leading colleges and universities.

We also introduced competition for assistant professor positions by having departments compete with one another. I would tell, say, six departments that they may search in competition with others, even though fewer than six positions would be filled. Only those departments that searched intensively, creatively, and with success, in other words, those that found great scholar-teachers, would receive a position. In the event every department had found a superb candidate, I had alternative strategies to locate the necessary resources, but that never happened. The innovation had several advantages, including encouraging departments to search for, instead of simply sifting through, candidates; raising the bar on faculty quality; and avoiding the politically awkward situation whereby the dean must veto a candidate. Under this system, the dean simply stated that the candidates in other departments were stronger. A university with a distinctive mission, say, a large array of integrative courses, can use such searches to ensure that considerations beyond disciplinary expertise play a role in hiring. One can also make the competition local. In some departments, two searches were authorized but only one line was granted; the fields within the department competed with one another to find the better candidate.

Problems and Challenges with Competition

Competition can lead to a number of problems and challenges. First, in imitating the best ideas of the competition and seeking to climb the rankings, universities may become too much like one another. This possibility is partly countered by the culture of diversity I described above, but assimilation is a danger. The pull of mainstream culture is so powerful that not only does a minority institution integrate many of its features, in doing so, it risks relinquishing its own distinguishing traits. Such a development would not only hinder opportunities for a university to flourish as distinctive, it would restrict the diversity of American higher education, which benefits from its religious and its nonreligious institutions, its liberal arts colleges and its research universities, its highly selective institutions and those with open admissions.

It is not always easy to find the right balance, so as to realize both aspects of distinction: difference and greatness. For example, Notre Dame long had a distinctive economics department, but its orientation toward social justice issues was not matched, as I noted in chapter 3, by an integration of state-of-the-art econometric and theoretical techniques. The situation involved an elevation of difference over quality; with considerable effort, we eventually moved toward a greater integration of the two. Yet as dean I often said that I would not want our philosophy or theology department to be ranked number one in the country. This partly tongue-in-cheek comment was designed to capture the ideas that if we were to become number one in philosophy, the department would have to be purely analytic, forgoing the history of philosophy and the larger questions that merit philosophy's special status at a Catholic university; and if we were to become number one in theology, that would mean having a religious studies rather than a theology department and adopting as our paradigm the disinterested study of religious phenomena instead of the theological concept of faith seeking understanding, which animates the Catholic tradition. I was not unhappy with each department being ranked in the top five or top fifteen and being recognized as the best of its kind. In truth, the danger here is not really competition but the temptation of letting rankings substitute for competition; Notre Dame's distinction, which may at times hurt its superficial rankings, continues to be a competitive advantage.

Second, internal competition must be attentive to both fairness and morale. It makes no sense if the departments and programs that are competing have not been given at least a base level of support that allows them to try to compete. A presupposition of the merit principle is that conditions must not be so absurd at the outset as to make fair play impossible. If a department is truly mediocre, with no prospects for development, then it is best closed down.

Further, if there are blatant winners and losers in the competition for selective excellence dollars, departmental morale can be devastated. This occurs if substantial dollars are taken from one unit and given to another and if the winners and losers are determined for too many years out, which destroys motivation. At Ohio State, an exercise was designed to determine which departments would receive targeted resources for the next five to ten years. That had the unintended consequence of sending the best faculty in the lesser departments packing. Ideal is a scenario where the competition continues over time, that is, incentives exist for departments to continue trying to improve. Introducing competition can also be bad for morale if the money is so modest as to make a competitive exercise meaningless. That is, the consequences are modest, but the workload is heavy enough that the lack of consequences makes the exercise counterproductive.

Third, competitions can be driven by bad criteria and can lead to category mistakes and poor judgment, for example, expecting a humanities professor to bring in significant research dollars when funding is less available in the humanities and more or less unrelated to quality of work. The goal to compete with other research universities can mean focusing limited resources on areas that count in such competitions while discarding others. SUNY Albany has over the years eliminated or reduced its faculty and course offerings in both ancient and modern languages, leaving intact only a major in Spanish, a bizarre development at a university that has as its motto "The World within Reach." In general, a tendency exists to invest dollars in what garners prestige and fosters further external resources instead of what advances knowledge and learning.

Fourth, competition could in principle lead to less cooperation and an erosion of community. The brutality of competition comes out in the following joke. As two hikers run from a grizzly bear, one yells, "Do you think we can outrun the bear?" The other responds, "I don't know, but I only need to outrun you!" Though the possibility of reduced cooperation across institutions exists in principle, in many years of engagement, including participation in more than twenty-five departmental reviews, I have never encountered this unhealthy phenomenon. Much as scholars read the essays of colleagues to make them better, faculty visit other universities to help them reach their potentials. It is simply part of the cultural and collegial ethos of the academy. Reviewing other departments can also be an opportunity to learn about effective strategies elsewhere. The competition for limited resources within a university is more likely to lead to the erosion of a common spirit and sense of common enterprise. The following can mitigate the problem: well-grounded criteria for the competition, including the avoidance of a reductionistic focus on merely quantitative factors; transparency about decisions; continual allusions to the common enterprise, which in the long run remains intact; gratitude for the continuing contributions of the faculty and departments that may not have received additional resources; and, as I noted above, continuing competition, so that further opportunities exist for those who may not have received additional resources or recognition recently.

Competition ensures that the best faculty are recognized, but it can also lead to market anomalies. For example, competition exacerbates the inequities that one sometimes finds at universities, especially between disciplines, as salaries are determined by the market. The increasing competition for new faculty members means that cases of salary compression or even inversion arise: newer assistants may make more than advanced assistants, and assistants may make more than some associates. Obviously such differences can tear at the fabric of a community.

Fifth, competition can drive up costs. As one university invests more in research, other universities follow and adjust to the market. A university that is not able to respond will lose out. The reverse side of competition demanding investment of more resources is that competition increases support, in cases where funding is available, and elevates those who are effective; it discourages spending money on weaker performers and encourages support for premier scholars. Because Notre Dame's newly configured economics department was at the time not as highly ranked as it has since become, we decided to add something distinctive to the start-up package in order to attract incoming assistant professors. We offered them a one-time research fund of $50,000, in addition to market salaries and a market teaching load. The following year the market adjusted, and every top program offered one-time research funds of $50,000 to junior economists. In this way the market goes up and up. Economists are particularly good at manipulating markets; each year they have a publication in which universities list the previous year's offers and support packages and their expectations for the next year. A strategic chairperson takes that list to the dean and makes the case for higher salaries and greater support. In addition to costing less, humanists tend to be less organized and strategic.

Finally, intensive competition and resulting migration from one university to another diminishes the loyalty faculty members might otherwise develop to their own institutions. They may be tempted to play the market to test their worth. At the same time, those who stay despite higher offers or those who never test the market show a higher level of devotion to their institutions than those who stay simply for lack of competition.

The market intrusion into disinterested knowledge has created justified unease, especially among humanists. A major reason for the academic's dissatisfaction with capitalism is its insistence on market value. Not only an attraction to social equity but also the intellectual's unease with market evaluations of one's own contributions (which are often quite low) contribute to the appeal of Marxism and neo-Marxism (and with it a less market-oriented economy that is more prepared to support intellectuals). A Marxist framework, however, is not likely to lead to a competitive university. The best solution would be a non-Marxist normative framework, which could resurrect the value of the intellectual. In a sense, a normative vision (of what should be) is essential to balance competition and an unfettered market, even if one needs to recognize the necessity and advantages of the market. Indeed, as one surveys the various challenges under competition, virtually every one can be countered by vision, greater resources, or both.

Incentives, or What the Second-Best Way to Motivate Faculty Members Is

The strongest motivation occurs when we pursue a good for its own sake. When the vision of a university is clear and compelling, faculty members want to participate and contribute because they identify with the goal and recognize its intrinsic value. However, one needs other strategies as well. At the next level are incentives. Whereas vision exerts power and influence through ideas, incentives serve the same purpose through a reward system that often, though not exclusively, involves funding.

Incentives, then, are a second strategy for motivating persons. We seek not only intrinsic goods but also goods that offer opportunities or recognition. Budgetary and academic priorities should be linked, and budgetary decisions should foster an institution's highest aspirations. Whatever priorities an institution might have, incentives can be introduced. Indeed, much of what I have already written about competition also involves incentives.

Creating competitions for faculty lines can function as an incentive for departments to search actively and creatively for superb candidates. Incentives can also be used for unusually strong hires or hires who advance diversity or mission. These can include upgrades, for example, elevating an assistant professor line to a tenured position, or prehires, that is, hiring someone in advance of a future retirement.

Incentives must sometimes be developed and consciously introduced. At some universities, administrators watch the bottom line at year end. They do not want to overspend (although often overspending has no serious consequences), but they also don't want to return money to the general pool, so just in case, they buy things they don't need—a new computer, copy machine, and so on. In a worst case scenario, those who spend less lose their money at year end, and those who overspend incur no penalties and possibly are even rewarded, since the next year's budget is based on the previous year's spending plus x percent. As a result, efficiency is not encouraged.

Addressing this irrational situation involves introducing flexibility and incentives. At other universities, money carries over at year end; this functions as an incentive to save, and one has the freedom to spend the surplus on strategic priorities the following year (one must simply report annually on how the money was spent). And if one overspends, one has to pay it back out of the next year's allocation; this accountability mechanism makes possible both incentives and negative sanctions.

At Notre Dame, when the policy was introduced, the college spent one-time money on bridging pre-hires for future years, so that selected departments could hire a particularly promising faculty member prior to the anticipated retirement of a current faculty member; as additional start-up funds for new hires; as matching commitments to help fund faculty research; as one-time allocations to faculty research accounts; for visiting appointments; and as top-off stipends for graduate students (to match competing offers). In one case, we even bundled $100,000 together to create a permanent endowment for undergraduate research, thus signaling to donors that we ourselves were investing precisely where we wanted them to invest.

Selective Excellence

Selective excellence is an important principle in any incentive system. A university will never become great if it offers incremental change across the board. Instead, it must identify a few areas for excellence and serious investment and then support others at reasonable levels. Once criteria for excellence are established and communicated and the administration begins applying them to make differential decisions, departments respond. Not only are new dollars awarded on the basis of this principle but departments that make consistently bad decisions lose funding.

An example of an incentive that integrates competition and accountability is a program we introduced at Notre Dame called midlevel graduate stipends. An important measure of scholarly standing is a university's ability to attract outstanding graduate students in head-to-head competition with other highly ranked universities. Financial considerations are an important factor in students' decisions about where to enroll. Like other good universities, Notre Dame has tuition waivers and regular stipends for graduate students, as well as some prize stipends, often called presidential stipends, set at a much higher level. The idea behind the initiative was to increase the number of higher and more competitive stipends by introducing a middle level between regular and presidential.

The design was as follows. An assessment mechanism was drafted and discussed with directors of graduate studies to measure strengths in graduate studies and overall research strengths. Each year graduate programs were reviewed. On the basis of a sifting of the information, some departments and programs were designated eligible to nominate incoming students for higher stipends to enhance both recruitment and support. Others were not eligible. The nominated students were then reviewed by a faculty committee, much as presidential nominees are sifted in competition with one another. Departments placed in the pool were told that they needed to address certain areas in order to remain in the pool for the next year. Departments that were not in the pool were informed of their weaknesses and told that they needed to address selected areas if they wanted to join the pool the next year. Examples of feedback included introducing a better review of graduate students to reduce late attrition, improving the departmental teacher-training program for graduate students, and developing a more distinctive profile that resonated with Notre Dame's mission.

Obvious advantages to this model (over other competitive models that choose programs for the long term) are that departments in the pool must continue to improve to stay in the pool and those that are not in the pool know that they can seek to make a case in the future if they improve. Funding for midlevel stipends increased the incentives for graduate programs to strive to fulfill higher aspirations and allowed the university to reward the best-performing programs. It also enhanced recruitment. Our intent was to strengthen the incentive system, enhance our competitiveness, and assure a wise and efficient use of funds, with an investment in core departments.

Harvard University, noting that doctoral students in the humanities and social sciences take too long to receive their degrees, introduced an incentive/accountability scheme, whereby for every five graduate students in years eight or higher of a PhD program, the department or program would lose one admissions/fellowship slot for a new doctoral student. As is wise when such penalty conditions are stipulated, new support was also introduced. Students were given funding for a full year, not simply nine months, of dissertation writing, and they were freed from teaching obligations during that year. The almost immediate result was more rapid movement of students toward degree completion. When the program was announced in 2005, sixteen of twenty-four departments ran the risk of losing thirty-three students. By the time the program was implemented, after a warning period, only two programs lost slots (Jaschik).

A recent Notre Dame initiative similarly works with incentives to help students finish their degrees on time, an issue that is important not only because students might run out of support or waste university resources by never finishing but also because hiring departments often interpret time to degree as an indirect signal of whether or not a candidate will be likely to develop a tenurable case on time. Called the 5+1 Postdoctoral Fellowship Program and partially supported by the Mellon Foundation, this program, which was introduced in 2016 by my successor, guarantees every graduate student in Arts and Letters who completes the doctorate within five years a sixth year as a postdoctoral fellow. The fellowships come with a very good stipend, professional development funds, and the health benefits of a university employee. Fellows have the flexibility to choose one of two options during this transitional year: to teach a relatively low load of two courses per year, which frees them to develop their research even as it allows them to expand their teaching portfolios in advance of entering the highly competitive academic job market; or to take a professional apprenticeship, for example, at the university press, in the center for the study of languages and cultures, in the office of digital learning, or with development, so that they are able to explore new areas, round out their skills, and develop meaningful professional experience in advance of becoming candidates for positions beyond the academic job market. Although incentives tend to function in tandem with competition, here the incentive reinforces community: all who satisfy the condition are eligible for the postdoctoral award. In guaranteeing support to all students who finish and in offering them either a relatively low teaching load or other career-enhancing and career-altering opportunities, the postdoctoral program is distinctive. It is not by chance that the initiative arose after graduate funding had been moved to the colleges, which increased the flexibility of each dean.

Incentives for Research

Universities often have targeted funds to encourage projects that make sense for the university as a whole. For example, a Catholic university might have research grants for projects that link the diverse disciplines with the study of religion or funding for guest lecturers who address mission-related topics. In this sense incentives in the form of funding opportunities can serve the university's overarching mission and motivate faculty research.

Faculty are eager for grants, which help them to pursue research, increase resources, and gain recognition, but grants also allow faculty to buy out courses. In the humanities, year-long fellowships release faculty members from their teaching responsibilities and provide recovery funding so that replacement teachers can be hired. At Notre Dame, we introduced the policy that if a faculty member earned, say, $120,000 per year and received a fellowship for $60,000, then the faculty member would receive his or her full salary, which was already budgeted; the dean's office would take $30,000 for its annual cash allotment in support of one-time projects; and the department would receive $30,000, which could be used for replacement teaching or, if it could manage the lost courses more efficiently, other purposes, such as faculty or student research. Here incentives existed for faculty to develop competitive proposals that would give them more research time while ensuring that the university had funds to replace them. Note that the incentive structure existed for both the faculty member and the department as a whole. At Notre Dame, any faculty member seeking a university-supported sabbatical must also apply for at least two national or international grants or fellowships. As a result of these incentives, along with a strong faculty and effective support structures, over the final decade of my tenure, we ranked first nationally in the number of National Endowment for the Humanities Fellowships and sixth among liberal arts faculties at leading research universities, behind Harvard, Berkeley, Princeton, Michigan, and Chicago, in the receipt of fellowships from agencies, such as the American Council of Learned Societies, the National Endowment for the Humanities, and the Guggenheim Foundation, used by the National Research Council in its rankings (Roche, *Dean's Report* 7, 26).

Enhancing Learning

If a university wants to see more courses of a particular kind, for example, ones that focus on the development of oral skills or that address ethical issues, it can offer course development grants for new courses. At Notre Dame these have traditionally involved summer stipends, with the idea that faculty are losing time from research by developing courses they might not otherwise develop. The incentive is to ensure that faculty interests line up with university needs and aspirations and to compensate them for shifting their plans. The following, for example, were offered at Notre Dame:

- Grants for courses on business and the liberal arts in order to persuade students that they can gain some understanding of the business world without having to major in business. The grants were for faculty outside of economics who wished to design courses that integrated traditional liberal arts areas with business-related concerns, for example, the anthropological study of corporate culture, economic sociology, literary portrayals of the business world, the psychology of leadership, or Asian cultures and business.
- Development grants for courses before or after students' study abroad in order to integrate the study abroad experience more organically with courses taken at the home university.

- Grants for faculty who wanted to develop an entirely new course in which diversity played the central role or partial grants for faculty who wanted simply to develop a few new units for an already-existing course that did not yet include diversity but could be enriched if it were expanded in this way.
- Grants to develop courses outside of theology that would enhance the university's distinctive mission. The goal of the initiative was to encourage faculty to think about their teaching in relation to the religious affiliation of the institution and to encourage students, in turn, to think about issues that touch on faith.

Colleges within a university often have the incentive to develop continuing education programs that bring in more resources. In such cases the tuition dollars normally go directly to the college that offers such classes, with the central administration taking a certain percentage for overhead.

At Notre Dame we offered an incentive for departments to encourage sophomore students to read a book, selected by faculty, over the summer and to have evening discussions about it early in the fall semester. The college purchased the books and covered refreshments for those evenings. Whenever a department wanted to bring the author to campus, we paid for that visit as well. The idea was not only to stretch learning into the summer and into the voluntary realm but also to foster community and peer learning. In the first year, faculty members led the seminars for the rising juniors. In the second year, the veterans of the previous seminars, after modest preparation by faculty members, were invited to lead the seminars for the next class of rising juniors. If it were a different book, the student leaders could discuss it first with a faculty member. Student-to-student engagement not only fosters the best learning, it mimics the learning that continues after college.

Alas, teaching and incentives are too infrequently linked. One reason for high failure rates in some fields relates to ineffective teaching methods, which do not make use of the latest science on student learning. Research on learning recommends that less class time be spent on straight lectures and more class time be spent on active learning—with students engaged in asking questions, giving immediate indications of knowledge (levels) by using clickers or other feedback methods, solving problems in groups, and discussing the material with their peers. The instructor's role is to give feedback (Freeman). Why do we see so little innovation along these lines? Because insufficient incentives exist to motivate faculty to change their teaching methods; here, the elevation of research over teaching represents a problem with an ironic twist: research on student learning is insufficiently integrated, at times even ignored.

Problems and Challenges with Incentives

The above example brings us to the first challenge associated with incentives: poorly designed, counterproductive, or otherwise bad incentives. Anticipating and avoiding bad incentives is as important as ensuring that good incentives serve an institution's highest priorities. At some universities, the best way to obtain a significant raise is to get an offer from another institution. Faculty are thereby motivated to spend their time applying elsewhere and lose their attachment to their home institutions; they may also leave. The best counterstrategy is, on the one hand, to have alternative incentives—in this case that means highly differential salary adjustments, so that persons who could obtain offers elsewhere receive adjustments in advance of their entering the market—and, on the other hand, to refuse occasionally to match offers. Some faculty members were taken aback when their chairpersons and I made decisions not to match external offers; in our eyes their contributions were not sufficiently excellent. Such precedents certainly give pause for reflection when one is considering whether to go into the chairperson's or dean's office prepared to bargain. Another example of a bad incentive: Some universities make faculty assessments on the basis of number of completed dissertations per faculty member; this elevation of quantity over quality creates an incentive for faculty members to accept and approve work that is mediocre instead of telling their students that the work is not sufficiently strong and needs to be revised.

In an effort to help build the faculty, Notre Dame once developed what were called target-of-opportunity hires. In the initial years, the university offered these as permanent add-on positions. If a department found two outstanding candidates, one of whom was a minority or a woman, it could hire both. The idea was laudatory, but the practice had three problems. First, aggressive departments would find sufficient candidates, so that the budgetary add-ons through tuition increases and other revenue were completely consumed by target-of-opportunity hires. Instead of being part of the picture, the target-of-opportunity hires replaced all other priorities. Departments had difficulty prioritizing, and colleges were forced to cover the salary and nonsalary expenses for these new hires from unfilled faculty positions until the provost could provide the additional funds, which in most cases came years later. Second, departments would sometimes game the system. For example, a department would conduct a search and suggest that the leading candidate was a white male Protestant, whereas the second-place candidate was Latina Catholic. Because the department would never consider dropping its standards with respect to quality, the chairperson would argue that the department needed extra funds so that it could hire two people, ensuring that the Catholic female minority would also be hired. Third, departments had no incentive to set a high bar for their target-of-opportunity hires, since the line was fully free.

Once having recognized these problems, the university abandoned the program, but the College of Arts and Letters decided to continue it with altered parameters. Now the college covers the salary of a new faculty member with temporary funding or cash until the department has a departure or retirement. In this way, target-of-opportunity hires no longer compete with other long-term initiatives, as they are no longer permanent add-ons. The department that makes a successful case receives the line but only as a temporary addition, that is, as a prehire for someone still to be replaced. Departments no longer have the absurd incentive of setting a low bar when evaluating candidates; they proceed with caution because the prehire would be a permanent replacement for a coveted faculty position. Departments have an incentive to search for prehires in order to ensure that the college does not reallocate its lines to departments that have more pressing needs or consistently produce higher-quality work. In addition, the departments that have prehires garner an extra faculty line for several years, during which time two faculty members technically occupy the same position.

Financially the situation is much better. The university is not committing to a second line in perpetuity but needs only soft funding or cash for x number of years, which is always easier to locate. If all existing lines in a college are funded, in any given year some positions will not be filled. Funding from such vacancies is available for one-time purposes.

Any change in academic policy usually involves long, drawn-out discussions, which are a disincentive for undertaking change. This is where the democratic structure of American universities is most vibrant and where entrenched interests are most at play. At Notre Dame, students take five courses per semester. We have an unusually heavy set of curricular requirements, which means our students have less freedom in course selection. If Notre Dame were to move to four courses per semester, as at some peer universities, faculty could expect more student focus on each class, and average class size would drop (the same size faculty would be teaching fewer enrolled students, that is, the number of students times four, not five). Proposals on the table a decade ago that might have changed both the number of courses and student requirements (going to four courses would have required reducing the requirements) were met with strong faculty resistance. Another idea put forward during the review was to move away from requiring two philosophy and two theology courses toward having students take one of each, with a third chosen from between the two, thus creating a bit of a market mechanism. Departments with better courses would be rewarded. The same idea was in play for science and mathematics. Instead of two of each, students would take one of each, with a third chosen in either area. Faculty in those departments strongly resisted, partly for academic reasons (how could any educated student get by with fewer than two courses in their areas?) and partly for self-interested reasons (departments would surely have lost faculty lines over time). A lot of effort went into the reform; still, only tiny changes were made around the edges. Another example of an incentive against undertaking change—and of faculty prominence in curricular discussions—was a course our college faculty discussed at *ten* different meetings (beginning under my predecessor) before it was eliminated and a replacement course identified. The time investment was staggering. One understands why major curricular changes are few and far between and why administrators simply let the status quo be.

The second challenge is that incentives can undermine the internal motivation that exists in the true scholar, making faculty members more outer-directed. This is in principle a legitimate concern. However, because good scholars want to be at good institutions and also want to be recognized for their good work, the concern is modest. Even if one works for internal reasons, external recognition can be uplifting and can add to one's motivation, enthusiasm, and sense of solidarity with the institution. Related to this, incentives can steer research to funding areas elevated by a university or foundation or federal agency. In many cases these represent objectively appealing areas, and when they do not, this is a modest price to pay as long as there are various sources of funding and not all funding is for applied areas.

CHAPTER EIGHT

Accountability, or
How Criticism Can Be a Gift

Although motivating faculty members through vision or, alternatively, incentives, is more desirable, accountability is no less necessary to the functioning of an effective organization. Universities are accountable to the board of trustees, and state universities are additionally accountable to the relevant state commission on higher education, the legislature, and indirectly the taxpayers. All universities are further accountable to donors, faculty, students, and those, often parents, who pay tuition. When universities take out loans to undertake building projects or cover unexpected drops in the endowment, they are also accountable to credit rating agencies.

In general, the universities must make clear that they are using their resources wisely and efficiently, not only to justify their tuition increases but also so they can receive continuing support from donors. Accountability is on the rise at American universities. In many states, funding for universities had traditionally been awarded solely according to number of enrolled students in the first weeks of classes; now it tends to be awarded on performance measures, such as graduation rates (Quinterno, *Making Performance*). In development offices, stewarding existing donors, with reports, has become as important as doing research on potential donors.

After vision, my most prominent goal as dean involved a cluster of issues having to do with enhancing faculty governance, clarifying policies, improving efficiencies, ensuring accountability, and garnering more resources. Clear and transparent policies and procedures help assure higher morale by guaranteeing fairness, and they can be crafted to increase faculty participation and responsibility. In turn, the effective use of resources inspires confidence among donors and others who may be capable of providing more resources. Linking accountability with new resources is effective not only for donors but also for faculty, because if faculty see that accountability serves a higher end, namely, more resources for priorities, they are more likely to be supportive of changes resulting from accountability.

Let me give a seemingly pedestrian example of a policy change—the introduction of enrollment management—that rendered resources more efficient. At Notre Dame, we consistently offered classes—both undergraduate and graduate—to as few as two or three students. At the same time we had far too many classes with more than fifty students, which limits discussion. We wanted instead to have more classes with twenty or so students. Proper reconfiguration of faculty assignments and course offerings helped us address a significant number of these cases. Some such lower-enrolled classes should, for a variety of reasons, be offered and subsidized, and they can be among a student's most memorable experiences, but the department should have to present a strong academic argument for these offerings; they should not stand simply for lack of oversight, for example, letting faculty teach whatever they want irrespective of student need. We introduced the policy that course enrollments below a certain number required justification. Within a few years, a majority of our undergraduate classes were in the ideal range, and the percentage with more than fifty students dropped more or less consistently. Because enrollment management resulted in fewer classes with tiny numbers of students, we were able to offer a smaller number of classes in total; this in turn reduced the percentage of classes taught by part-time faculty. Adjunct-taught classes were at 18 percent when I arrived, then fell annually—in the new policy's first year to 9 percent, and then to 8 percent, 7 percent, 6 percent, and, finally, 5 percent, where they stayed more or less stable through the end of my term. Our number of underenrolled classes remained in the single digits each semester, as departments thought more carefully about offering courses that resonate with student needs and interests and rotating those that were likely to attract fewer numbers.

Because of their greater external oversight and fewer resources per student and faculty member, state universities have tended to excel in efficiency. Some of them, such as those in the Committee on Institutional Cooperation (CIC)—thirteen large public universities plus Northwestern and the University of Chicago—are part of a consortium and so share policies on various issues. Being part of a consortium has the advantages of allowing members to share data, trade best practices, provide fora on common challenges, and foster connections for potential collaboration. In addition, such a group provides an audience for sharing one's story. Decisions fostering efficiency have greatly helped these institutions remain competitive despite limitations in funding. When I was chairperson at Ohio State, the annual meetings with chairs of the other CIC institutions, which took place on a different campus each year, were rewarding: we discussed common puzzles, shared best practices, and gave each other updates on new developments.

Over time I learned to distinguish between what I called a culture of responsibility and a culture of accountability. In the former, one believes others will follow through on requests and simply expects that to happen. In the latter, one ensures, through various strategies, that initiatives have been completed. As dean I discovered that even with very good subordinates, the second model was necessary. I met with each of my associate deans individually on a weekly basis to discuss their areas of responsibility and think out loud together about puzzles and strategies. In addition, my executive assistant kept a list of all special projects that I had assigned to the person or that the person had initiated and said would be a priority. The executive assistant also met once weekly with the persons privately to review progress, and if a project was not being completed, I would be notified, so that I could ensure accountability or shift priorities. The system worked extremely well and was, furthermore, efficient. The subordinates were actually grateful for being kept on track, and if there was a reason to push back a deadline, place a project lower in the hierarchy, or drop it completely, that could be done consciously. To ensure the tracking of projects, I simply needed to ensure that my assistant was present at group meetings, where tasks were distributed, and inform her of agreed-upon projects after private meetings took place. One of the most frustrating things for an administrator is to assign a project to resolve a problem or advance a priority, assume it has been carried out, and then discover later that it was never addressed. Such situations waste time, leave problems or opportunities unaddressed, and wear on the administrator psychologically. Revisiting issues that one has already addressed is one of the most tiresome aspects of being dean.

One of the challenges I had when I started as dean was that almost all authority and responsibility were with the dean himself. There was an associate dean whose main goals were to oversee staff and keep the spending on track, an associate dean who ran the research support office, and an associate dean who oversaw scheduling and advising. As one associate dean put it, they had been asked to keep the trains running on time. As new initiatives emerged, my job became more complex, and over time I asked the various associate deans to assume more responsibility. Eventually, because of new initiatives, greater accountability, and expanding size, we moved to four associate deans and a budget person. A new position was created for a dean of faculty affairs, and one dean assisted with development. Since the associate deans were defined by function, not field (e.g., arts, humanities, and social sciences), there was greater unity. In a sense all four associate deans had new or radically redefined positions and were engaged in tasks and responsibilities that I had spun off from my own work as dean. That is of course a one-time issue. As they worked longer, I learned more and more from them, and the meetings focused on collective thinking out loud as they brought me their most complex issues. Although I wanted to accomplish much, my goal was not to have changes associated with my person but instead to have them built into the way we did things.

In the academy one often needs to phase in change. A policy I adopted essentially subconsciously, but which moved us from a culture of responsibility to a culture of accountability, was to introduce good ideas, suggest their usefulness, and then over time, as one or the other department adopted them on a pilot basis, make them mandatory. These sometimes included issues that were modestly controversial, such as including a reference to Notre Dame as a Catholic university in our job ads, or that involved more work, such as preparing written annual review letters for junior faculty members; introducing departmental honors programs, which meant offering special courses for academically stronger students and advising more senior theses; and arranging departmental receptions or ceremonies for graduating seniors. It takes time to let a culture adjust and evolve. Before one knows it, a foreign idea becomes a best practice and then simply part of the culture in every department. The phase-in process from suggestion to pilot projects to universal expectation serves three purposes: it helps with the reception of the new idea, permits one to learn from the best and worst pilot projects, and allows time for cultural change.

Some things I required take place immediately, yet virtually every change took some time to gain support within the ranks. I received several angry memos about enrollment management; then they ceased over time, and enrollment management became part of the culture. On my first day I announced that all vacant faculty positions would return to the dean and could be reallocated to other departments; they would not automatically return to the departments. At first faculty did not believe me. Then they protested. Eventually, faculty would inform one another that of course the line goes back to the dean, and we need to try to build a compelling case for retaining it. Annual faculty evaluations and merit raises were also introduced right away, as I outline below, but they were not formally endorsed by the faculty until years later.

As a university grows in size or range of initiatives, it becomes more complex. Decisions can no longer be made on an ad hoc basis. Instead, policies and procedures need to be introduced. How quickly all of this evolved in the American landscape is remarkable. It was not always the case. A senior colleague at Ohio State told me an amusing story that had happened decades back. As chairperson he one day received a call from the dean, asking him who had tenure in the department. There were no records in the college office. His eyes twinkled, and he smiled as he told me the story, noting the temptation, which he resisted, to decide who in the department at that time should have tenure and who should not, instead of informing the dean of what really was the case.

One of the first things I did when I became chairperson was carefully read *Robert's Rules of Order*. The intention was fairly basic—to ensure as the moderator of our discussions that they followed our stated guidelines. But I discovered something more—and it was amusing. Under the previous chairs, authority for interpreting the rules had been implicitly granted to a senior colleague, who told the chairs how certain complex votes were to be conducted, which kinds of motion trumped others, and so forth. But he was often wrong, and no one had bothered to check. To know the rules inside and out and be able to guide colleagues was a huge advantage.

To ensure appropriate articulation and dissemination of policies and procedures, I developed at Notre Dame a *Reference Guide for Chairpersons and Faculty*. It grew each year until it was well over 250 pages. The development of such a document and the creation of corresponding committees and structures to ensure its implementation are to some degree one-time events, needed as a university moves from a smaller operation guided by informal and often ad hoc procedures to a more professional organization, even if such documents need to be edited or adjusted by associate deans on a regular basis thereafter, the result of new initiatives or policies emerging from complexities one had not previously encountered.

Standardization of policies and procedures serves multiple purposes. It increases faculty participation and governance and ensures communication with faculty on standards as well as on opportunities and obligations. It ensures due process and fairness, as opposed to ad hoc and idiosyncratic decision making. In many cases, it also enhances efficiency and saves resources. I was told by a colleague, who had moved from Ohio State, that she was eager to see policies created in her new department, as she had learned to what extent clear and transparent policies protect the majority against those who seek unique favors or are so enamored of themselves that they insist on special treatment. Finally, not just rules, suggestions, and best practices but our normative vision and aspirations were embedded in the *Reference Guide* and so were present to all. While such policies may seem to counter the principle of flexibility, with good arguments the policies could be changed in house, and the *Reference Guide* opened by my inviting good counterarguments that would encourage us to reconsider the soundness of any policy.

Every university benefits from leaders who can craft a compelling vision, but a university is also enhanced by administrators, whose focus may be ensuring efficiency and accountability. Two examples of simple management expectations involved requiring each administrator to develop a position manual and conduct meaningful and productive staff evaluations.

A position manual, the initial creation of which should be delegated to the administrative assistant, details the tasks of the position, the schedule of responsibilities by date, and sample documents for each task. That way, the administrative assistant prompts the administrator when it is time to start an annual project, and the administrator has the previous year's letter, report, or memorandum on the subject as a starting point. In addition to a section organized by date, thematic sections are created on such topics as searches, faculty evaluation, visitors, conferences, student awards, donor stewardship, and so on. The position manual serves at least two purposes: it ensures that the administrator is not reinventing the wheel each year as repetitive tasks arise and that a new person could step in and assume the responsibilities without starting from scratch; in either case, it saves time. Moving chairpersons and staff to accept this innovation was not easy, but we collected the manuals, and with the assistance of my staff, I gave chairpersons feedback through an iterative process. When I discovered, after having been dean, that some departments had in the interim more or less abandoned the project, I realized I had not communicated well enough its rationale and had not been strict enough in insisting on compliance.

Meaningful staff evaluations are also essential. Some obvious best practices exist: review the position description, acquire copies of previous reviews, keep notes during the year, provide honest and candid evaluations, give specific examples of both excellent and substandard performance, and initiate a development plan. Administrators depend heavily on staff persons, and helping them develop to their full potential is imperative. This can be done only through a healthy relationship in which honest feedback is provided in a supportive environment, during the year as well as, more formally, on an annual basis. Faculty, most of whom do not regularly supervise others, need help when they transition to administrative positions, where such reviews are expected. Early in my tenure, one chairperson said that he absolutely needed to replace his assistant, who had been underperforming for years. I asked to see the annual reviews: they were all glowing.

An important principle of accountability is that the budget be in line with priorities. When academic priorities and budgetary allocations diverge, cynicism results. One of the worst institutional experiences I ever had was to participate in a curriculum review at Ohio State that was animated by a profound vision of what a liberally educated person in the twenty-first century should know and be able to do and what courses would lead to that outcome. Then after exerting both hard work and extensive political capital to help implement the ideal in my department, I was informed that the university was scrapping extensive parts of the ideal, including the language and culture component, for lack of budgetary resources. The lesson I took from this travesty was clear: vision and budget must always work in tandem. Asking in what ways the budget matches one's vision and priorities is appropriate for an oversight board; such questions ensure that those at the top of any hierarchy are also held accountable.

Negative Consequences

Accountability can also be linked to consequences or negative sanctions as a third means of motivation, beyond vision and incentives. Persons do not wish to be wounded or hurt; they seek to avoid harmful consequences. Without negative consequences for poor performance, however, the full range of motivational strategies is not utilized. Though less appealing than the carrot, the stick is sometimes necessary. Yet it should never be used when an incentive will work instead. A mundane example makes this clear. Since 2007, Notre Dame has offered an annual incentive to faculty and staff and their spouses: they receive a modest reduction in their monthly contribution to health insurance if they take some relatively harmless tests and fill out a health-risk questionnaire as part of a wellness initiative. The initial rollout was uneventful. Many looked forward to a free and confidential assessment of their current health status and recommendations for improvement, and most were happy to save a few dollars a month. In 2015, for example, 62 percent of faculty and staff took advantage of the opportunity. In 2013 Penn State did something analogous, but they chose not to offer an incentive but instead to impose a penalty: those who did not participate paid a fine. The Penn State questionnaire was also much more invasive, asking faculty about their plans to become pregnant and about problems relating to separation or divorce. Even beyond these transgressions, the contrast is in principle valid. The incentive model is slightly enticing, whereas the negative consequences model is taken to be objectionable and coercive. Penn State, not surprisingly, backed off its plan (Wilson).

Departments that fall short of expectations should be at risk of losing lines when faculty members resign or retire. A dean should be willing to close programs that are weak and to say no to departmental requests for searches or hires that are not compelling or do not match priorities. Ideally, the chairperson is willing to say no if the department hesitates to set an appropriately high bar for a promotion-and-tenure case or wants to settle on a mediocre candidate simply to fill a faculty position and avoid the work of another search. However, the dean, being more distant from the action, should be prepared to take a certain number of hits for chairpersons. In some cases, I offered to be the one who said no after hearing the chairperson's discontent; some were willing to be honest with me for that reason; others, even more admirably, were willing to take tough public stands on their own.

Most academic administrators, one hopes, will be able to satisfy their goals with vision and incentives, but when they can't, one advantage of negative sanctions is that they rarely need be complex. One need not be creative; one simply needs to be willing to say no and have the courage and willingness to weather the consequences when resistance arises.

The negative consequences that I used the most were vetoes of potential hires, negative tenure decisions, removal of faculty lines from departments, the closing of graduate programs and interdisciplinary centers, increased teaching loads for nonresearchers, and 0 percent raises. Virtually every one of these strategies, however, can be countered in advance by the use of incentives or other creative structures. When other strategies fail, one must simply appeal to the criteria for excellence and make the necessary decisions, recognizing that it is not a personal issue but a decision on behalf of the institution's vision and standards. Failure to make tough decisions, burdening one's successor with one's mistakes, is among the greatest sins an administrator can make.

Faculty Evaluation and Mentoring

An obvious area for differential adjustments involves merit raises. The raises I awarded annually spanned a range from 0 to 20 percent or more, even when the base increase was relatively modest. Reviews encourage faculty development and ensure well-grounded salary adjustments. The evaluation involves a collection and review of materials on teaching, research, and service. Critical is that one have clear principles and goals, that one be transparent about what materials are important and will be reviewed, and that the review culminate in meaningful feedback. Beyond providing guidance to faculty members, such reviews afford faculty members the opportunity to express concerns about their progress to date and suggest ways in which the chairperson, colleagues, and university can assist them in achieving departmental goals and university standards. Ideally, the spirit of reviews is to be candid and constructive. When people are not performing well, they are often unhappy themselves and might well be grateful for avenues to improve or other ways in which to contribute. The conversations can also help with collective efforts at thinking through areas of common concern.

In universities where merit raises are now the norm, some faculty members initially and vocally opposed them. Because state universities are more accountable to the legislature, they tended to move more quickly toward merit raises. When I arrived at Ohio State in 1984, raises were already differential. Indeed, all the funding was differential; there was no across-the-board increase whatsoever, even for satisfactory performance. One of the deans wanted to make sure that the raises were sufficiently differential and so required that every year, 60 percent of the money go to 40 percent of the people, a seemingly modest but in fact significant modification of the salary scale over time.

When I served as chairperson, I became concerned about some faculty neglecting their teaching or service or not being engaged in research and so introduced the radical concept that a faculty member who had a substandard rating in any of the three areas of the profession would receive a 0 percent raise, no matter how impressive the other areas were. We could not survive and flourish as a community, I argued, if people did not meet minimal expectations. The policy certainly motivated faculty to perform appropriate service and not to neglect the classroom, not least of all because raises were public. I also discovered that service, which tends to be underrated, could be a difference maker with those whose teaching and research were modestly similar. Although I received resistance in one or more specific cases, with threats of lawsuits and the like, none of which actually occurred, the idea in principle was simply accepted as the way things are done at an ambitious state university. Great variety in performance led over time to great variation in compensation.

One of my early challenges at Notre Dame involved faculty evaluations. At the time, with the exception of one department out of the twenty in the college, systematic evaluations of faculty members did not exist. One or two chairpersons had clearly warranted recommendations for salary adjustments, most simply asked for across-the-board raises, and a few responded to the squeaky wheel. When I met with the chairpersons and then again with faculty during my first weeks as dean, I explained the importance of systematic faculty evaluations and asked chairpersons to begin departmental discussions on criteria. I asked that three principles be followed: that appropriate materials be collected to evaluate performance, that differential recommendations be made, and that feedback be given to the faculty members.

The idea was so foreign that virtually no one took me seriously. My announcement, it turned out, had fallen on deaf ears. It simply did not register as something that would or could be translated into reality. Some months later, the chairpersons confessed unease and hesitancy in dealing with faculty on this issue, and those in favor of the policy asked me to write the faculty to explain it again. Although I had already communicated with the faculty in person, I chose to back up the chairpersons. I did so, using in my paper memo (the year was 1998, and the shift to all e-mail correspondence occurred a month or two later) the strategically infelicitous phrase, "highly differential raises, where appropriate." No one at my previous university, which had a much more competitive internal economy, would have blinked at the phrase, but Notre Dame was different. Within twenty-four hours, more than fifty faculty members had written the faculty senate protesting this imposition of state-university accountability and differentiation on a Catholic university. The faculty senate held a public forum, at which perhaps thirty people spoke vociferously against the scheme. One person spoke in favor. Given by the moderator the final word, I identified about seven different arguments against and sought to counter each one, reiterating my plans to go forward. The moderator, one of our most distinguished endowed chairs and a liberal and well-liked professor, closed the meeting by recalling his arrival at Notre Dame from an Ivy League university. He asked the chairperson at the end of the year for his evaluation and was told that, at Notre Dame, no such evaluations were done. He indicated to the audience that was not necessarily a good thing.

The mandate had come not from the provost but from my own sense of what was appropriate, and I was told by more than one person in the higher administration that I might want to back off so as to avoid a revolution of some kind. What I did instead was twofold. First, I changed my rhetoric from "merit raises" to "mentoring," which was indeed part of the process. Mentoring had been weak, which is inevitably the case in a culture where no evaluation takes place. It was difficult to argue against the moral obligation of mentoring assistant professors and associate professors who were long in rank. In making the argument, I could also draw on the words of the prominent colleague who had chaired the faculty senate forum. This shift in rhetoric worked amazingly well. The goal became to congratulate those who were performing well, to mentor those who needed guidance, and to try to address the overlooked situation of so many persons not succeeding at promotion. Second, I agreed to move away from the system I liked at Ohio State, where 100 percent of the funding was granted simply on merit, and toward a system where those faculty who were already meeting the very high expectations of a premier research university would receive a base increase, which I would set each year, on the basis of a combination of inflationary indicators and the size of my allocation. The remainder would be 100 percent merit. It was still a 100 percent merit scheme, as many failed to qualify for the base increase, but the distribution paid homage to the local culture and climate.

There continued to be much wrangling over the policy, and most of the persons who privately expressed support were uneasy about publicly defending the unpopular policy. Naturally, the stronger faculty for the most part wanted differential adjustments, but they were less vocal. Women, who were fewer in number, were on the whole supportive, recognizing that they would only benefit from greater transparency and fairness. Resistance to change is always intense among those who have done well under a previous system, whereas support among those who simply hope for something better is invariably modest (Machiavelli 19–20). In my fifth year, I charged a faculty committee to review the policy. The review took two years and included visits with every department. The committee report endorsed the policy with two suggested changes. First, some departments were not implementing the policy fully, that is, they needed to do a better job of fulfilling the guidelines, especially in terms of giving feedback to faculty members. Second, chairpersons did not like setting the raises for their colleagues, so the committee recommended that the dean set all five hundred salaries, on the basis of conferences with each of the twenty chairpersons. The policy passed unanimously at the College Council, our legislative body, seven years after it had been vigorously attacked as unjust, unworkable, foreign to Notre Dame, and anti-Catholic. This was a sobering sign of how slowly cultures change but a promising sign that cultures do change.

The process was as follows: chairpersons submitted in advance of their meetings with me three pieces of information: a ranking of faculty members, with a brief rationale for each decision, on the basis of performance in the previous calendar year; a list of important cases of salary equity, that is, a ranked list of persons whose salaries had not kept pace with their contributions over time, independently of their performance during the previous year; and a ranked list of persons for possible one-time research support. The meetings were significant, as it was the one occasion each year to reflect systematically on every single faculty member and to ask how we might help each one to reach his or her potential. An external review I had arranged of my office had recommended eliminating the meetings and replacing them with only paper submissions, since twenty meetings, ranging from thirty to sixty minutes each, seemed to them excessive. I followed their advice for a year but noticed that they were wrong and reintroduced the practice: The annual meetings with chairpersons to discuss the progress of every faculty member were essential for mentoring and for strategic as well as evaluative purposes. One might fear that with differential raises, one would want weaker colleagues, but this was not the case: stronger colleagues attract better students and stronger departments receive more resources, including more salary funding. Over time we had enough money to reward good performance, independently of comparisons.

One of the essential parts of a faculty review process is the conversation with faculty members, including the question, How can I help you better reach your goals? Every faculty member, including every administrator, benefits from constructive feedback on issues both large and small. Faculty want to be thanked for their contributions, and they enjoy thinking out loud with others about their current trajectories and priorities. I can recall in my first year as chairperson at Ohio State giving a faculty member a 0.6 percent raise. He made a point to thank me, not for the raise, which he noted was paltry, but for my having reviewed his materials carefully and having written him a letter about his performance; I had taken him seriously and acknowledged his work. Still, many administrators are not keen on awarding merit raises, which is why the chairpersons wanted to delegate authority back to me. Telling faculty that they are not doing superior work can lead to conflict, for a human tendency exists to see ourselves as better than others see us. In a study at the University of Nebraska, 95 percent of faculty rated themselves as above average in teaching, and 68 percent placed their teaching performance in the top 25 percent (Cross 10). Negative feedback is invariably a surprise.

While most salary adjustments were highly differential, the differences among endowed chairs tended to be modest. In other words, where radical differentiation is not appropriate, it is not undertaken. Among the endowed chairs, there were exceptions: those who were simply off the charts in the quality and extent of their scholarly activity; those whose salaries were lower in relation to performance and needed to be raised over time; and those who were in fields, such as economics, where the interuniversity competition was radically escalating.

The different measures of performance must be developed by the departments themselves, with appropriate checks for weaker departments to ensure that their incentives are in line with disciplinary standards or, if they differ, that compelling arguments exist for the difference. In economics, for example, journal placements are far more important for impact and rankings than grants, which can involve industry hiring persons for relatively low-level work. Indeed, not simply journal publications but publications in specific journals are essential: there are more than two hundred refereed economics journals, but not all journals are equal in impact. Rankings of economics journals have been developed on the basis of the average number of citations received by a typical article in the journal (Kalaitzidakis, Stengos, and Mamuneas). Such studies show that the three highest-ranked journals account for about 30 percent of all citations to articles in economics journals. Similarly, the ten highest-ranked journals account for more than 50 percent of all citations, the twenty highest-ranked journals account for more than 70 percent, the thirty highest-ranked journals account for more than 90 percent, and the forty highest-ranked journals account for more than 95 percent. This is important information for a dean and needs to be ferreted out if the department is not on board with the expectation that faculty attempt to publish in premier journals. However, the default is that the criteria come from the bottom up and are then reviewed and approved at the higher levels. Trust but verify is a reasonable procedure in assessing criteria for faculty evaluation. Matters can become more complicated if departments give compelling intellectual arguments against deferring to disciplinary expectations, insofar as they may constrain methodologies and questions, but these arguments should be openly discussed and weighed, not simply assumed to be valid.

An objection I sometimes heard was that in any merit scheme one would have to publish something each year to get a raise, but the process was much more sophisticated. First, one considers work in progress, which ensures that faculty members are not motivated to publish too quickly but can instead develop larger and more comprehensive projects. Ensuring documentation is appropriate, however, so that the same work in progress is not credited year after year after year. Second, one recognizes major publications over multiple years. In history, books are more important than articles, and books in history, which almost always require substantial archival work, tend to take longer than in most other fields. One of the history chairpersons with whom I worked argued that he wanted to focus his evaluation not on annual performance but on the previous ten-year period. I accepted his rationale. Some money needs to be held back for equity/excellence adjustments, that is, for faculty who for one reason or another did not receive sufficient annual adjustments along the way but whose overall performance exceeds their salary ranking. Also it is important that the chairperson's recommendations be reviewed at higher levels, and that the dean construct cascading charts of high-to-low salaries, so as to note inappropriate anomalies. We did this also by gender, discipline, and rank, with appropriate analyses of the high and low, the mean and median.

Another concern I heard was that evaluation of performance would place freedom of research in jeopardy and force scholars to follow trends. That would be possible only if an administrator judged research by its immediate currency. Basically I have seen the opposite, that is, a concern to recognize meaningful scholarship that transcends passing trends.

Notre Dame introduced a policy, whereby a committee, partly elected and partly appointed, oversees an annual quantitative analysis, using regression analyses recommended by the American Association of University Professors, of teaching-and-research faculty salaries, with identifying name information removed. It reviews the results of this analysis to determine whether a pattern of inequity exists on the basis of gender or minority status. These proceedings are confidential, but the committee is obliged to prepare an annual public report of its findings and conclusions with respect to gender and minority salary equity. The committee also studies the results of the quantitative salary analysis in order to identify salaries that seem anomalously low and which suggest the need for further review by the provost's office. The provost's office, in turn, requires a written explanation of any such salaries from the relevant dean, and, if appropriate, calls for the development of a plan for salary adjustment. The provost's office summarizes the results of this review and the adjustment plans, if any, for the committee.

Not only must one allow variation for the diverse disciplines, one can allow options in terms of who reviews candidates, the chairperson or a committee, and how feedback is given, orally or in writing or both. There are advantages to both individual and collective reviews. A collective review benefits from a range of perspectives, and it unburdens the chairperson slightly (although even when a special committee assigns ratings, the chairperson still makes the salary recommendations). A collective review also has disadvantages, as it can, in some cases, become political, and it increases the collective departmental workload. In assessing options, one also needs to consider contingent factors, such as the scholarly standing of the chairperson, the size of the department, and the department's traditions.

The issue of oral versus written feedback is also complex. On the one hand, oral communication offers an opportunity to think out loud together with a colleague and may permit the chairperson to be a greater mentor and problem solver. It may seem less formal, which could appeal to some colleagues. In a conversation, you needn't worry about precise, written formulations for every issue that invites reciprocal dialogue. Oral communication may also allow you to interpret your colleague's reactions and adjust your rhetoric accordingly in order to make it more effective. In addition, oral communication is more conducive to a welcome give and take. On the other hand, oral feedback may not be as precise as a well-considered written evaluation, which has the further advantage of allowing one to offer supporting evidence. Because of the immediacy of oral transmission, colleagues' responses to feedback may be less considered than if they have had time to reflect on a written statement. In addition, written communication offers a better record of performance over the years, especially when problems have surfaced. At the very moment you review the materials, you can search for the proper words and examples to give more nuance to what you would like to say. It also permits you to say things that might be more difficult to say in person than they are to formulate on paper. Another possibility, the one I prefer and adopted over time, is a combination of the two: a meeting in person, at which time you articulate some of your own thoughts and questions in response to the review you have conducted—these comments can serve as an initial opening to a meaningful and reciprocal conversation—after which you can then finalize a letter that has already been drafted but not yet shared and has formed the basis of your opening comments and questions.

Another option, in this case with regard to frequency and kind of review, is the following: an annual oral discussion and, across the years, that is, at least every three to five years, a written evaluation that involves, before the final formulation of the letter, an initial oral consultation. In the case of probationary faculty members, an annual letter that also includes feedback from the senior faculty members who will eventually conduct the promotion-and-tenure review would seem obligatory. Also, any faculty member whose performance has been substandard should receive a written evaluation. Even in such a case, one need not simply draw attention to deficiencies, one can also try to articulate gratitude for accomplishments, when they exist in limited areas, and strategies for improvement as well as opportunities for assistance.

All three areas of the profession (research, teaching, and service) are considered in annual reviews, with appropriate weights assigned to each area. These weights can be determined by departments and will differ for individual faculty members, depending on their teaching and service responsibilities. At Notre Dame, which takes both research and teaching seriously, my generic recommendation for tenured faculty was 40 percent for teaching, 40 percent for research, and 20 percent for service. Obviously, the percentage allocations will depend on mission and priorities.

Some faculty members express unease about the evaluation of teaching because it seems more difficult to assess than research and service and because some false indicators exist (popularity with students does not necessarily mean that students are learning). The most common strategy at virtually all universities is indeed to turn to student evaluations. Crucial here is the formulation of the questions. Students are not without insight into good and bad teaching. Above all, they can recognize how clear, well-organized, and responsive an instructor is and whether the course is intellectually challenging or stimulating. They can report how many hours they study outside of class each week. And they can comment on the extent to which they believe that they have made progress. Students are less equipped, however, to judge whether the course content is appropriate, to what extent the course contributes to the overall curriculum, whether the workload is suitable, and whether the standards for evaluation and grading are appropriate.

For the most part, student evaluations help to identify the best and worst teachers (from the students' perspective). Fine distinctions in the middle are usually not very helpful. Student evaluations can be biased, lifted up by expectations of higher grades (Johnson), and so teaching needs to be reviewed in the light of course demands and grading. Student evaluations can easily be misused, and such misuse saves administrators time. It also saves faculty members time when doing peer assessments. Reviewing a fuller array of materials, such as a teaching portfolio that includes a statement on teaching goals and strategies, course syllabi, sample assignments, and graded student work can be hugely time consuming and is one reason why faculty members feel burdened by service. An overemphasis on student evaluations caters to a poor understanding of the student-faculty relationship, one driven by a corporate model of student satisfaction instead of educational models of what is expected in a demanding and ambitious learning environment.

One needs, therefore, a multifaceted approach to the evaluation of teaching. Are the learning goals meaningful, ambitious, and clear? Is the course design current and relevant to the university's and department's missions as well as to the students' needs? Are the course materials, concepts, and activities rigorous? Review of syllabi and other materials, including assignments, can help address such questions. The implementation also matters. Does the faculty member create a stimulating environment that is conducive to learning and effective in the use of students' time? Are students being inspired and encouraged to think analytically and creatively and to develop knowledge, skills, and appropriate habits of mind? Peer visits can shed partial light on such puzzles.

The most important question is: are the students learning? Here one can look at student performance on exams and papers, on standardized tests, and in subsequent semesters. In disciplines where courses tend to be tiered, each presupposing and expanding the knowledge developed at earlier levels, the attainment of learning goals is easier to evaluate. In many cases one must look for indirect indicators. Does the faculty member set high expectations for student performance, provide students with helpful feedback, and apply appropriately demanding standards when evaluating student work?

Another factor involves the faculty member's contributions to the collective. Does the person offer broader courses or only specialized courses, required courses or only elective courses? Does the faculty member offer to create new courses when a need is identified? Does the person mentor students well? Is the person advising a reasonable share of dissertations or theses?

Of course one needs to find effective strategies to economize in the review of such materials, which is a serious puzzle. Although not to review teaching is unacceptable, to spend so much time reviewing that faculty are drowned in committee work and service assignments is equally unappealing and nonsensical. Whenever administrative positions are filled by persons who are not active faculty members, the danger of overburdening faculty with service expectations will rear its ugly head.

The investment in evaluating teaching, in order to be justified, also needs to serve the purpose of improving the collective teaching of the department. Many faculty find that reviewing materials of colleagues, visiting their classes, and engaging in follow-up discussions give them new ideas for their own teaching. That has certainly been the case with my own reviews of others. Feedback to faculty, especially those at the junior level, can help them tremendously. Many faculty also undertake voluntary midterm evaluations. Several weeks into each semester, I ask students to take a few minutes to answer three questions: What are the two or three most effective elements in helping you achieve the learning goals of the course? If the course has helped you learn, to date, describe the nature of that learning. Can you suggest some changes for the remainder of the semester that would better help you learn?

Mentoring is one of the most basic responsibilities of both chairpersons and senior faculty. This involves not only sharing information but also helping more actively, for example, asking, "What can I do to help you improve your teaching or to move your research along?" Because it can be awkward to move directly from mentoring to evaluation, some universities keep a list of faculty members who have expressed their willingness to mentor faculty members from other departments, noting the areas in which they are willing to try to help others: teaching, research, administration, navigating the profession, or even broader issues, such as balancing work and family.

Accountability to Students

The university is also accountable to its students. Indeed, students and their families, who pay tuition, expect universities to offer the best possible learning experience. Small classes, effective teachers, and a variety of curricular options and opportunities, as well as a supportive environment, are a part of this culture. One should not forget that the culture of high student expectations tends not to arise in countries such as Germany, where students pay no tuition and teaching is less valued.

I can remember a tiring trip in the winter of 1984, as I was completing my dissertation and interviewing for assistant professor positions. I drove first to Vassar, then to Williams, and then, in a blizzard, on country roads, to Dartmouth, for a series of finalist interviews. I was exhausted by the time I arrived at Dartmouth, but the meetings were relentless and provided no time for rest. I can remember the first breakfast at Dartmouth. I was asked, as a candidate always is, what courses I would like to teach. I had a wide array of options in my mind and for some inexplicable reason spoke about a course on the philosophical novel, in which students would read the most ambitious works of Thomas Mann, Hermann Broch, and Robert Musil. Faculty members counseled that might be too much for one term. They were of course right (the novels I mentioned are very long), but I decided, rather stubbornly and again inexplicably, to defend the choice. Within seconds I could practically watch myself making a fool of myself, almost like being in a Woody Allen movie, and I could see that, though the campus visit would last another day and a half, I had already eliminated myself from contention. Teaching counts, as does common sense.

In many departments, a finalist candidate for a faculty position is asked not only to give a public presentation but also to teach a class. I did that at a variety of institutions, private and public, small and large. When the candidates do not teach a class, the question-and-answer period after a talk is viewed as a partial window onto teaching. Submission of a teaching portfolio, with at a minimum a teaching philosophy, sample syllabi, and student evaluations, is routine at the finalist stage at many universities. When I was dean, I delayed several possible appointments because departments neglected to do a thorough review of teaching before making their recommendations.

Although I alluded to the potential tension between teaching and research, one should not overdramatize. Even as American universities have become stronger in research, teaching has become an unmistakable part of faculty evaluations. Certainly, there is the frequent lament that at some premier American universities the pendulum has swung too far toward research, but the concept is still present that teaching and research are both pillars of the modern university, and at some universities they are in fact treated equally. When I became dean, I quickly sensed that the push toward research had led in some quarters to insufficient emphasis on teaching. I insisted on the value of both, and faculty knew that I would ask about the teaching credentials of every potential faculty hire and would begin every promotion-and-tenure evaluation with an analysis of teaching quality in order to ensure that it would not be undervalued.

At some universities, the students publish their own guide to courses. Already in the 1920s, Harvard students were releasing a student guide to college courses (Doyle 4). I can recall being in a class in Tübingen, Germany, more than thirty-five years ago that seemed to me to be one of the most poorly taught classes I had experienced on either side of the Atlantic. I was shocked that the students were not active in complaining to the teacher or the administration about the waste of time and resources. In a university system where students pay for their education, the response would have been radically different. I may have been the only student to visit the faculty member and express my concerns. When Notre Dame introduced substantial reforms at one of its study abroad locations, students were surprised at the unexpectedly high academic demands placed on them. They chipped in together and paid for a return flight, so that one student could bring her complaints to the home campus. In this case, the university stood firm, but the incident illustrates the seriousness with which students approach their experiences and their willingness to provide feedback.

First-year students at Notre Dame receive nonbinding midsemester grades to help them grasp any challenges they must rise to meet, and advanced students receive midterm deficiency reports if they are failing. Such early academic warnings can be effective in helping students succeed. Students may be asked to submit weekly essays for their classes, in some cases even two or three brief essays per week, which are then returned with comments by the next class; this is not a common practice in other cultures. In general one of the important principles of good learning is that students receive helpful and well-grounded feedback; students receiving such feedback view their college experience more favorably (Light).

Russell Berman, former president of the Modern Language Association, suggested during a panel discussion in 2011, at which I was speaking, that language, literature, and culture teachers might think of themselves as coaches, so that every language student has a personal coach. I like this idea for at least three reasons. First, as Berman noted, student–faculty ratios in language departments permit teachers to engage students in this way. Second, the requirements for effective language learning have analogies in athletics: beyond guidance or coaching, language students need motivation, discipline, practice, and an intuitive sensibility for the activity. Think, for example, of the abilities to make educated guesses about meaning on the basis of cognates, context, and the component parts of words and to intuit which words are more vital to learn than others. Third, the metaphor emphasizes the extent to which language learning must take place beyond the boundaries of the classroom and the time frame of the semester. One could easily extend the analogy beyond language study. A professor who adopts a small number of students can easily become an informal coach, guiding them in their overall studies and helping them to realize that the idea of study and scholarship is also the idea of a life form, which is not restricted to satisfying curricular tasks but addresses the whole person in terms of cognitive interests, normative values, and life goals. A teacher-coach helps students on their journey in a specific discipline and beyond. Such a role can be demanding, but it is certainly also rewarding.

Graduate students are offered at least the same high level of attention and mentoring that is given to undergraduate students. Because of the high investment in these students—the opportunity cost of choosing one student instead of another, the financial investment in stipends, and the faculty time devoted to a small number of students—the philosophy is to get the right students admitted. If a department is going to lose them, it should happen early, since late attrition means wasted resources for the university and lost time for the students. Common at many institutions is an annual meeting of the departmental faculty at which all graduate students are discussed, important feedback for each student is debated, and decisions on continuation of support in difficult cases are weighed.

To foster mentoring and professionalization in our graduate department at Ohio State, I initiated a weekly three-hour class for doctoral students. The first half of every class was devoted to one student's dissertation project and the broader issues and common concerns it evoked. Students beginning their dissertations would speak informally for twenty minutes, whereas the advanced students would give twenty-minute versions of their campus job talks. The next seventy minutes consisted of nothing but questions and discussion. I asked a question only after every single student had asked one, since stretching into other people's areas of expertise and asking intelligent questions are expectations for faculty members. This tactic allowed for a range of questions and gave students practice in what would be expected of them later in the profession: knowing how to elicit a good discussion after a public lecture. Anticipating questions—in this case through practice—is the best strategy for performing well and ensuring higher-level discussion. After each session, I met privately with that week's presenter to discuss additional questions that could arise and to offer informal advice.

The second ninety minutes of every class stressed practical concerns and professional development: defining, researching, and writing a dissertation; writing job application letters and preparing an effective curriculum vitae; investigating professional organizations and presenting conference papers; obtaining fellowships and writing grant proposals; approaching publishers; writing effective book reviews; drafting meaningful course syllabi; preparing for interviews; developing a compelling dissertation abstract; upholding professional ethics; anticipating future concerns, such as how to negotiate an offer, balance teaching, research, and service, and prepare for promotion-and-tenure reviews; and evaluating current debates in foreign language and culture departments.

Considerable research has been done that explores student learning and development in college, including classic works by Astin (*What Matters in College?*), by Pascarella and Terenzini (*How College Affects Students*), and by Kuh et al. (*Student Success in College*). The research elucidates a number of principles that help to ensure student success. Among them are the following: high academic expectations, frequent student-faculty contact, independent research or collaborative research with a faculty member, ample humanities courses with writing assignments, a residential environment, and adequate support services and safety nets. These research findings and resulting policy recommendations have had a tremendous impact on colleges and universities as they have developed their curricula and teaching strategies.

Further principles with which we are familiar from these and other works include that students learn more when they have an existential interest in the subject matter, are actively engaged in the learning process, learn from their peers, encounter diverse perspectives, and receive meaningful feedback toward their learning goals. Every one of these principles is present in a good discussion class, where students engage a fascinating topic, experience give and take with one another and with often diverse readings, and receive feedback from faculty members and peers.

One measure of accountability to students involves graduation rates, which at America's premier universities are among the highest in the world. How are retention rates so high at good American universities? Several dimensions must coincide. The university must have clear goals, including the priority of graduating students; the right students must be recruited, admitted, and encouraged to attend; an appropriate student–faculty ratio and faculty mentoring of students must be valued; and funding must be allocated for support structures, such as residential advisors, a counseling center, a writing center, a career center, and student activities.

Also essential to high graduation rates is a successful first-year experience. This is especially the case for vulnerable students from lower-income families as well as for black and Hispanic men (Bowen, Chingos, and McPherson 56). Very valuable are orientation sessions, often with students and parents, which introduce the college's mission, its expectations, the purpose of various requirements, and helpful information on, for example, navigating the library and finding academic and counseling support services. At colleges that reach out to less prepared students, a one-credit course is often offered to assist with time-management skills and proper study habits. Many universities have higher numbers of advisors working with first-year students. Also common are smaller seminars for first-year students, so that they have close contact with a faculty member early. Student engagement in smaller classes that involve close contact with faculty members helps with retention, especially for students who enter college with lower levels of academic achievement (Wolniak, Seifert, and Blaich; Kuh et al.).

Some courses are specifically designed with students, not faculty, in mind. For example, the College Seminar at Notre Dame requires faculty to reach beyond their disciplines, so that students have an opportunity to address great questions from a variety of disciplinary perspectives. Restricted in size, each seminar is oral-intensive. In addition to various writing assignments, the course includes student-led discussions, classroom debates, oral interviews, and oral exams, all of which are designed to help students develop the capabilities to formulate clear questions, listen carefully and attentively, explore ideas through dialogue, argue for and against differing positions, and express their thoughts eloquently and persuasively.

During my second year as dean, we held a series of three open meetings, fully voluntary, to discuss a report that had recently been published on undergraduate learning at America's research universities (Boyer Commission). The invitation was designed to have faculty think about, and discuss together, how the report might apply to us. At each session, a significant number of faculty members came to discuss the issues: commenting on the report itself and emphasizing various points in the light of our situation, reflecting on areas in which we already excelled and which should be further developed, identifying topics we should communicate to prospective students, considering current obstacles to a better integration of teaching and research or difficulties to be weighed as we sought to realize the ideals of the report, and discussing innovations that might be welcome. A summary of the discussions was then posted on the college website. Among the ideas stressed in these discussions were more opportunities for capstone experiences, such as senior theses, in the humanities; more emphasis on student-faculty research teams in the social sciences; more possibilities, such as integrative seminars, for students to integrate or synthesize knowledge; and greater emphasis on communication skills, especially on oral expression and the ability to write, for persons who are not experts in a field. These discussions led to initiatives in linked courses and learning communities, honors tracks, enhanced spending on undergraduate research, and, some years later, the College Seminar, with its focus on oral skills and integrative learning.

Core requirements should match the university's vision of itself. In that way, the curriculum is accountable to both vision and students. But other offerings should also reinforce vision. At Notre Dame, where the idea of the unity of knowledge is vibrant, we offered students interdisciplinary minors, most of which had a connection to mission: Catholic social tradition; education, schooling, and society; international development studies; journalism, ethics, and democracy; liturgical music ministry; peace studies; philosophy, politics, and economics; philosophy, religion, and literature; philosophy within the Catholic tradition; poverty studies; public service; and science, technology, and values.

Accountability to students should not be confused with affirming student preferences. Students sometimes make inappropriate requests, for example, for less demanding courses and higher grades or for more practical or vocational courses. This student culture is best countered by ensuring that students realize that they are not customers but students and apprentices, who must in fact follow faculty expectations, assuming that these are well grounded, articulated, and communicated. An important factor is administrative leadership, which should encourage faculty to be responsive to students but should also be strong in countering students and parents who make inappropriate and poorly grounded requests or demands.

Another presupposition of accountability to students, as opposed to giving in to student preferences, is countering grade inflation. The problem can be dealt with in several ways. As with other challenges, the most desirable strategy rests on vision—convincing faculty and students of the value of rigorous grading and asking students to stretch to meet their full potentials. Evidence shows that faculty who expect more of their students tend to be more successful in helping them learn (Bain 68–97). Extensive feedback, which helps learning, also makes lower grades more acceptable; students see how much they still have to learn. Especially early on, students need to see that what they think is good is not good enough (Tinto 54). An essential character skill, ideally fostered in college, is the ability to learn from criticism. Karl Jaspers notes perceptively, "Whoever evades criticism really doesn't want to know" (28). If convinced, faculty may make the adjustments themselves, but that is not easy. The focus on vision can be supplemented by the sharing of best practices. For example, one can articulate grading criteria to students in the sequence B, A, C, D, F. If the faculty member begins by explaining the quality of work that defines a B grade, making clear that an A is reserved for the highest achievement—work that is above and beyond very good performance—the student might think, "If I do really good work, I can get a B." The burden shifts from the faculty member answering the student's question, "Why did I not get an A?" to he or she asking the student, "What in the paper was above and beyond very good work?" A third strategy is some level of informal oversight. When I was a dean, I periodically reviewed grading patterns across the college; in courses where, for example, 80 percent or more of the grades were A or A-, I spoke with chairpersons about such anomalies. The more aggressive strategy of allowing only a certain percentage of grades in the A range has often been met with student unease as well as faculty discontent; it removes the value of flexibly responding to student performance. Princeton, which experimented with such a policy beginning in 2004, reversed course a decade later.

A genuine challenge is that, to teach well and provide the kind of constructive criticism that is ideal, faculty members must spend lots of time grading and providing feedback. That can steal time from research. The best strategies to combat this challenge are small classes, a low number of classes per semester, and a generous leave policy.

Measuring an Institution

A prominent aspect of accountability involves institutions measuring themselves. This involves three simple steps. First, the university must articulate its goals and aspirations. Second, it must gather data to answer the question whether or not the articulated goals are being met. Third, it must make adjustments—in personnel, resources, curricular offerings, and so forth—in order better to meet those goals.

What are some of the measures a university can use to assess its performance? On the one hand, it is important to keep in mind that the more measures one has, the more dispersed one will be in attending to them and the less of a priority any one measure becomes. On the other hand, one cannot become so focused or narrow that research always trumps teaching or that one attends to only one criterion in evaluating a discipline or that one forgets in how many different areas a complex university must advance simultaneously.

Data need to satisfy three central conditions. First, we need to have confidence that the data we are collecting are reliable, a nontrivial issue. Second, the data need to be meaningful, that is, we want to collect data only if they tell a story that we could use to ensure accountability or foster advancement. The last thing we need are reams of useless data or, perhaps worse, data that are interpreted with inappropriate measures. Of course, sometimes the story is hidden, so it helps to be patient and thorough with the data initially collected. Third, the data need to be such that they could be gathered without so much effort that the cost in time would outweigh the benefits of having the data.

I was a huge fan of data as a tool to help me analyze problems and puzzles. I had my budget and operations person create so many charts that it became a bit of a running joke: What chart would he ask for next? I wanted information on staff size per faculty member, faculty size per major and credit hour, research space per faculty member. I wanted a chart, in cascading order, of the number of years associate professors had been in rank. I had multiple salary charts. I had charts of student evaluations of teaching by department as well as grading by department. I had charts of definite, likely, and possible hires each year, so that I could track diversity, gender, mission, and start-up costs. For every development project, I created a chart of funding opportunities at different levels, depending on the donor's likely preferences and capacities. I had charts on the movement of faculty lines from and to departments, charts on the number of doctoral advisees each faculty member had, and of course budgetary charts of all kinds.

Beyond tracking basic categories, colleges will want to track institution-specific ones. For example, a university that elevates internationalism might track the percentage of international students and faculty members; the percentage of students who study abroad; majors in foreign languages and literatures; students pursuing summer language study, service projects, internships, or advanced research in non-English speaking countries; and the percentage of alumni living or working abroad.

Some measures will not be quantitative but will instead involve narrative or anecdotal descriptions, such as the quality of recent faculty hires. It is a matter of finding the appropriate balance. I can recall an amusing exchange between two faculty members in a group forum on assessing student performance. A chairperson from engineering insisted on quantitative measures for everything, adding, "If you can't quantify it, it doesn't count." A poet sprang to his feet and countered, "No, just the opposite, if you can measure it, it has no value. Is love something you quantify?" The obsession with quantity over quality is also evident in the story of a Cold War delegation traveling in the Soviet Union. The delegation was regaled by the guide in Tula about an impressive cultural development: "We have today within twenty kilometers thirty-four writers. In the previous century there was only one." "What was his name?" "Leo Tolstoy."

An ambitious university keeps annual charts that benchmark its own institution against peers and aspirational peers and its own institution against itself over time. Three main strategies for self-evaluation exist: quantitative comparison with others; quantitative comparison with one's own past; and nuanced, nonquantitative evaluation and assessment. One does not have to be overly systematic; one can often rely on common sense. Counting recently published books, for example, strikes me as an absurd practice, since some books are clearly superior to others. If such a figure were used, say, for an institution where fewer books are written, in which case the number might indeed tell a story, the information would still need to be carefully sifted. At the same time, an institution should think creatively about what it might track that could be overlooked. Every institution knows its number of Fulbright awards, because these are collected nationally, but not all track the number of placements at the leading law and medical schools or the percentage of bachelor recipients who have received doctorates in the past ten years.

On many campuses, graduating students fill out a survey, which is required for them to receive their diplomas and which asks a range of questions. For example, Did you regularly discuss course content with students outside of class? Have you been a guest in a professor's home? In what skills did you develop much stronger capabilities during college: writing skills, leadership abilities, public speaking ability, understanding of global issues, and so on? If you could make your college choice over, would you still choose to enroll in your current college? The data can also be tracked longitudinally, so that one knows over time whether the university is improving in response to such questions as: Were you mentored well? Were your classes intellectually stimulating? Do you feel part of a college community? And so forth. In departments that are truly interested in self-assessment, individual exit interviews or focus groups are conducted in order to determine to what extent their students have flourished.

To undertake this data collection, each university needs an office that can gather and present such data. That office should also include experts in strategic planning, as the two are, ideally, linked and relevant data may affect goals and action items. Note that these data are obtained not for any external agency. Instead they serve the simple but important purpose of helping the university assess its own effectiveness.

Critical are detailed departmental reviews, which occur every seven to ten years or so. As part of the process, the department goes through a self-study exercise, in which it articulates its vision and priorities, goals and strategies, challenges, indicators of success, and synergies with other departments and programs. It also notes the financial implications of its goals and ranks any new requests. It is also normally asked to reflect on, to varying degrees and depending on various factors, the activities of peer departments, availability of talent, and opportunities for funding. Data and information are gathered of various kinds, from program requirements and course offerings, with descriptions and enrollments, to information on faculty research. The department also presents as part of its self-study the puzzles and questions it most wants the reviewers to address. A full packet of materials is quite extensive. Outside reviewers, usually two to four, read the documents, along with general information on the university, and then visit the campus for two days. There, they meet with all relevant parties, offering an oral report to the dean and provost at the end of the visit and sending a written report soon thereafter. On some campuses, they are accompanied by an internal reviewer from a neighboring department, who can explain aspects of the local culture and, in some cases, is asked to prepare an additional report.

At Notre Dame, we arranged for a meeting after every external review to decide what actions would be taken and what issues would receive continuing reflection. A member of the administrative staff prepared a summary of to-do items along with who was responsible for each one; it was then reviewed by the dean and distributed. Three years later we met again to revisit those earlier decisions and to-do items to gauge follow-through, monitor progress, and consider new needs. Such accountability is essential both for a university to advance and to ensure continuing faculty investment in such reviews.

One of the fascinating aspects of external reviews is how open persons are with third parties in identifying problems. Many faculty members are shy about speaking out directly to senior administrators, in some cases even to their own colleagues. When third parties or external reviewers are brought to campus, faculty open up. Also, external reviewers tend to be frank in telling us how we are doing. Similarly, exit interviews for departing faculty members are best handled not by current administrators but by trusted faculty members who are not involved in the negotiation process or chain of command. Such interviews are a wonderful source of information on how a university can improve.

To ensure progress toward such goals, one needs to search for faculty members and not simply sift applications. I sent an annual letter to each chairperson on the department's previous hiring record and on goals for quality, mission, and diversity. Departments were held accountable for candidates they advanced as finalists; that is, a department had to submit finalists to the dean for approval before on-campus interviews could be scheduled. If the pool did not include any women, for example, the department had to answer the question, "Who was the strongest woman in the pool, and why did she not make the cut?" We cancelled searches midstream if the pool was unjustifiably narrow or the quality unusually low.

Accountability for Administrators

Little unnerves faculty members more than lack of accountability among administrators, for example, when an administrator appoints a task force but does not ensure a report has been completed; or a task force report is received but never publicly addressed because the administrator has moved on to other topics or crises or because the budget prevents the implementation of suggestions; or a faculty member who has made a suggestion, written a complaint, or asked a question never receives a response. These are inexcusable errors that demotivate faculty members and breed cynicism.

Accountability requires that goals be stated publicly and that reports on progress toward those goals be communicated widely. As dean, I set goals for various demographics in hiring, each of which I divided into minimal (the bare minimum I wanted to reach each year), expected (what I hoped could be achieved regularly), and aspirational (a more ambitious figure toward which we would strive). For Catholic faculty hiring, the figures were minimal, 50 percent; expected, 55 percent; and aspirational, 65 percent. For minority faculty hiring, the figures were minimal, 20 percent; expected, 25 percent; and aspirational, 35 percent. And for women faculty hiring, the figures were minimal, 40 percent; expected, 45 percent; and aspirational, 55 percent. I reported the results for each year, as well as those for the past x number of years. Releasing the data annually, both at a public meeting and on paper, reinforced my commitment to the self-identified goals.

Much of accountability means simply ensuring that we measure ourselves against our own aspirations. After about seven years as dean, I arranged for a voluntary review of myself and my office, so that our structures and my time allocation would more effectively advance our vision and academic priorities. I perceived the need for such a review, and one of our donors offered to fund it. The college had grown dramatically in faculty lines, we had introduced more due process and accountability, and we had undertaken a significant number of initiatives. As a result, with the existing level of staffing, we had begun to fall behind in meeting all our aspirations. I did not want to miss out on proactively pursuing all possible development opportunities, I wanted to quicken the turnaround time for written annual reviews of chairpersons, and I felt the need to be visible for the kind of informal conversations that bind a community together. If we as a college were to consider any changes in how we organized ourselves, I wanted us to think systematically about our responsibilities and reporting structures, so that we could maximize our efficiency, ensure clarity, and create a structure that would ideally last for years to come.

As part of the review, I prepared an array of materials for the external evaluators: a sitting president of a liberal arts college, who had also served as provost of a major research university; a former president of an Ivy League university; and a prominent businessperson, who later joined our board of trustees. The materials ranged from annual reports and addresses articulating vision and goals to reporting structures and data of all kinds. I was very open about my challenges and weaknesses. As part of the preliminary exercise, I dictated my use of time for two weeks and had my assistant sort the activities into Excel charts. Time management was far and away my greatest challenge. There was never enough. I was amazed at how splintered my activities were. The reviewers read the materials, came to campus, and spent time not only with me but also with the university's leaders and all of my coworkers, including the chairpersons. They then recommended adjustments. The review sharpened my sense of which priorities I should keep and which I should delegate. The changes I made meant that I could devote more time to what really mattered.

In addition to recommending one additional staff person, some structural reorganization, and some adjustments in daily and weekly practices, the reviewers recommended I focus on eight responsibilities and delegate all else. Four tasks involved focusing on vision and implementation of vision through budget and accountability: overall vision and strategic planning, fund raising and external representation and advocacy, major budgetary priorities and decisions, and departmental reviews and evaluation. Three tasks related to personnel: the hiring of tenured faculty members, including external recruitment to full professorships and endowed chairs; promotion-and-tenure decisions, including renewal appointments; and the appointment and review of associate deans and chairpersons. The final task involved leadership development within the college, including my playing a broadly pastoral and community-building role.

It is not as if, as a result of the review, I simply sat back with my feet on the desk, saying to my staff that this and that were no longer my responsibilities; instead, the changes meant that I could devote more time to what had the highest priority. Implementing the change involved delegating more and altering the culture of expectations for chairpersons and faculty. That meant not every issue that had previously gone to the dean still went to the dean, for example, interviewing and recruiting junior candidates, allocating funding for part-time faculty members, addressing space issues, awarding funding for conferences, and the like. As I look back at my time as dean, my biggest challenge was without question finding enough time, in other words, prioritization and efficiency; most of my mistakes derived from my not devoting enough time to an issue that mattered.

In some cases my time had been wasted. One of the tasks I disliked involved dealing with academic dishonesty appeals. A student is accused of cheating, and the faculty-student committee finds the student guilty and assesses a penalty. The student has the right to appeal either the judgment or the penalty to the dean. The Academic Articles stipulate that the appeals go to the dean, and the cases demanded considerable time. I eventually reinterpreted the articles, at the suggestion of the president, to mean that the appeals went to the dean or to his or her designated associate dean. It makes no sense for a dean to spend time on issues for which his or her expertise is not needed and which others could easily decide. Another task I was delighted to unburden myself of involved adjunct appointments. The dean should set the principles, but concrete decisions should be made by persons on the dean's team who can thoroughly and patiently study the existing faculty resources and projected enrollment numbers.

One successful president with whom I had an engaging conversation on leadership and priorities told me that he had only three: develop and foster the vision and mission of the university, ensuring that all that is undertaken is related to the core mission; identify, mentor, and maintain a leadership team; and enable others, which he indicated increasingly meant raising resources. I was impressed by the focus and elegance of his response.

The right support staff is essential. In my first five years, I went through three different administrative assistants, two of whom left after stern reviews. Along the way, our Office of Human Resources was not in the least helpful. They simply forwarded the applications without doing any sifting, and there was no staff to assist me in the dean's office. For a longer stretch, since I did not have time to find the right person, I used temps, who were quite uneven. It was not until about halfway through my work as dean that I found a superb assistant, who was some years later promoted to special assistant for the provost. Fortunately, I was able to find another superb assistant. It was not until I located a great person that I realized how significant a difference the right assistant can make. Since I did not want to make any mistakes once I decided to hire an executive assistant as well—someone at the doctoral level, who could undertake more complex tasks—when I brought the finalists to campus, I set the candidates up in an office and gave them various writing assignments as part of the interview process.

Another example of voluntary accountability arose with new faculty members. Each year I and eventually one of my associate deans, to whom I delegated the task, met with new faculty members and asked them two sets of questions: First, what did we do well and what did we do poorly in recruiting you? What recommendations would you have concerning changes for the future? Second, how was your transition? What worked well, and what problems occurred? What recommendations do you have for changes? We summarized the recommendations each year and shared them with chairpersons, so that they could help implement the good ideas. Our improvement was visible over time, as some of the early recommendations simply became part of the culture. The ideas were mainly common sense, for example, ensuring that our distinctive identity be used as a recruitment tool for all prospective faculty members; introducing job candidates to persons in neighboring departments, who might be interesting interlocutors or helpful mentors; arranging a student-led tour of our attractive campus; preparing a small departmental orientation booklet covering practical issues for new faculty members; and having pictures of all faculty and staff in the departmental area or on the Web. Still, we needed to be reminded of commonsense practices.

Reviewing Chairpersons

While I was dean at Notre Dame, the chairperson traditionally served a three-year term, though most stayed for six years. During the three-year cycle, the annual review worked more or less as follows: In addition to filling out annual activity reports on teaching and research, chairpersons answered various questions that helped me to understand their service and leadership contributions. In a sense the materials also provided a useful record of departmental advances and challenges. The questions communicated the priorities under which performance was to be evaluated. Chairpersons were free, instead of answering question by question, simply to prepare a holistic narrative.

Toward the end of the chairperson's first year, we sat down together for one hour to brainstorm on successes but mainly challenges, the two of us thinking out loud about how the department could advance and how the chairperson could work through various challenges, as well as how I or my colleagues in the dean's office could help. It was an enjoyable strategic conversation that helped set an agenda for the following year. At times I also had in the back of my mind the issues that had arisen in advance of the person's having been appointed chairperson. Before I made an appointment, I invited every member of the department to submit confidential reflections, which are an excellent source of information on departmental challenges. The focus for the most part was on broader and collective issues, as we had already met a month or two earlier to review every faculty member.

Halfway through the second year, I gave the chairperson a 360-degree evaluation, which included feedback from faculty and staff. These midterm evaluations were designed for self-development. Reviewers were asked to rate the administrator on various categories, such as vision, initiative, integrity, courage, accountability, teamwork, communication, accessibility, timeliness, and so on. The forms also offered ample room for narrative comments, with an invitation to address strengths, weaknesses, and suggestions. The purpose of the peer evaluation was not to report to the chairperson that she or he scored a four overall on a five-point scale. In some cases, the chairperson might have been making complex and difficult decisions that naturally led to her using up some political capital with departmental colleagues.

The goal of a peer evaluation is to determine whether, on a comparative scale, faculty members report that the chairperson is, for example, very strong in "fostering research" but very weak in "communication." If the score for "support of mission" is low, then the dean needs to ask the chairperson, "How can I help you become stronger in mission?" The goal should not be to have the chairperson land a five in each category. At times a weak chairperson who is not challenging his faculty might get close to a five, and a very good chairperson who is willing to make difficult decisions might have upset some persons and garnered lower scores. The goal was to diagnose strengths and weaknesses from the perspectives of the faculty and staff and to brainstorm on strategies to improve, be it in reality or in perception. We placed each category in a cascading chart from high to low to see which areas received the lower scores and thus were most likely in need of attention.

At the end of three years, I gave chairpersons a formal letter, usually about five pages, rarely shorter and sometimes much longer, that articulated three areas: strengths, areas for development, and departmental challenges. These letters were, in a certain sense, a deep statement of gratitude for the past and a guide to the future. The sense of gratitude is not unimportant because colleagues are unlikely to express gratitude to an administrator; they view administration as work of secondary importance, and they expect to be supported in their primary work as teachers and scholars. The letters also articulated expectations and reaffirmed to chairpersons what they were doing well. The letters served as road maps for chairpersons' reappointments. Initially, I wrote letters only for continuing chairpersons, but then I resolved to write also, if more briefly, for exiting chairpersons. Such letters take considerable time, but they were important documents for the chairpersons, as well as significant opportunities for me to ensure that I was being sufficiently grateful for the person's good work and clear, in concert with the chairperson, about our goals and strategies for the coming years.

A Decanal Review

At my five-year reappointment as dean, an elected faculty committee reviewed my performance. On any objective scale, the college had made enormous progress; still, the review was scathing in stretches. There were several problems. At a most basic level, I had changed too much too fast. Normally, an administrator listens for one year and changes nothing. There are at least two reasons for this standard practice: first, this more patient process helps one avoid mistakes, as one gets to know the institution and the new role; second, it allows people time to adjust to the new administrator and for that person to gain a social base, which is important for the reception of change. Contrary to this common wisdom, I moved ahead immediately in making changes and bringing forward new initiatives, and I did so for three reasons. First, I had studied the institution carefully for some time before deciding to move to Notre Dame and had been there for a semester as a regular faculty member, so I knew it better than someone who was a complete outsider. Second, I found some things, such as the lack of faculty evaluation, simply unacceptable and refused to sit tight for a year, which would have involved awarding salary increases without a review. Third, I wanted us to move ahead quickly and, even more importantly, I wanted to do my administrative work for five years and get back to the faculty ranks, so I didn't want to waste any time.

The net result was that we did advance very quickly, but for a number of persons, it was too much change, too fast. This partially negative reception was exacerbated by my being too much of an outsider. Many of the changes had a ring of foreignness in the local climate: merit raises, enrollment management, monthly meetings of chairpersons, a merit-based sabbatical policy and peer review of sabbatical requests, a peer review process for support of new journals and continuing support of existing journals, a reference guide on policies and procedures, statistical data on each department's performance and resources, and the replacement of an associate dean with a staff person to work with me on budget and oversee operations. Comically exacerbating the situation was that in the early years, whenever I got very tired, I tended to make substitution errors in my speech. Saying "Ohio State" for "Notre Dame" or "Columbus" for "South Bend" or "quarter" for "semester" did not endear me to anyone, especially as the mistakes seemed only to accentuate the foreign, public-university character of my changes. When on my first day I visited the provost with a copy of the *Undergraduate Bulletin* in my hands, he rightly guessed that I was carrying it around so as to be able to look up which departments were under my purview and where they were located.

Many of my ideas were recognized as very, very good. These involved, for example, honors tracks in departments to encourage undergraduates to stretch intellectually; marketing initiatives to recruit students into the arts and sciences instead of business; the introduction of competitive postdoctoral fellowships to help enhance graduate placements; public fora on promotion-and-tenure issues for junior faculty and associate professors to enhance mentoring; and, so as to move people through the faculty ranks, an annual competition for full-year leaves for up to two associate professors who had been in rank for twelve years or longer, had outstanding teaching credentials, and had a research project on the horizon that could trigger a promotion to professor. But these ideas, to name just a handful from among dozens, were my ideas; they did not stem from the faculty. I did not trumpet that, but I did not adopt the wise strategy of hiding their origin. Senator Claiborne Pell once wittily suggested, "The secret is always to let the other man have your way" (Wilkinson 95). I was tone deaf on that score.

Implicit in each change was the idea that what we had been doing was not good enough. I reacted very strongly against an objection I often heard—"But we don't do it that way at Notre Dame"—to which I would reply, much too publicly, "That is not an argument." Moreover, new initiatives not only challenge the status quo and disrupt the routine, they cost time and work. I failed to present change as sufficiently embedded within the (best of the) existing culture. An outside person with new ideas is not always a welcome combination. New ideas take hold best when they are attached to what already exists, and intrinsic motivation comes not only from vision but also from a sense of community and belonging. The latter should not be underestimated.

Not unrelated, many of the decisions reduced departmental autonomy: the idea that all lines return to the dean, the introduction of zero-based budgeting, and, most importantly, the overturning of academic personnel recommendations. In some cases, that meant rejecting hiring recommendations, but more frequently the decision involved turning down (or literally recommending against) departmental promotion-and-tenure recommendations. In my eyes many of the recommendations were simply not ambitious enough, and it was clear to me from the high number of associate professors long in rank (one of the first things I had noticed at Notre Dame) that we had not been tough enough in the past. In the case of our two weakest departments, I took away virtually all of their power to hire. I used too much language about how we were not yet what we should be instead of noting how good we were. I criticized too much and praised too little. I saw in Notre Dame too much self-approbation and not enough honest assessment of genuine weaknesses; that lens came partly from my character—I tend to look for contradictions or unfilled promise in order to address problems and gaps—but also from my being in the advantageous position of coming from another culture and bringing that external perspective to bear on Notre Dame's situation. The very idea of merit raises was seen to be a criticism of many faculty members for their performances to date.

And yet, as I look back upon eleven years of being dean and count up my many mistakes, arguably the greatest ones—the ones with the deepest ramifications for the institution—arose in those cases when I did not overturn a departmental recommendation for a faculty hire or for tenure. In other words, although one obvious and objective mistake involved my pushing too hard and too fast and not sufficiently embracing local practices and standards, another equally objective mistake was not pushing hard enough and not adjusting standards quickly enough. Almost every case on which I was deeply hesitant, but which departments favored, and which eventually fared positively, were in retrospect bad decisions, paving the way for long-term, less productive associate professors. A wise colleague once said about difficult tenure decisions, "When in doubt, say no." It was good advice. Departments did not always make the tough calls, and a few times I trusted them too much or did not push effectively or hard enough to gain support for a negative vote at the upper levels. Low standards weaken an institution for generations, as faculty tend to perpetuate their own standards.

The contradiction of pushing too hard and too fast and not pushing hard enough or quickly enough may be inevitable in a transition period when two goods collide. Vision, which necessarily takes us beyond what is, and accountability, which holds us to task for reaching that vision, can come into conflict with community, even though community is part of any meaningful university vision. Conflicts can work in both directions. The administrator can hold the departments and faculty accountable to high standards, but accountability can also fall back on administrators who violate principles of community. An administrator cannot survive without the community's partial support and cannot flourish without its strong support. There is a complex dialectic between defiance, which often means elevating one's own autonomous judgment, and deference, respecting the autonomy and judgment of others.

Sometimes I held back. I'm confident that I did so for good reasons, having to do with respect for autonomy and hope for development. Besides deferring to departments at times when they favored tenure cases that were in retrospect weak, I also occasionally made the mistake of being too patient and leaving in rank less effective administrators, thinking they might change when in fact past behavior was, sadly, a reliable predictor. Most character flaws are not corrected but instead magnified over time. Exceptions exist, but the number has been, in my experience, low. The insight is shared by Bowen: "Once it is evident that someone is just not working out, it rarely, if ever, pays to just hope that things will improve" (29). I did let some persons go in the middle of their terms, and, whenever I did, I lost a colleague.

Finally, I had invested too little in social time with the faculty. I underestimated the social and communal dimension of leadership. I thought, perhaps a bit like an engineer, that one needs only to put the right parts in the right place and implement the good ideas to improve an institution. My strengths in administration were related to vision (optimism, energy, initiatives, courage, and communication) and management (efficiency, accountability, feedback, knowledge of variables, and ensuring effective structures). Over time I learned to place greater emphasis on the social and emotional dimensions of fostering community (blending change with tradition, creating more communal events, enhancing opportunities for reciprocal dialogue, spending more time listening, communicating more in person and informally, praising as much as challenging, and delegating more and more to others). An interesting puzzle was fairness and integrity: these were never in principle questioned, but since I had voted against a number of positive promotion-and-tenure recommendations, departments sometimes felt in practice that they were being treated inappropriately.

The courage I had demonstrated was not rewarded but criticized. I had three options. (1) I could, say, forget the hassles of administration, and go back to my first love, full-time teaching and research. After all, I had not actively sought the position and would have been happy to be free of the burden. (2) I could become defensive and highlight all of the objective achievements, so as to underscore the combination of new ideas and tough decisions as the essential presuppositions of our progress, which was in fact admired by most of the best faculty members. (3) I could view the criticism as just, indeed as a gift, however much it might have stung at first, and learn from it. I could put myself in the roles of the faculty members I had criticized as not yet having reached their potentials. I chose the final option, not least of all because my motivation was to help the college, and we still had much unfinished business.

I met with the entire faculty and expressed my gratitude for the review, indicating some changes that would be forthcoming while upholding most of the core concepts I had advanced, such as high standards and accountability. I would continue to address quality gaps instead of overlooking them. At the same time I empathized with them. They were concerned about my challenging their view of academic quality, about disruption in the community, and a general sense that their autonomy had been violated. I acknowledged that the introduction of new policies and procedures, many of which were necessary for our increasing complexity or for fairness and justice (especially toward women and minorities), were nonetheless alienating. I acknowledged the difficulty faculty had in accepting merit raises at a time when salary allocations were modest. I noted that my greatest challenge was time. My many activities—from raising resources and interviewing all faculty candidates to working with chairpersons and solving problems—quickly consumed the seven days of the week.

I spoke honestly and directly, expressing my apologies for not having done all I could to make everything work sufficiently well. I felt a deep sense of melancholy that not all had been done as well as it might have been, but I acknowledged we are human, and we gain strength by recognizing our limits as well as our advances. Notre Dame, too, is an evolving community, I stressed, and some tensions—for example, between distinction as excellence and distinction as difference or between challenging and affirming faculty—will inevitably arise. Ideally, there is a balance between these creative tensions. Notre Dame has had a great history and a distinguished tradition, yet it had also not yet reached its full potential. I closed my comments with a Hasidic saying, which could apply to Notre Dame, could apply to me as dean, could apply to all of us as faculty members and persons: "We need a coat with two pockets. In one pocket there is dust, and in the other pocket there is gold. We need a coat with two pockets to remind us of who we are."

The final six years went very well, both objectively and socially, and I left on a high note. I made myself more available, and I shifted my rhetoric toward a greater balance between criticism and praise. Time allowed people to get accustomed to some of the changes and also made evident our objective advances. I learned to develop greater patience for change and resolved not to use up political capital on minor issues and instead to focus ever more carefully on which goals to pursue when. I also spent much more time with the faculty.

Previously, we had one meeting of the entire faculty per year, a dean's address in December, a tradition I inherited. I had done that a few times, but I eventually recognized that it made more sense to speak informally and give the faculty time to ask questions and make comments. I decided not only to change the format but to move to three such events per year. Each time I spoke informally for about twenty to thirty minutes, leaving at least thirty minutes during which we had open microphones for the 250 or so faculty members present, followed by a vibrant two-hour reception with refreshments. This gave me direct access to faculty members. The meetings were well attended and went well, not least of all because there was some drama as to what kinds of questions and topics might be raised. I had read a book on leadership and management, which had strongly counseled against answering any questions in an open forum that were not written down in advance (so that questions could be screened and answers carefully crafted). I ignored the advice. I tried to ensure that at each meeting some interesting information—about budget, ongoing initiatives, new opportunities for faculty, or other important issues—would be released for the first time. Faculty could come forward to the microphones to ask or say anything they wanted, and they did. Some younger faculty told me that it meant something to them that I was able to identify each faculty member by name and department as they approached the microphone. With a faculty of under 500, that is still possible; with a larger faculty, the sense of community, which presupposes knowing one another, wanes. The value of the meetings included the elevation of transparency, the focus on the continually evolving story of our advances, and the fostering of a common or collective identity. The reception with beer and wine didn't hurt either.

Instead of eating lunch quickly at my desk whenever I did not have a luncheon meeting scheduled, I visited the faculty cafeterias, so that faculty would have informal access to me and would see me among them. Not long after the review, I invited the chairpersons to my home. Culture, I increasingly realized, is based on conversations, for which one needs to make time. I also sought to cultivate community by having a simple box lunch with a randomly selected group of seven or so faculty members about three times a week (the only sifting process involved disciplinary and gender diversity). I opened the meetings by saying that they served four purposes: I wanted the faculty members to get to know one another, and they left with brief bios of each person present; I asked how the college could improve; I invited their questions; and I welcomed a discussion of whatever was on their minds. The full hour was devoted to whatever topics faculty members wished to discuss. Over time, hundreds of faculty members joined me. Various useful ideas arose from these lunches. They were enjoyable, a nice and efficient way to eat lunch. The more conversational dimensions were often about issues of teaching, which we all had in common, and since I was still teaching, those conversations reinforced our common bond.

Direct access to faculty was reinforced by my visiting more departmental meetings. Although I had told chairpersons I was available anytime, I had visited only some departments. I regularized the visits, putting myself on the agenda but allowing the faculty to choose the discussion topics. My goals were to touch base, listen to ideas and suggestions, answer any questions, and respond to comments. In short, to be visible and available. I held more fora: informational fora, such as on how the budget works; and brainstorming fora, for example, on how promotion-and-tenure documents might be enhanced. In addition, I restructured how I conducted meetings of the College Council, our legislative body of some seventy faculty members and a few students. Previously I had opened each meeting by making a few announcements. I shifted those announcements to an e-mail a few days in advance, started the meeting by asking if there were any questions, quickly had the minutes approved (assuming no objections), and then moved on immediately to discussion items. Essentially all of the meeting time was reserved for discussion. Any guests wanting to make presentations were given a strict five-minute limit, after which they either exited or engaged in discussion. Colleagues whose comments were not on the subject were, out of respect for others, not permitted to hold the floor. I adopted the technique of structuring a time-limited brainstorming session for complex topics, after which a committee would work to develop a recommendation. That gave everyone a voice, allowed changes to be arrived at more deliberatively, and also made the meetings more interesting. The meetings of deans and chairpersons likewise focused more on discussion, and we increased the time devoted to the sharing of best practices.

The college's strategic plan was developed not simply by me or by me and the associate deans and chairpersons. Instead I charged four faculty committees, each one chaired by a faculty member elected by the committee, to draft sections. I served on each committee and attended each meeting, so it was actually more work for me, but it was an important strategy to share the direction of the college, ensure that the full range of good ideas would be sifted, and spend meaningful time with key faculty.

I appointed two special committees. One reviewed the situation of full-time faculty not on the tenure track, a group that naturally felt dispirited since they did not satisfy the link between research and teaching that I regularly stressed and were paid on average considerably less than tenure-track faculty. The other, a greater gamble, was the committee of chairpersons to review my faculty merit-raise policy. In addition, I announced that the agenda items for the dean's advisory committee, a group I had created some years earlier, would be chosen by the membership, not by me.

In an age when pictures were less common on the Web, we undertook a little initiative to assist with staff morale: a brochure, with pictures, so that people could better identify the staff who worked in central offices by name. We also introduced several annual awards for the outstanding contributions of staff members.

I also worked to ensure more support structures to match our higher expectations. As a result of a series of complex events, partly deriving from our taking advantage of various university incentives and partly from our provost's having very high ambitions that at times outstripped annual-rate funding (the resulting shortfalls I covered temporarily with cash or one-time funding), the provost's debt to the college in terms of promised annual rate funding amounted to more than $2.2 million, which arrived in the college a few months after I signed on to another term; that sum was equivalent to an endowment of more than $50 million. In addition to increasing funding for research and more space, which had been early priorities, we put greater stress on salary increases and higher graduate stipends. Some of our internally competitive awards were transformed into so-called "interim awards," that is, faculty could apply at any time, and any worthy proposal would be approved—for example, selected course development grants, faculty seminars, and grants to aid long-time associate professors in getting their research back on track.

Over time, I became more strategic about how to ensure faculty quality. Instead of vetoing searches, I introduced more competitive searches, as I outlined above.

In my eyes, the five-year review was a blessing. The college had objectively advanced, and the accomplishments were unambiguous, but I had failed in important ways. I had moved ahead in advance of faculty support. I had been impatient, concerned about getting things done and getting out. I had not spent enough time with faculty socially. I had introduced too many foreign ideas, some of them too quickly. Still, my actions came from a love of the institution. Even if that love was not immediately visible, it became more visible over time. The Socratic concept of love includes a consciousness of incompleteness and a striving for more, a longing to bridge the gap between what one is and what one might yet and should become; this more complex dimension of love was gradually appreciated, even as it was combined on my part with greater recognition of what was already present.

Problems and Challenges with Accountability

The most common danger of thorough efforts at accountability and assessment is too much busywork and paperwork that draws attention to what one wants to do and what has been done but gets in the way of actually doing x, y, and z. Too much data and too many reports and strategic plans obscure what is most important and steal time from the highest priorities.

Any time new processes are introduced, they are unusually time consuming, as the patterns need to be developed and approved, for example, criteria to evaluate research and teaching. However, universities are constantly becoming more complex and accountable, as they seek to ensure due process and fairness, which means more and more faculty involvement. A competitive climate means an ever-greater number of time-consuming initiatives. Support offices can gather most relevant data. Still, administrators and faculty need to be involved to guide the questions and rationale.

Contingent factors can make matters worse. Many senior administrators who initiate requests for accountability have themselves been effective and efficient chairpersons and may have little empathy for those who are not equally efficient; they might thus underestimate the demands on chairpersons' time. Other senior administrators have never served as chairpersons and are clueless about such demands. Or in choosing to become senior administrators, they are devoting themselves to service and the institution and may inflate the importance of service (over teaching and research) and of institutional concerns (over faculty goals). I once suggested to our provost that no new requests for additional burdens on chairpersons should be made without corresponding reductions in previous standing requests. Such a model can keep an institution accountable in relation to the ever-bourgeoning growth of bureaucracy.

The challenge of misplaced priorities is exacerbated whenever an institution develops a professional bureaucracy for data collection and analysis that sees its raison d'être not in serving the higher mission, in which accountability plays an appropriate but limited role, but instead in developing more and more work for its office, expanding its staff, and increasing its budget. Even as a professional staff, the numbers of which are increasing at most universities (Schuster and Finkelstein 123), frees faculty to focus on teaching and research, it runs the risk of moving academic decision making away from the faculty. Thus, it is essential that such persons play a supportive role under faculty members, not an independent role that serves administration more than teaching and research. Ensuring that vision guides everything requires faculty leadership. To guarantee full accountability, moreover, a university needs to track administrative budget and administrative staff, that is, bureaucracy size per student, faculty member, and total university expenditure both across time and in relation to other institutions. An office of accountability must itself be accountable to higher goals.

A second danger is the tendency to focus on what is easy to calculate, not on what matters most. Still worse is a recognizable trend whereby what one is able to count becomes the new norm, such that goals are set not by ideals but by what one is able to measure empirically. The measurement results in a new incentive: scholars produce work in order to fulfill the quantitative expectations (Münch 102). But studies have shown that some essays may garner many citations shortly after publication and then none subsequently, whereas other essays may receive very few citations early but many over time (Fischer 14–15). This phenomenon is not unrelated to the problem that normal science, which involves modest progress within established paradigms, makes its way into the highly cited mainstream journals, whereas a revolutionary idea, introduced perhaps ahead of its time, may not be well received and may not garner immediate recognition (Kuhn). For this reason as well, one needs to be attentive to a qualitative assessment of arguments without succumbing completely to the legitimate recognition that most scholars do in fact work within the mainstream. Quantitative figures can be used, but they need to be sifted by a discerning mind and supplemented with judgment.

Applying inappropriate measures is related to the problem of misinterpreting what data mean. High graduation rates are normally a goal for an institution, but one can raise graduation rates with two simple strategies, which may not match other institutional goals: become more selective in admissions and lower grading standards. Rarely is the latter the right strategy, and the former is an inadvisable option for community colleges, whose raison d'être involves open access. Normally one wants to have a high yield among graduate students, but this is not necessarily an indication of quality. If a department is not good enough to attract students who are also accepted to the very best programs, it may indeed have a good yield. If it becomes better and attracts more and more students who are also applying to, and being admitted by, the very best programs, its yield will drop because it is now competing with better departments. This need not be bad; it can be the natural result of a better pool and a higher level of competition, even if one still wants to improve further. So here, too, one needs to approach accountability with considerable nuance—in choosing objective measures, determining strategies to realize them, and interpreting the results.

A third danger, which results from a misunderstanding of the ultimate purpose of accountability, is the reduction of accountability to one of its necessary elements, efficiency. Accountability always presupposes assessing action in accordance with an ideal. Pure efficiency can violate all kinds of ideals. It is surely more efficient to have adjunct or part-time teachers; to order fewer books for the library; to have larger class sizes or heavier teaching loads; and not to teach subjects, such as languages, that tend to call for smaller classes, but these efficiencies come at the cost of higher values, and so are incompatible with an intelligent accountability.

The final danger is aesthetic. Even if efficiency is not the highest value, it is a value and it can be employed to assist an institution. However, there is no need to introduce the language of business management. I cringe every time I hear expressions such as "total quality management" or "continuous quality improvement." Such terms are unappealing, and they tend to be counterproductive with faculty. I once heard a staff person speak of the academic side and the business side of the university. Such seemingly innocuous rhetoric actually changes our values. There is no academic side to a university. There is an academic *core* and a support *side*.

Community, or How Something Can Be Both an End and a Means

Community is an end in itself, but it can also be a means toward fostering other ends. The sense of belonging in a community makes us more relaxed as well as more attentive, opens our minds to others within the community, and gives us energy and resilience for new challenges. Good learning presupposes that students are being challenged; as students confront these challenges, a sense of community helps. A vibrant extracurricular life both bonds a community together and offers learning opportunities. Collective rituals and ceremonies are important whenever there is the possibility of isolation and alienation, for faculty as well as students.

Small classes, close mentoring relationships, a communal atmosphere, and meaningful activities throughout the day are part of what makes an overall college experience successful. I have noted in chapter 2 that online education offers some benefits, but it can hardly replace community. It can offer only parts of learning. The holistic college experience will not be replaced by online education or broken down into learning modules. Meaningful and sustained interactions with faculty members are crucial to student flourishing. When I became dean in 1996, most boards of trustees in the country were eager to pursue online learning, as a means to cut costs, make money, or both. While there have been isolated success stories in the past twenty years, the idea of online education replacing academic community has had little argumentative force. Trendy and flimsy are rarely opposites.

Community can be fostered or damaged by leadership. If the institution's identity is in some way distinctive, persons are more likely to remain in their positions. Consistency in leadership can be encouraged by a sense of community and can further encourage such community. If an institution's identity is interchangeable with that of any number of similar universities, one tends to find professional administrators, who move among universities. Such persons may be qualified and perform useful service at each stop but rarely are they beacons for the building of community. Indeed, such changes in leadership can trigger shifts in focus, which are then abandoned, thus resulting in faculty cynicism as each administrator arrives with a new vision. At Ohio State, I had in my six years as a junior faculty member four different chairpersons. While serving for five years as chairperson, I worked for three different deans. During my twelve years there, the university had five different provosts. The contrast with a more distinctive university is remarkable. The two presidents under whom I have served at Notre Dame, one of whom is still in office, have to date served a total of twenty-nine years. The two provosts during my tenure have served to date a total of twenty years, and one is still in office. My own tenure as dean was eleven years. It is not by chance that the Technische Universität München, Germany's highest ranking and most innovative university, and the one with the most compelling vision, has Germany's longest-standing president, Wolfgang Herrmann, who is in his twenty-first year. Great changes are not possible without a vision for the long term.

Universities often fail to groom future potential presidents, provosts, and deans, knowing that they can compete for such persons nationally. But as a result, universities may end up hiring someone from outside who has become a career administrator and readily leaves after a short time for another position, as the first years are always easier. It is less trouble to repeat those years while making more superficial advances. Here one can admire a number of administrators, especially presidents, who remain loyal to one institution, turning away the aggressive and potentially lucrative requests of search firms, and provide stable leadership with a view toward the institution's long-term future.

One mark of a great institution is that it finds the appropriate balance between, on the one hand, preserving its collective identity with the past, drawing on its accomplishments and traditions; and, on the other hand, recognizing fresh opportunities and adjusting to new challenges triggered by internal developments, contemporary issues, increasing aspirations, and the insights of new colleagues. To address the new while honoring the past helps ensure that initiatives are well embedded in the culture and endure. To honor the past is also to ensure a strong sense of tradition, which is in many ways a diachronic analogue to community. To keep in simultaneous focus an institution's distinct past and its unwritten future is to ensure both community and change, a living tradition.

Alma Mater

At many liberal arts colleges, incoming students across all disciplines read a common book over the summer and discuss it with one another and with faculty members when they arrive, creating a context for intellectual friendships. Not surprisingly, students who live on campus as part of the community tend to be more engaged academically (Keup and Stolzenberg 42). Being involved and having a sense of belonging are crucial for retention: "The more students are academically and socially engaged with faculty, staff, and peers, the more likely they are to succeed" (Tinto 7).

For a student at a good American college or university not to know many other students and to eat most meals alone would be unimaginable. Americans may forget how distinctive this is. When I was studying in Bonn in 1976, our program was set up in such a way that the Americans took classes by themselves, in German, with faculty members from the university. There was little integration with German students, and meeting other students was not as easy as it had been at my small American college. One day I placed myself about three blocks from the student cafeteria, noticed a German student approaching, and asked her where the cafeteria was. Fortunately, as I had hoped, she invited me to join her, as she was also on her way there. The shock was not that it required some creativity on my part to connect with a German student (that could easily be explained by my being a foreigner). No, the shock was that in the course of several subsequent conversations, I discovered that I was the first student she had gotten to know. She had been at the university for a semester but had not really made any friends, and yet she had no language hurdles to overcome; she had grown up less than sixty miles from Bonn.

Because Notre Dame's graduation ceremony is large, we phased in more intimate departmental convocations or receptions for graduating seniors, which mean a great deal to students and their families. Such events provide a fitting conclusion to a student's experience and send the students off in a personal way. In some departments these take place at the homes of faculty members who live near campus. Such activities cultivate a feeling of belonging, of collective identity.

Community is as important to graduate students as it is to undergraduates. When I was applying to graduate school, I submitted my applications from Germany and therefore did not visit any of the campuses. Upon arriving at Princeton, I discovered that most of the other students in our class of seven had narrowed their choices the previous spring to Princeton and Yale. Several had visited Yale and told the same story. They had sensed at Yale, in contrast to Princeton, little sense of community among the students or between students and faculty members. As a result, each of my colleagues chose Princeton.

In the early 1990s, we resolved at Ohio State to cover the costs to bring the top prospective graduate students to campus before they made their decisions, the result being that the yield of accepted students rose dramatically. One year the department invited six students to campus; five agreed to visit, and five enrolled. Prospective students also received at least two personalized letters from graduate faculty members whose areas of interest overlapped with theirs. We offered them a community of learning they could visualize.

In the penultimate year of my tenure as dean, Notre Dame's theology department garnered a yield of 91 percent from the pool of those admitted at the country's best universities, consistently winning in head-to-head competitions against Chicago, Duke, Emory, Princeton, and Yale. The department was not only strong academically (9.6% of the applicant pool was offered admission that year), but the coordinators of the different fields arranged to invite the prospective students to faculty homes; surely, the students could imagine a supportive social and intellectual environment.

Not surprisingly, community has a strong effect on graduate student completion rates and graduate student flourishing (Lovitts 107–8, 118, 176; Walker et al.). Partly for that reason, one needs to ensure a strong community once students arrive. I can recall hearing some student complaints at Ohio State and calling a meeting of all graduate students, so that I could listen to their concerns. I reformulated them as positive suggestions for faculty members, essentially recommending guidelines in areas ranging from accuracy in course descriptions and consistency with deadlines to offering early feedback to students and working cooperatively with other faculty members on dissertation committees. Addressing such challenges helps students finish their studies and helps attract future students.

Athletic events can bond a community together, strengthening emotional attachment to the institution (Toma). Participation in sports can also help to develop leadership, cooperation, and perseverance. In 2008, about five times as many undergraduates participated in club sports as in varsity sports, a number that will surprise those who tend to be familiar only with higher-profile varsity teams (Pennington). Club sports, which allow students with modest resources to run their own teams, are less formal. Students coach themselves, set up the schedules, and manage modest budgets. Audiences may be small; the sports, such as rugby and water polo, are often less mainstream; and the esprit de corps is usually quite high. With club sports, the amateur ideal is vibrant, and the educational experience of leading and managing a team can be meaningful, as I recall from my own experience at Williams. Intramural sports engage students who might have competed in high school but do not have the talent or time to invest in athletics at the varsity level. For these students, participation is more important than competition. Each of these options helps fill a need for ritual and community.

Research shows that the larger the institution, the less likely it is that a strong student orientation is visible (Astin, "How the Liberal Arts" 84). The smaller its size, the easier community is fostered. A recent survey of alumni thirty years after graduation made evident that the graduates of liberal arts colleges rated their overall undergraduate experience much more favorably than did graduates of larger universities (Hardwick

Day 9). Here as well, faculty scholarship and devotion to student learning are interwoven (Astin and Chang), and undergraduates are more likely to be engaged in research (Hardwick Day 22). Not surprisingly, given the intense student-faculty relations, a higher percentage of liberal arts graduates than research university graduates go on to receive doctorates (Oakley; Bourque; Cech; Burrelli, Rapoport, and Lehming).

If students have an excellent experience, they become the university's best ambassadors in recruiting other students, partly by chatting exuberantly on a variety of relevant topics while conducting campus tours. Notre Dame, for example, has at any given time more than 150 undergraduates trained to give campus tours to groups of 8–10 visitors. Current students are also far and away the most successful speakers when it comes to making the case to alumni for the value of supporting the university, especially through scholarships. And of course the current students themselves become prospective future donors.

Because the baccalaureate experience is not only about disciplinary learning but also about discerning one's values and becoming a person, continuing identification with the university is not unusual. Students enter college when they are still quite young and find there lifelong friendships, an engagement with great questions across the disciplines, and a holistic education that tries to address their minds and their hearts. "Much more than as a stepping stone to later careers, the alma mater is a continuing affective focus for many Americans" (Knox, Lindsay, and Kolb 175). This identification is reinforced by campus traditions, school colors and symbols, and a distinctive ethos, all of which contribute to a student's sense of collective identity.

Bringing parents to campus on an occasional basis helps them feel part of the university. Notre Dame speaks unabashedly of the Notre Dame family, meaning faculty, staff, students, parents, alumni, and donors. Such visits help parents understand better what collegiate learning and extracurricular life involve. On such weekends parents hear from administrators about their vision for the students' education; are told about opportunities, such as the career center, of which parents should be aware; listen to entertaining talks by popular faculty members; and connect with their son's or daughter's peers, as well as with their parents and, in many cases, their professors. I have often found it to be a special experience to meet the parents or even grandparents of my most engaging students, just as I can recall introducing my Williams and Princeton professors to my parents. All of this fosters a sense that students matter and that college is a community experience.

The sense of community for students runs not only across the students (and faculty) of a given time, it extends across time, as the institutional bonds remain after graduation. The students' communal experiences help immeasurably when the university later seeks resources in order to reach its highest aspirations. The more university graduates identify with their alma maters, the greater their alumni donations (Mael and Ashforth). According to the *U.S. News and World Report* ranking of best colleges, only three American universities—Princeton, Dartmouth, and Notre Dame—had annual alumni giving rates above 40 percent in each of the past two years (2015 ed. 72–73; 2016 ed. 74–75); what these three have in common is a strong residential, undergraduate culture and a focus, in numbers, more on undergraduates than graduates. Interestingly, seventeen first-tier liberal arts colleges can claim rates above 40 percent (2016 ed. 82–88). The highest figures among all institutions belong to Princeton University at 63 percent, Thomas Aquinas College at 58 percent, and Williams College at 57 percent (2016 ed. 74–75, 82–83, 86).

Collegiality and Leadership

A sense of community is also important for faculty. Working in an environment in which one can collegially discuss one's teaching and research with others is appealing. Faculty want to work at an institution with which they can also identify emotionally. And it is clearly in the university's best interest for faculty to identify with the institution as well as with the discipline. The more distinctive the university's identity, the easier it is to cultivate this social and emotional connection and the easier it is to attract new faculty and students, who perceive a connection to the institution. Were Notre Dame not a Catholic university, its faculty, along with its students and its resources, would not be nearly as impressive. Notre Dame would be just another generic midsized Midwestern university without a hospital.

While community can help scholarship, tensions within departments can steal time away from scholarship. A department that suffers from infighting is likely to have its lines frozen or see them lost to other units. In short, even community can be related to accountability and incentives; a dean is not likely to invest in a unit that cannot function effectively.

Small things can make a difference in fostering a welcoming community. Ideally, an institution introduces a sense of collegiality at the earliest stage, when it seeks to attract faculty, ensuring, for example, that prospective women faculty meet with other women and that younger faculty meet with other younger faculty, even if that means reaching out to persons in other departments. How one is first treated when one arrives at an institution is not easily forgotten and is psychologically significant for one's sense of long-term well-being at, and emotional identification with, an institution. When new faculty members enter their offices for the first time on some campuses, basic information on the college, from the overarching to the most practical, may be on their desks in an attractive handout, along with selected supplies. Some colleges welcome each new faculty member by publishing the newcomer's picture, his or her educational background and previous positions, and a quotation about what attracted him or her to the university in the campus newspaper. At the end of the college's fall meeting at Notre Dame, new faculty come forward, whatever their rank, and briefly introduce themselves.

The wisest American universities seek to hire people to whom they would like to grant tenure, even if tenure will not be granted whenever the high expectations of the institution have not been met. Still, everyone is supported, and everyone has a chance. Persons who do not have a strong sense of the future find it difficult to invest in a community. While the dominant factor in any faculty search is the combination of scholarship and teaching, new hires can reinforce or hinder a sense of community. For that reason some departments weigh the potential service and leadership contributions of new hires. One of Notre Dame's departments employs what the colleagues call the n-factor as a fourth element beyond teaching, research, and service. They want to hire only "nice" people, knowing what a drain difficult persons can be on a departmental sense of community. In such cases, one needs to guard against the n-factor becoming a kind of illicit and unacknowledged bias, but after having seen so many problems in their own past and at other universities, they found it equally absurd to ignore it completely. Interestingly, in a 2015 survey, 84 percent of provosts strongly agree or agree that civility is a legitimate criterion for faculty hiring decisions (Jaschik and Lederman, *2015 Inside Higher Ed Survey* 13).

Some institutions have internal awards to recognize community building. Notre Dame's arts and letters college, for example, introduced an annual award of appreciation designed to honor an outstanding colleague outside the college whose work adds immeasurably to the college and enriches its life. Recipients have included, among others, the director of the career center, who worked successfully to find internships and job opportunities for liberal arts majors; a professor of mathematics, who developed a new course for humanities students; a museum curator, who effectively integrated museum visits into classes; the director of the center for social concerns, who worked imaginatively to foster links between academic and experiential learning; the university's investment officer, whose success helped to ensure that our endowments grew even in difficult times; and a development officer, who was crucial in helping to raise funds for the college.

At Ohio State the development campaign also included a so-called campus campaign. I found the slightly counterintuitive idea appealing and, when asked, agreed to help organize the campaign. Faculty members were invited to contribute to the university, and many did. In the first ten years of the campaign, faculty and staff contributed $25 million. Faculty could choose to give to areas, such as undergraduate scholarships, departmental research funds, staff development, or the university's public radio station, that were meaningful to them. Some funds were named for deceased colleagues, and faculty contributed to those funds. Giving deepened their emotional bonds to the university, and it certainly helped with the pitch to external prospects, as we could say that our own faculty were investing in priority projects. During the year I was actively engaged in the campaign, 100 percent of the faculty and staff in my department contributed to the campus campaign, which helped greatly when I met with donors. At my current university, many retired faculty members devote, in their last wills and testaments, a portion of their estates to the university. That is a sign of great loyalty and affection, which reinforces the idea of the college as a community.

Fostering community also helps an institution retain the top faculty by strategies that emphasize more than simply salary. Studies have shown that across professions voluntary departures are driven less by compensation and prospects elsewhere than by disengagement from one's current place of employment and its values. This is not often recognized: whereas 89 percent of managers believe employees leave for more money, 88 percent of employees say they leave for other reasons (Branham 3). Identification with one's firm or institution comes from experiencing trust and confidence in leadership, vision, and values; feeling that one's contributions are advancing worthy goals and being recognized; having one's expectations and hopes for oneself and the institution fulfilled; receiving appropriate training, experiencing meaningful challenges, having opportunities to develop and advance, and obtaining regular feedback (Branham).

If one recognizes the centrality of community, then promotion-and-tenure decisions need to take some account of service and leadership contributions or leadership potential. At Notre Dame, in fact, we saw negative decisions made on the basis of inadequate service at all levels: the renewal of assistant professors, tenure, and promotion to full professor. Such decisions can negatively affect the pure elevation of research, on which most rankings depend. But a university is more than individual researchers doing their work, and I view such decisions as in principle appropriate—even for the overarching research enterprise. Fortunately, they are rare.

Mentoring fosters community because it makes one feel valued and recognized and helps one to flourish. Mentoring affects faculty productivity and retention, particularly for women and minorities. In small departments, asking for mentors outside the department and even, when necessary, beyond the university is often useful. Chairpersons can provide small incentives for such mentoring—for example, reimbursements for breakfasts and lunches. Also, mentoring can and should involve programs to develop future leaders in administration by providing faculty with opportunities to participate, learn, and develop new skills, as well as to discover whether they like administration sufficiently to take on a greater role.

Toward the end of each academic year, I invited chairpersons and spouses to a dinner away from campus. The event involved primarily expressing gratitude for their service, including recognition of their sacrifice, as well as more humorous comments, which encourage the bonding experience and can be ends in themselves. Whereas scholars tend to align themselves with those in their subfields, being an administrator forces one to think of the discipline in its widest sense; such a role also encourages faculty to identify with the institution and thus deepens their sense of collective identity. To identify with the department, college, and university is to expand one's sense of self. Such events can contribute to that higher purpose.

The spirit of community manifest at American colleges is not always common elsewhere. Any faculty member who has given a lecture in both Germany and the United States could comment on the differences. The American model of academic discourse after a lecture tends for the most part to be communal and supportive, even if one disagrees with the thesis. One says, "Linda, I disagree with you, but if you were to add the following point to your argument, you could perhaps strengthen it further." In Germany, faculty are prone to two tendencies: offering a strong critique of the speaker's thesis and, often, a minipresentation from the questioner's own area of expertise. In an American context the German method can be amusing: a *New Yorker* cartoon once showed a faculty moderator announcing that the floor was now open to short lectures disguised as questions. The American model can offer more help to the speaker, while the German model is more likely to lead to intense debate; one can certainly see the difference in terms of community.

When I gave my job talk at Ohio State in 1984, I spoke about laughter in Thomas Mann's novel *Doctor Faustus*. The job talk was in English, but I delivered the quotes in German. I began with a short joke, which elicited laughter; I then stepped back and noted that the laughter in *Doctor Faustus* is of a different kind, a diabolical laughter. After the presentation, I handled a half dozen or so questions. Then came a question in German. I assumed that this was a test of my linguistic abilities and so responded in German. My German was quite good at the time, so I spoke with good diction and without seemingly making any grammatical or stylistic mistakes, but I eventually realized that I was not saying anything substantial. Why? I was not responding to a question because there was no question. I stopped and said, "What exactly is your question?" The speaker looked befuddled, paused, and then withdrew his question. Afterward, he introduced himself. His speaking German was not a test of my German, it turned out. He was a visiting professor from Germany and he spoke German because he felt more comfortable speaking his native tongue. In a moment of self-reflection over dinner, he confessed that he indeed did not have a question but having seen me begin with a joke, he had given a little *Referat* on the Baroque concept of laughter and its relation to rhetoric. I was right. It was not a question but a minilecture.

In the German university, there is a much stronger sense of hierarchy. Assistants are cautious about the kinds of questions they ask after lectures so as not to appear to be undermining the position of one or the other professor. The first few questions are typically asked by the chairs; then others follow more or less according to rank. In the United States, questions are asked on a first come, first served basis, independently of rank, though at some lectures, the moderator may say, I would like the first two questions to come from undergraduate students (as a way of encouraging them to participate before they become intimidated by more complex questions from faculty members). It has been said that in the United States, where the students are front and center and where the professors care for the development of their characters and souls, the professor is a bit like a minister. Because Russia invested so heavily in research institutes divorced from the university and its students, the professor can be viewed as analogous to a monk. In Germany, where the professor oversees a hierarchy of underprofessors and assistants and has complete power over his or her domain, the professor is more like a bishop.

Incentives can be employed to enhance a sense of community. At Notre Dame we introduced a program encouraging every newly tenured faculty member to invite three colleagues to a meal and celebration at the college's expense. The condition was that all three guests must be from outside the tenure recipient's home department. They could be senior colleagues who had been mentors, faculty members they had wanted to meet or engage more fully in conversation, or junior faculty with whom they could imagine developing or had been developing a mentoring relationship.

Also in support of collaboration and community, Notre Dame introduced funding for multiyear exploratory seminars, which bring together faculty from at least three departments and which focus either on integrative scholarship across disciplines, such as the environment or developing countries, or on community challenges, for example, integrating academic and residential life or balancing career and family obligations. As an institution becomes larger or enhances its research profile, it must continue to look for ways to foster meaningful dialogue across disciplines and emphasize the ways in which the university is a communal and hospitable environment.

Every year I hosted an annual dinner that brought together the college's newly tenured faculty members. The event served three purposes.

First, being together fostered a sense of community among the cohort. (Cohorts can be hugely important. More than fifteen years after a particular class of new faculty arrived at Notre Dame, they still have an email listserv, where they communicate with one another about professional and social events as well as share questions and requests for information.) Second, it ensured that at this crucial juncture in their development, they felt recognized. I prepared for each faculty member who was present the equivalent of a page of comments, the kind of paean a person would want his or her parents to hear and which the person's colleagues did hear. Third, I wanted to send them a message about their new roles, particularly an invitation to dream big on behalf of the university and to carry the university forward with their dreams. It was a pep talk about our expectations for them. I wanted to encourage those who now had a greater stake in our future to help us advance to a higher level of distinction. I asked, how can we improve together? What can we collectively change in order to realize our highest aspirations? What one action could we undertake in the dean's office to improve things? What one action could you take to improve things?

A sense of community has the additional advantage of helping to cultivate an interest in administration. Scholarship, especially in the humanities, is often a private enterprise. In administration, one works collectively: with other administrators, faculty, students, and staff, as well as with colleagues from around the university in various support offices. If one identifies with the collective, one is more likely to sacrifice and to work on its behalf. To take joy in the success of others is a privileged and often neglected virtue, one that tends to surface only when one has a meaningful sense of collective identity; and the exercise of that virtue as one assumes a leadership position further reinforces one's identification with the community.

Staff Morale

Meetings among support staff—to keep them in the loop, to give them guidance, and to let them know of professional development opportunities—are good for morale. An initiative by Notre Dame's leadership to orchestrate town hall meetings at which the university's goals are articulated and the results of staff surveys are revealed and discussed has had excellent success. The surveys identified what staff found outstanding and deficient, what they liked and disliked about their positions, how they might serve Notre Dame better, and how the administration could communicate with staff more effectively. These surveys, which have been repeated at regular intervals, have been exceptional in helping to foster change, including some changes one might not have anticipated. In the first year, staff complained the most about other staff members who were not carrying their weight and encouraged fuller, more critical, and consequential reviews of staff so as to address such issues.

Cultivating an atmosphere in which staff feel as much a part of the broader mission as do the faculty and students is important. This requires mentoring, workshops, and regular reviews. It also means creating bridges so that staff benefit from, and are stimulated by, the university's full set of resources. One of the most welcome innovations at Notre Dame was the introduction of a university newspaper for faculty and staff—*ND Works*—which comes out once a week during the semester. It highlights new hires and faculty research of interest to a broader audience; announces special initiatives, events, and opportunities; and lets people know what is happening on campus, such as upcoming construction projects and the ways they will advance institutional goals. It has since been supplemented by a weekly e-mail, with updates, events, opportunities, and even coupons for discounts at local establishments; and a website, separate from the university website, with relevant information on events around campus, news, features, staff recognition, and a link to the university's online calendar. These various messages communicate the university's determination to foster collective identity, celebrate the individuals who make the university special, and highlight benefits and opportunities.

Staff reviews can lift morale and encourage a sense of community, insofar as they clarify the person's role in the larger enterprise, involve praise for work well done, and suggest ways the staff person can develop. Above all, they are the context in which to speak about the university's or department's ambitions, how we expect to arrive at those objectives, what we want the staff person to contribute toward goals, and how he or she is doing in that effort. Guests from Europe invariably comment on how polite the university staff is in the United States. Staff feel part of the project and are eager to help students and faculty; they view their jobs as a privilege and a responsibility. At the end of the academic year, Notre Dame's president has a dinner for all of the faculty, but he also holds one for all of the staff. In addition, university policies and initiatives, such as flex-time options, on-campus child care, and back-up care for unexpected child care or elder care needs, that support both work and family help immeasurably with community building.

Problems and Challenges with Community

The dangers of community are, first, that it can delimit the level of autonomy desired of every educated person. Scholarship is closely bound with dedicated and focused study, which is not always compatible with a strong sense of community. The faculty time needed to foster a sense of community is in modest opposition to the freedom and independence that scholars justly prize. Also, community can weaken autonomy among students, which is crucial for their development. Balance is appropriate in terms of ensuring that neither independence nor community is supported at the expense of the other.

Related to the above challenge is another defining characteristic of professors, cosmopolitanism (Engels 304). Research reputation arises from colleagues in the field, who are spread around the globe and not centered on the local campus. Any shift toward the higher value of research tends to move allegiance away from the local community to the discipline's international framework. Any sense of community, of identification with one's campus culture, must respect that need for a wider horizon and so seek an appropriate balance.

A third danger of overvaluing community is that faculty align themselves with junior colleagues, protecting the local community against the idea that some of its members might not be strong enough to warrant tenure. Here community can be disadvantageous for maintaining high standards. To cultivate a strong sense of community and collective identity is already difficult, which makes it all the more precious, but one cannot let that sense of hard-won community infringe on autonomy, cosmopolitanism, and high standards.

Fourth, some campus activities, for example, athletics and other nonacademic events, that foster community and an emotional connection to the university, can detract from the primary focus of a college education, intellection. An amusing exchange in the Marx Brothers film *Horse Feathers* addresses the relative priority of academics and athletics:

> GROUCHO (Dean Quincy Adams Wagstaff). Have we got a stadium?
> FACULTY. Yes.
> GROUCHO. Have we got a college?
> FACULTY. Yes.
> GROUCHO. Well, we can't support both. Tomorrow we start tearing down the college.

The witty line one occasionally hears on college campuses, "Don't let your studies interfere with your education," can be read idealistically to imply that students learn greatly outside the classroom. But its more common reading is cynical, suggesting that admission to the college's curricular programs is essentially a ticket to its vibrant social life.

Fifth, to foster community at larger universities is a challenge that is best accomplished through a combination of rituals for the entire university and circles of community fostered within the larger university. Still, even though liberal arts colleges are more successful in fostering community, two-thirds of the alumni of large public universities in the United States recall experiencing a sense of community even thirty years after graduation (Hardwick Day 26).

Conclusion

The two great transformations in the history of the modern university—
the German invention of the modern university, where teaching and research overlap and where academic freedom is prominent, and the great
American university, aided by a huge infusion of resources and directed
toward the goals of educating a majority of young Americans and developing world-class research—were characterized by distinctive, indeed
revolutionary, visions.

As communication and mobility across universities increase and as
rankings measure what is common, the tendency arises for each college
and university to adopt the best practices of the competition and thereby
begin to resemble the institutions from which its faculty members have
come and those colleges and universities that rank more highly.

But one of the great dimensions of the American university landscape is its diversity. Ohio State has a different vision of itself than does
Williams College. Notre Dame is different yet again. Each university
benefits from being able to articulate in meaningful and not simply inci-
dental ways why a particular student or faculty member should be drawn
to that institution. This diversity is the best brake on the homogenizing
tendencies of rankings. It offers students, faculty, and others additional
opportunities for intrinsic motivation and emotional identification.

I have argued that developing, sustaining, and realizing a distinctive vision require tremendous effort in terms of faculty socialization, support structures, communication, incentives, and leadership. What also distinguishes the American university today are tremendous resources. These come partly from federal research funding and federal student loans but also from the tuition paid by students, who for the most part want to study at that particular college or university, and from donations from the alumni, who are wedded to the distinctive vision of their alma maters. Distinctive identity involves, therefore, not only vision but also embodiment and resources, and each contributes to the other.

A handful of principles have helped to foster the acceleration and success of the great American university. I've experienced these principles—flexibility, competition, incentives, accountability, and community—firsthand in my own administrative work. The American administrator has tremendous flexibility, which of course varies slightly by institution, but to the extent that administrators have opportunities for innovation, the institution is capable of advancing more quickly.

The constant competition, which is greater in America than in most other countries, including Germany, with its once-great universities, has played a tremendous role in advancing our colleges and universities. Above all, competition for students and faculty has been a distinguishing hallmark of the American landscape. Competition is a double-edged sword that encourages institutions to mimic and conform to the practices of others, but only their distinctive capabilities allow them to stand out and thus garner a competitive advantage. Vision is the best counter to the tyranny of the market, yet it can, paradoxically, itself be marketable.

Although we tend to think of competition above all between institutions, competition can be embedded also within institutions. In the latter case we sometimes speak of incentives, which go hand in hand with competition, though incentives, unlike competition, do not always dictate some getting more and others getting less of the same. Incentives to advance a vision can be supported without necessarily leaving anyone behind.

A category that has gained tremendous importance in recent decades is accountability. At times it is severed from vision, but when vision and accountability work together, when the question asked is whether we are using our resources efficiently and effectively in order to advance our vi-

sion, then the university can measure itself against the competition and
its own aspirations for itself. Accountability tells us whether the vision is
actually being realized or whether we need to change and work more
strategically to bring us closer to that vision.

Competition, incentives, and accountability are more palatable when
a university embodies the original meaning of the term university, a
community of faculty and students. The wise administrator does as
much as he or she can to foster a sense of community without allowing
it to hinder academic quality.

If I were to step back and ask what are the most compelling personal or
philosophical insights I developed during my time as dean, I would name
the following three.

First, do not waver from vision. Central to this book is the idea that
everything revolves around vision and setting priorities according to vision. Without an overarching vision, motivation is weakened and clarity
of purpose diminished. Certainly, a vision can be complex, and at times
choices need to be weighed with a great deal of ambiguity. Some mistakes
I made derived from weighing conflicting goods and misjudging which
decision would most support the long-term aspirations of the institution.

Serving in administration has little purpose if one does not have a
vision of what one hopes to accomplish, even if that involves simply providing greater support for students and faculty. Still, one can shoot higher
and imagine ways in which one can greatly enhance academic community and provide truly new opportunities. Most importantly, one needs
to ensure that all decisions, especially those affecting the use of one's time,
the appointment and evaluation of personnel, and the allocation of budget, serve the overarching vision. The adjustment of my responsibilities
halfway through my tenure was strongly effective, not least of all because
it clarified the importance of priorities in support of vision. Not losing
time on what is unimportant or inessential is an important principle.
And here vision can run counter to tradition, that is, to established procedures and expected practices.

Effectiveness in response to a higher vision, not business efficiency
in support of instrumental goals, should shape a college. Economic and
business principles are essential, but they cannot themselves be a telos.

Developing a distinctive vision is not one and the same with marketing a brand. Entrepreneurship is essential, but that need not mean elevating the corporate drive for the commercialization of research over its intrinsic value or its capacity to address social problems. Vision should drive business plans and business strategies, not vice versa. A blurring of vision is likely to mean at the very least a weakening of donor support and a redirection of precious resources to tangential areas.

Administrators serve briefly in comparison with the long life of an institution and so have the responsibility to prioritize long-term flourishing. The long-range perspective that governs the management and payout of college endowment should drive administrators as well. I recounted above how tenure decisions, even if they create immediate conflict, need to be made in the institution's long-term interests. One is serving more than the present, and one needs to keep in mind one's responsibilities to the future. Leaving mistakes to one's successor, while inevitable, should be curtailed as much as consciously possible, even when that means difficulties in the present. Vision can give one the strength to face conflict.

I could add under advancing vision any number of related but subordinate principles. Listening closely as other persons enhance or challenge the vision, spending extensive time in informal conversations, communicating the vision effectively to multiple audiences, investing in priorities, using resources efficiently, ferreting out and confronting gaps, and developing practical means for measuring competency and success—all are examples of further important principles, but almost all valid administrative principles, these included, are subordinate to and part of either forming or realizing the vision.

Second, round out your weaknesses. Everyone has strengths and weaknesses. An academic leader receives a position on the basis of strengths (and despite recognizable or as yet unseen weaknesses). At some institutions at certain stretches of time, an administrator may be able to help advance or maintain a university without the full repertoire one wants to see. A chairperson, dean, or other academic leader without vision or without strong communication skills or without the capacity to listen or without efficiency or without organizational skills or without mentoring capabilities or without a willingness to face conflict may well survive but is unlikely to succeed as well as he or she might on behalf of the institution. I could almost divide chairpersons into those who used cogent critical feedback to reach a still higher level and those who turned away from the advice and either stayed in place, struggled, or exited more quickly than they had intended or wanted.

Helped by a bracing review, I was able to reflect on ways to stretch my repertoire and shift some of my emphases. In my case, this involved, after first having focused on standards and structures, devoting much more time to the social and emotional elements of leadership. The voluntary review that sharpened my priorities gave me the capital to hire an additional person, delegate more, and focus on essential issues. These changes were crucial to my reaching a higher level of effectiveness. In the case of the external review, the weaknesses identified were as much structural as personal. Just as a college moves forward by focusing on its gaps, so my own work improved when the lens was turned inward—to me and to my office. One can identify weaknesses in oneself or one's office in many ways—through introspection or with the help of trusted staff and candid faculty members, by undergoing obligatory or voluntary reviews, and by assessing progress made in targeted areas. The number of ways to identify gaps and develop strategies to address them is countless, which brings me to my next point.

Third, identify best practices. It makes little sense to reinvent the wheel on every issue. Most institutions wrestle with analogous issues. One can visit other campuses and consult other leaders. One can reach out to those on one's campus who might have faced analogous problems. One can ask faculty for their ideas, engage in brainstorming sessions with staff, skim relevant literature on higher education puzzles, and draw on one's own creativity. One can question faculty who have arrived from excellent universities, asking, from what aspects of your previous university can we learn and what do we do that strikes you as deficient. Although I have stressed distinction, all universities can learn from one another concerning their common challenges—from recruiting and mentoring faculty to fostering peer learning and intellectual community. This commonality, I hope, will allow my book to appeal to administrators and faculty members at a diverse array of colleges and universities.

Developing a repertoire of ideas and ways to address various kinds of problems is important. I was helped to some degree by having previously been at different kinds of institutions, so I brought new perspectives to the table. Many ideas emerged from thinking in the back of my mind about puzzles before us. The costs of that—not uncommon among administrators—is that one's work is always part of one's subconscious. The same of course applies to faculty members who are truly devoted to scholarship and teaching, but it is slightly different when an active faculty member is consumed by administrative conundra.

My own thinking was sharpened as I thought out loud with myself while reading selectively, especially early in my tenure, in the leadership literature on higher education. A variety of books were helpful in stretches, most prominently as I filtered their thoughts through the lens of my own situation. No less helpful was reading classic works—by Sophocles, Plato, Hegel, Dickens, Fontane, Mann, and others—that explored some of the wider issues at play in any complex intellectual or human situation.

Just as there are multiple strategies for almost any kind of situation, dilemma, or crisis, so, too, are there multiple means for identifying strategies and options. Over time, experience ensures that one or more options are already at one's disposal. Early on in particular, the stories of others bring newer administrators up to speed more quickly.

In speaking of best practices, I have been thinking primarily about academic puzzles such as moving graduate students toward timely completion of their degrees, hiring for diversity, making wise promotion-and-tenure decisions, helping associate professors progress through the ranks, adopting enrollment management strategies, developing sensible policies for annual evaluations, reviewing chairpersons, and so forth. But best practices pertain also in the neighboring and arguably equally important realms of surviving the wear and tear of administrative work, allocating one's private time, and finding strategies for resilience. As dean I swam five days a week. When a faculty member once asked me how I had the time to go for a swim, I answered immediately, "I don't have the time not to swim." Physical exercise, with its accompanying clearing of the mind and renewed energy, was necessary to give me more meaningful, focused time for work. I managed my research and teaching time effectively, finishing some books in the early years and shifting my faculty time to teaching in the later years. However, I did not pace myself at all for longer service. That was not my goal, but if it had been, I would have been out of luck, and one certainly wants to keep options open. I wisely let go of my disciplinary ties for the most part (one has to sacrifice some things), but were I to start fresh, I might try to spend more time networking with deans at analogous institutions. One can learn from peers, as I knew from my days on the Committee on Institutional Cooperation, trading best practices and thinking out loud together about common problems.

There are also best practices when it comes to one's use of language. One of my early insights, seemingly mundane but actually quite important, was that language and rhetoric can make or break a reform or an initiative. I finally gained some traction or at least had less resistance on the introduction of annual evaluations when I shifted my language from merit raises to feedback and mentoring. Small changes can make a huge difference. The shift was from the culture of money to the culture of support, from a more business-style language to a more academic language.

The reader may have wondered about the image that adorns the cover of this book. The oil painting by Maria Tomasula, a Notre Dame faculty member and contemporary artist represented by Forum Gallery in New York and Los Angeles and Zolla/Lieberman Gallery in Chicago, was commissioned by the Notre Dame College of Arts and Letters Advisory Council at the end of my tenure as dean and presented as a gift to my wife and me. Tomasula paints still-life motifs in a realistic but also highly stylized and symbolic way. Her paintings are technically sophisticated, with saturated colors, glistening surfaces, and intriguing value shifts. Often in unexpected combinations, the objects in her paintings tend to be complex and ambiguous. In the painting, titled simply *For Mark and Barb* the gloved hand pulls together a tapestry of gold on which various items are arranged; these symbolize diverse qualities and characteristics that are brought together in the distinctive university and in academic leadership.

The painting can partly be interpreted as suggesting an ideal of academic leadership. The compass symbolizes the vision essential for any administrative position. The white at the center of the work evokes integrity. The tapestry includes a book, representing scholarship. The petals of the iris traditionally allude to wisdom, faith, and courage. The number of water droplets on the iris—thirty—symbolizes dedication to a calling. The clock recalls the need for leaders to use their time well and to hold themselves and others accountable. The stirrup, a tool for elevating one-self onto a horse, is symbolic of the assistance provided by others to any-one in a leadership position. The herbs can be associated indirectly with the qualities of personality that members of a community contribute to one another. The blue, representing contemplation, and the gold hand, signifying power, complement one another in stressing two essential as-pects of academic leadership, the *vita contemplativa* and the *vita activa*.

The images are both general and particular. The blue and gold over-all and in the compass and class ring in particular combine to represent the colors of the University of Notre Dame. The fleur-de-lis on the com-pass, which echoes the more prominent iris, is a symbol of the Trinity as well as an indirect allusion to the French order that founded L'Université Dame du Lac. The iris is associated with the Virgin Mary and thus with Notre Dame, an allusion reinforced by the blue background, which is the color of Mary's cloak or robe. The fire and light of the red garnets can be associated with the Holy Spirit, whose illumination is essential to the idea of a Catholic university. The gold hand and then the pearls, iris, and gold above the iris form a vertical axis, suggesting connection to a higher pur-pose, while the horizontal of the gold tapestry implies community. To-gether there is the hint of a cross.

The painting contains various symmetries and images of balance, which supplement one another. Spatially, the triangular composition is reinforced by the circle of pearls that extends upward and outward to the compass and the clock and by the red of the garnet and the purple herbs, which together form an analogous triangle. More subtly and in reverse, the soft blue of the iris is linked in a triangle with the blue on either side of the hand. The circularity of the compass and the clock balance one an-other, as do the gold scale and the gold ring. The leather of the book has a common bond with the stirrup. Thematically, both the gold and the pearls are images of the self-luminous, the capacity to radiate a vision. Faith is represented by the iris and the pearls. Both the rain droplets and the iris (the flower's name having been taken from Iris, the female mes-senger of the gods) link the heavenly and the earthly. The ring expresses union, a symbol of what binds us to one another and to a higher purpose. Much as the ring conveys circularity, and thus continuity and wholeness, so does the circle of eight pearls. Whereas the scale of justice seeks to balance out decisions, the gold hand, also a symbol of justice, holds together diverse qualities. The eight pearls represent pairs of opposites, which, however, mirror one another; in forming a circle, they imply balance as well. Not only the book and the iris are associated with wisdom; so, too, one of the herbs, sage.

The painting is not without its evocation of the challenges of administrative leadership. The hand is the left hand, which is often viewed as sinister, a common perception of administrative leadership. Although gold can symbolize justice, it has less appealing associations as well. The number thirty is ambiguous and recalls not only the age when Christ began his ministry but also the thirty silver coins for which he was betrayed. The red of the garnet is symbolic of blood and thus of sacrifice. The water droplets can be read as tears. One of the herbs, basil, is traditionally used at funerals and rites of the dead, though as a symbol of love. Ambiguity is further evident in the traditional image of herbs as both poisonous and medicinal. The compass does not point precisely north, which suggests that the direction may be slightly off course. The entire painting, when placed upside down, has a loose association with Notre Dame's Main Building, the so-called golden dome. This idea is reinforced by the association of the iris with the Virgin Mary, who sits atop the dome. Change elicited by an active administrator can seem to turn an institution upside down.

The multiple images of regeneration and rebirth imply both a passing away and a renewal. The garnet is above all a symbol of regeneration; so, too, are the pearls. The number of pearls, eight, is symbolic of rebirth. In Christian vocabulary eight is the number of resurrection, for on the eighth day after his entry into Jerusalem, Christ was said to have risen from the grave (which is why Christian baptismal fonts are octagonal in shape). The water droplets, too, can be said to suggest a kind of rebirth. The clock, which signifies the passage of time, is joined by the iris, which is at its peak, and so hints at the end of a person's tenure as a leader.

Having completed my work as dean, I now live with the decisions we made over a period of eleven years. If there is a policy under which I suffer, I say it is because of the incompetence of the current dean's predecessor.

As a former administrator, I am sometimes asked to help think through puzzles or serve on university committees. As I write these pages, I am serving as a member of the decennial committee to review our core curriculum and chairing a committee charged with thinking through the core requirements pertaining to our Catholic mission.

I am struck by how much of what I explored above has been present in these discussions. What administrators must think through is for the most part also what its university citizens must contemplate as they weigh in on university issues. We began our deliberations with vision. A Catholic liberal arts university should have core liberal arts requirements like other universities but also distinctive Catholic requirements. The core is one of the most visible ways in which a distinctive vision becomes incarnate.

Catholic higher education has traditionally sought to embody its distinctive mission by requiring a certain number of courses in theology and philosophy. Notre Dame's core, which requires two courses in theology and two courses in philosophy, has been stable in that regard for more than forty-five years. To some this vision stands clear, and these requirements should be untouchable, beyond any discussion.

Others have asked whether the vision that these requirements are intended to support, including the expectation that the courses will provide a level of integration essential to the Catholic idea of the unity of knowledge across disciplines, is being met, since both disciplines have, in faculty research and teaching, moved away from integration and toward specialization. Further, as teaching loads have been reduced since the last reform in 1969, fewer courses have been taught by faculty. Could the goal of integration be met in other ways? Could other faculty contribute more to mission?

The discussion has been contested, not because there is any desire to move away from our distinctive mission, but because there are conflicting ways of understanding how that might best be articulated and realized. Some who support the status quo sought to advance their case by reaching out to alumni and conservative Catholics, partly by triggering media coverage, including in the *Washington Post*, and they turned to social media and letter-writing campaigns (Bailey). Such national press underscores the idea that Notre Dame does indeed have a distinctive identity with strong emotional allegiance.

Beyond the conflict in vision, questions of accountability have arisen. If requirements are passed on to departments, who is responsible for ensuring that all of the courses meet the university's expectations? Our strong push toward greater accountability, which involves pointing out gaps between where we are and where we should be, has led to considerable consternation and tension. And yet precisely this pressure has led to internal departmental reforms that otherwise might not have been made. In the wake of our discussions, universal agreement has surfaced that the first courses in philosophy and theology need to be taught by faculty and that all of the core courses need to be reviewed by the university and improved on a regular basis, not every ten years.

One proposal to reinforce flexibility, incentives, and competition advanced the idea that students who have taken an initial course in philosophy and one in theology might be allowed to have some choice between the two disciplines, along with the opportunity to choose courses in other departments that combine disciplinary knowledge of Catholicism with faith questions or normative questions: a course, for example, on the history of the Catholic Church that would require students to reflect on their faith more fully as a result of this new historical understanding or a course on Catholicism and politics that would not focus simply on issues such as party affiliations and voting patterns but would also address the normative question, "How should Catholics think about the political order and political issues within it?" A course such as economics and Catholic social thought, to take another example, would allow students to integrate normative Catholic perspectives with disciplinary knowledge and so contribute to deep learning.

By drawing on faculty in other departments, the university could offer more faculty-taught courses in the Catholic core than are currently available. Faculty would have opportunities to imagine new courses, and departments would have incentives to try to keep or expand faculty lines by contributing to the core and proposing new faculty members who can offer such courses. One wants to see a fuller, more holistic, truly integrative concept of a Catholic university, in which faculty from multiple departments participate (Roche, "Principles"). Competition for courses would function as an added incentive, beyond intrinsic motivation, to encourage the two traditional stewards of Catholic mission to perform at the highest possible level.

But such change also involves risk. If goals are realized by faculty across departments, how do we know that they will be realized in ways that will avoid mission drift over time? Given that these four courses in theology and philosophy have come to be seen as a barometer of our support of Catholic mission, would reconfiguring them be viewed as backing away from our Catholic identity, would doing so in fact be a move toward secularization?

After I had been highly critical of the status quo and argued strongly for the more innovative model, I was told by a colleague who supports very little change that if I pushed much further, I would irreparably damage the community. I was reminded of similar comments years earlier concerning merit raises and the reform of economics. Change tests community.

Although the discussions have yet to be concluded, it seems likely that we will see at least modest change that enhances vision and embodies principles essential for the flourishing of any university, including a distinctive university: flexibility, competition, incentives, and accountability. An enduring and continuing sense of community despite disagreements also seems likely, given a common overarching vision and a communal campus ethos. In any case, the entire debate, in which I am now engaged as a faculty member and not as an administrator, underscores that the categories above are relevant not only for administrators but for all faculty members interested in ensuring distinction, with its twofold meaning of excellence and difference.

Works Cited

2013 College-Bound Seniors. Total Group Profile Report. New York: College Board, 2013. http://media.collegeboard.com/digitalServices/pdf/research /2013/TotalGroup-2013.pdf.

AAUP Contingent Faculty Index 2006. Washington, DC: American Association of University Professors, 2006. www.aaup.org/aaup-contingent-faculty -index-2006.

Abowd, John M., V. Joseph Hotz, and Valerie Ramey. *External Advisory Report on the Department of Economics.* University of Notre Dame, 30 April 2013. www3.nd.edu/~rjensen1/External%20Advisory%20Report%20on%20 Economics-FINAL-Signed.pdf.

Academic Ranking of World Universities 2015. Shanghai: ShanghaiRanking Consultancy, 2015. www.shanghairanking.com/ARWU2015.html.

Advisory Committee on Student Financial Assistance. *Empty Promises: The Myth of College Access in America.* Washington, DC: Advisory Committee on Student Financial Assistance, 2002. http://files.eric.ed.gov/fulltext/ ED466814.pdf.

Altbach, Philip G., ed. *The International Academic Profession: Portraits of Fourteen Countries.* San Francisco: Jossey-Bass, 1996.

American Association for Higher Education. *On Assuming a College or University Presidency: Lessons and Advice from the Field.* Washington, DC: American Association for Higher Education, 1989.

American Bar Association. *Section of Legal Education and Admissions to the Bar. Statistics.* Chicago, IL: American Bar Association, 2016. www .americanbar.org/groups/legal_education/resources/statistics.html.

American Council on Education. *The American College President: 2012.* Washington, DC: American Council on Education, 2012.

American Council on Education. *Putting College Costs into Context.* Washington, DC: American Council on Education, 2004.

Anderson, Nick. "Default Rate for Repayment of For-Profit College Loans Hits 25%." *Washington Post,* 4 February 2011. www.washingtonpost.com/wp-dyn/content/article/2011/02/04/AR2011020400015.html.

Angulo, A. J. *Diploma Mills: How For-Profit Colleges Stiffed Students, Taxpayers, and the American Dream.* Baltimore: Johns Hopkins University Press, 2016.

Arum, Richard, and Josipa Roksa. *Academically Adrift: Limited Learning on College Campuses.* Chicago: University of Chicago Press, 2011.

Ashburn, Elyse. "The U. of Arizona's President Finds an Unexpected New Field of Employment." *Chronicle of Higher Education,* 1 July 2011, A11.

Astin, Alexander W. "How the Liberal Arts College Affects Students." *Daedalus* 128, no. 1 (1999): 77–100.

———. *What Matters in College? Four Critical Years Revisited.* San Francisco: Jossey-Bass, 1993.

Astin, Alexander W., and Mitchell J. Chang. "Colleges That Emphasize Research and Teaching: Can You Have Your Cake and Eat It Too?" *Change* (September/October 1995): 45–49.

Aud, Susan, et al. *The Condition of Education 2011.* Washington, DC: U.S. Department of Education, 2011.

Avery, Christopher N., Mark E. Glickman, Caroline M. Hoxby, and Andrew Metrick. "A Revealed Preference Ranking of U.S. Colleges and Universities." *Quarterly Journal of Economics* 128 (2013): 425–67.

Axtell, James. *Wisdom's Workshop: The Rise of the Modern University.* Princeton, NJ: Princeton University Press, 2016.

Bailey, Sarah Pulliam. "Why Notre Dame's Curriculum Review Raises Far-Reaching Catholic Identity Questions." *Washington Post,* 17 February 2015. www.washingtonpost.com/news/grade-point/wp/2015/02/17/notre-dame-is-reviewing-its-curriculum-which-could-have-far-reaching-effects/.

Bain, Ken. *What the Best College Teachers Do.* Cambridge: Harvard University Press, 2004.

Baker, Ray Stannard. *Woodrow Wilson: Life and Letters. Princeton. 1890–1910.* Garden City, NY: Doubleday, 1927.

Bastedo, Michael N., and Ozan Jaquette. "Running in Place: Low Income Students and the Dynamics of Higher Education Stratification." *Educational Evaluation and Policy Analysis* 33 (2011): 318–39.

Ben-David, Joseph. *Centers of Learning: Britain, France, Germany, United States.* London: Transaction, 1992. First published 1977 by McGraw-Hill.

Bender, Thomas. "What's Been Lost in History." *Chronicle of Higher Education,* 17 February 2012, B4–B5.

Benne, Robert. *Quality with Soul: How Six Premier Colleges and Universities Keep Faith with Their Religious Traditions.* Grand Rapids, MI: Eerdmans, 2001.

Bennis, Warren. *On Becoming a Leader.* Reading, MA: Addison-Wesley, 1989.

Bes-Rastrollo, Maira, Matthias B. Schulze, Miguel Ruiz-Canela, and Miguel A. Martinez-Gonzalez. "Financial Conflicts of Interest and Reporting Bias Regarding the Association between Sugar-Sweetened Beverages and Weight Gain: A Systematic Review of Systematic Reviews." *PLOS Medicine* 10 (2014). http://journals.plos.org/plosmedicine/article?id=10.1371/journal.pmed.1001578.

Beyerchen, Alan D. *Scientists under Hitler: Politics and the Physics Community in the Third Reich.* New Haven, CT: Yale University Press, 1977.

Bildung und Forschung in Zahlen 2015: Ausgewählte Fakten aus dem Daten-Portal des BMBF. Bonn and Berlin: Bundesministerium für Bildung und Forschung, 2015.

Bok, Derek. *Higher Education in America.* Princeton, NJ: Princeton University Press, 2015.

———. *Our Underachieving Colleges: A Candid Look at How Much Students Learn and Why They Should Be Learning More.* Princeton, NJ: Princeton University Press, 2006.

Bolman, Lee G., and Terrence E. Deal. *Reframing Organizations: Artistry, Choice, and Leadership.* 3rd ed. San Francisco: Jossey-Bass, 2003.

Bouchikhi, Hamid, and John Kimberly. "Micro Processes and Isomorphic Adaptation: Insights from the Struggle for the Soul of Economics at the University of the Holy Spirit." *Social Science Research Network* (May 2014). http://papers.ssrn.com/sol3/papers.cfm?abstract_id=2441138.

———. "Subversion from the Top: How Transgressive Leaders Produce Change." *Academy of Management Proceedings* (January 2013). http://proceedings.aom.org/content/2013/1/10246.short.

Bourque, Susan C. "Reassessing Research: Liberal Arts Colleges and the Social Sciences." *Daedalus* 128, no. 1 (1999): 265–72.

Bowen, Ezra, and Barbara Dolan. "His Trumpet Was Never Uncertain: Hesburgh Retires from Notre Dame after 35 Distinguished Years." *Time,* 18 May 1987, 68–69.

Bowen, William G. *Lessons Learned: Reflections of a University President.* Princeton, NJ: Princeton University Press, 2011.

Bowen, William G., Matthew M. Chingos, and Michael S. McPherson. *Crossing the Finish Line: Completing College at America's Public Universities.* Princeton, NJ: Princeton University Press, 2009.

Bowen, William G., and Sarah A. Levin. *Reclaiming the Game: College Sports and Educational Values*. Princeton, NJ: Princeton University Press, 2003.

Bowen, William G., and Michael S. McPherson. *Lesson Plan: An Agenda for Change in American Higher Education*. Princeton, NJ: Princeton University Press, 2016.

Boyer Commission on Educating Undergraduates in the Research University. *Reinventing Undergraduate Education: A Blueprint for America's Research Universities*. Stony Brook: State University of New York, 1998.

Branham, Leigh. *The 7 Hidden Reasons Employees Leave: How to Recognize the Subtle Signs and Act before It's Too Late*. New York: American Management Association, 2005.

Bright, David F., and Mary P. Richards. *The Academic Deanship: Individual Careers and Institutional Roles*. San Francisco: Jossey-Bass, 2001.

Brint, Steven, Mark Riddle, Lori Turk-Bicakci, and Charles S. Levy. "From the Liberal to the Practical Arts in American Colleges and Universities: Organizational Analysis and Curricular Change." *Journal of Higher Education* 76 (2005): 151–80.

Burns, James MacGregor. *Leadership*. New York: Harper, 1982.

Burrelli, Joan, Alan Rapoport, and Rolf Lehming. "Baccalaureate Origins of S&E Doctorate Recipients." NSF 08-311. *InfoBrief SRS* (July 2008). www .nsf.gov/statistics/infbrief/nsf08311/.

Bush, Vannevar. *Science: The Endless Frontier*. Washington, DC: Government Printing Office, 1945.

Campbell, Peter, and Michael C. Desch. "Rank Irrelevance: How Academia Lost Its Way." *Foreign Affairs*, 15 September 2011. www.foreignaffairs.com/ articles/united-states/2013-09-15/rank-irrelevance.

Carnevale, Anthony P., and Stephen J. Rose. *Socioeconomic Status, Race/ Ethnicity, and Selective College Admissions*. New York: Century Foundation, 2003.

Carnevale, Anthony P., and Jeff Strohl. *Separate and Unequal: How Higher Education Reinforces the Intergenerational Reproduction of White Racial Privilege*. Washington, DC: Georgetown Public Policy Institute, 2013.

Caulfield, Marie, Geoffrey Redden, and Henry Sondheimer. "Graduation Rates and Attrition Factors for U.S. Medical School Students." *Analysis in Brief: Association of American Medical Colleges* 14, no. 5 (2014). www.aamc.org/ download/379220/data/may2014aib-graduationratesandattritionfactors forusmedschools.pdf.

Cech, Thomas R. "Science at Liberal Arts Colleges: A Better Education?" *Daedelus* 128, no. 1 (1999): 195–216.

Center on Philanthropy at Indiana University. *Giving USA 2011: The Annual Report on Philanthropy for the Year 2010*. Indianapolis: Giving USA Foundation, 2011.

Chronicle of Higher Education. Almanac 2011–12. 26 August 2011.

Chronicle of Higher Education. Almanac 2013–14. 23 August 2013.

Chronicle of Higher Education. "Trustees: More Willing Than Ready." 11 May 2007, A11–A21.

Chronicle of Higher Education. "What Presidents Think: A 2013 Survey of Four-Year College Presidents." 2013. http://results.chronicle.com/PresSurvey P1?elid=CLP2013print.

Clark, Burton. *The Distinctive College.* Piscataway, NJ: Transaction, 1992. First published 1970 by Aldine.

Clark, William. *Academic Charisma and the Origins of the Research University.* Chicago: University of Chicago Press, 2006.

Clotfelter, Charles T. *Buying the Best: Cost Escalation in Elite Higher Education.* Princeton, NJ: Princeton University Press, 1996.

Cohen, Arthur M., and Carrie B. Kisker. *The Shaping of American Higher Education: Emergence and Growth of the Contemporary System.* 2nd ed. San Francisco: Jossey-Bass, 2010.

Cole, Jonathan R. *The Great American University: Its Rise to Pre-eminence, Its Indispensable National Role, Why It Must Be Protected.* New York: Public-Affairs, 2010.

———. *Toward a More Perfect University.* New York: PublicAffairs, 2016.

College Board. *Trends in Student Aid 2011.* New York: College Board, 2011.

College Board. *Trends in Student Aid 2015.* New York: College Board, 2015.

Council for Aid to Education. "Colleges and Universities Raise Record $40.30 Billion in 2015." New York: Council for Aid to Education, 2016. http://cae .org/fundraising-in-education/survey-results-other-research/annual -press-release/.

Council of Graduate Schools. *Ph.D. Completion and Attrition: Findings from Exit Surveys of Ph.D. Completers.* Washington, DC: Council of Graduate Schools, 2009.

Cowley, W. H. *Presidents, Professors, and Trustees: The Evolution of American Academic Government.* San Francisco: Jossey-Bass, 1980.

Cross, John G., and Edie N. Goldenberg. *Off-Track Profs: Nontenured Teachers in Higher Education.* Cambridge: MIT Press, 2009.

Cross, K. Patricia. "Not Can, but *Will* College Teaching Be Improved?" *New Directions for Higher Education* 17 (1977): 1–15.

Delbanco, Andrew. *College: What It Was, Is, and Should Be.* Princeton, NJ: Princeton University Press, 2012.

Deresiewicz, William. *Excellent Sheep: The Miseducation of the American Elite and the Way to a Meaningful Life.* New York: Free Press, 2014.

Deutsche Forschungsgemeinschaft. *Jahresbericht 2014: Aufgaben und Ergebnisse.* Bonn: Deutsche Forschungsgemeinschaft, 2015.

Douthat, Ross Gregory. *Privilege: Harvard and the Education of the Ruling Class.* New York: Hyperion, 2005.

Doyle, Kenneth O., Jr. *Evaluating Teaching.* Lexington, MA: Lexington Books, 1983.

Dunham, Stephen S. "Government Regulation of Higher Education: The Elephant in the Middle of the Room." *Journal of College and University Law* 36 (2010): 749–89.

Eckel, Peter D., Bryan J. Cook, and Jacqueline E. King. *The CAO Census: A National Profile of Chief Academic Officers.* Washington, DC: American Council on Education, 2009.

Economist. "Jailhouse Blues: California Must Reduce Its Prisons' Overcrowding and Cost. But How?" 11 February 2010. www.economist.com/node/15500687.

Edmundson, Mark. "Do Sports Build Character or Damage It?" *Chronicle of Higher Education,* 20 January 2012, B6–B9.

———. *Self and Soul. A Defense of Ideals.* Cambridge: Harvard University Press, 2015.

Ellwein, Thomas. *Die deutsche Universität: Vom Mittelalter bis zur Gegenwart.* Wiesbaden: Fourier, 1997.

Engels, Maria. *Die Steuerung von Universitäten in staatlicher Traägerschaft: Eine organisationstheoretische Analyse.* Wiesbaden: Deutscher Universitäts-Verlag, 2001.

Esch, Camille. "Higher Ed's Bermuda Triangle." *Washington Monthly,* September/October, 2009. www.unz.org/Pub/WashingtonMonthly-2009sep-00038.

Evans, Richard J. *Cosmopolitan Islanders: British Historians and the European Continent.* Cambridge: Cambridge University Press, 2009.

Fichte, J. G. "Deduzierter Plan einer in Berlin zu errichtenden höheren Lehranstalt." In *Die Idee der deutschen Universität. Die fünf Grundschriften aus der Zeit ihrer Neubegründung durch klassischen Idealismus und romantischen Realismus,* edited by Ernst Anrich, 125–217. Darmstadt: Gentner, 1956.

Field, Kelly. "Faculty at For-Profits Allege Constant Pressure to Keep Students Enrolled." *Chronicle of Higher Education,* 13 May 2011, A1–A12.

Fischer, Klaus. "Fehlfunktionen der Wissenschaft." *Erwägen Wissen Ethik* 18, no. 1 (2007): 3–16.

Fisher, James L., and James V. Koch. *Presidential Leadership: Making a Difference.* Phoenix: Oryx Press, 1996.

Freeman, Scott, et al. "Active Learning Increases Student Performance in Science, Engineering, and Mathematics." *Proceedings of the National Academy of Sciences USA* 111, no. 23 (10 June 2014): 8410–15.

Gallup. *Great Jobs Great Lives. The 2014 Gallup-Purdue Index Report.* Washington, DC: Gallup, 2014. www.luminafoundation.org/files/resources/galluppurdueindex-report-2014.pdf.

Geiger, Roger L. *The History of American Higher Education: Learning and Culture from the Founding to World War II.* Princeton, NJ: Princeton University Press, 2014.

———. *Research and Relevant Knowledge: American Research Universities since World War II.* New York: Oxford University Press, 1993.

———. *To Advance Knowledge: The Growth of American Research Universities, 1900–1940.* New York: Oxford University Press, 1986.

Ginsberg, Benjamin. *The Fall of the Faculty: The Rise of the All-Administrative University and Why It Matters.* New York: Oxford University Press, 2011.

Gladieux, Lawrence E., and Watson Scott Swail. "Financial Aid Is Not Enough: Improving the Odds for Minority and Low Income Students." In *Financing a College Education: How It Works, How It's Changing,* edited by Jacqueline E. King, 177–97. Phoenix: Oryx Press, 1999.

Gleason, Philip. *Contending with Modernity: Catholic Higher Education in the Twentieth Century.* New York: Oxford University Press, 1995.

Golden, Daniel. *The Price of Admission: How America's Ruling Class Buys Its Way into Elite Colleges—and Who Gets Left Outside the Gates.* New York: Three Rivers Press, 2007. First published 2006 Crown.

Gouldner, Alvin W. "Cosmopolitans and Locals: Toward an Analysis of Latent Social Roles, I and II." *Administrative Science Quarterly* 2 (December 1957 and March 1958): 281–306, 444–80.

Grafton, Anthony T., and Jim Grossman. "No More Plan B." *Chronicle of Higher Education,* 9 October 2011. http://chronicle.com/article/No-More-Plan -B/129293/.

Graham, Hugh Davis, and Nancy Diamond. *The Rise of the American Research Universities: Elites and Challengers in the Postwar Era.* Baltimore: Johns Hopkins University Press, 1997.

Greene, Jessica A. "Survey of Catholic College Presidents." In *American Catholic Higher Education in the 21st Century: Critical Challenges,* edited by Robert R. Newton, 124–37. Chestnut Hill, MA: Linden Lane, 2015.

Green, Kenneth C. *The 2011 Inside Higher Ed Survey of College and University Admissions Directors. Inside Higher Ed,* 2011.

Hall, G. Stanley. *Life and Confessions of a Psychologist.* New York: Appleton, 1923.

Hardwick Day. "The Value and Impact of the College Experience: A Comparative Study." Commissioned by the Annapolis Group (November 2011). http://mroche.nd.edu/assets/204648/the_value_and_impact_of _the_college_experience.pdf.

Hart, James Morgan. *German Universities: A Narrative of Personal Experiences.* New York: G. P. Putnam's Sons, 1874.

Hartley, Harold V., III, and Eric E. Godin. *A Study of Chief Academic Officers of Independent Colleges and Universities.* Washington, DC: Council of Independent Colleges, 2010.

Heft, James L. "Leadership in Catholic Higher Education." In *American Catholic Higher Education in the 21st Century: Critical Challenges,* edited by Robert R. Newton, 89–115. Chestnut Hill, MA: Linden Lane, 2015.

Heinzel, Matthias. *Anforderungen deutscher Unternehmen an betriebswirtschaftliche Hochschulabsolventen: Zur Marktorientierung von Hochschulen.* Wiesbaden: Deutscher Universitätsverlag, 1997.

Hesburgh, Theodore M. "The University President." In *The Hesburgh Papers: Higher Values in Higher Education,* 3–16. Kansas City: Andrews and McMeel, 1979.

Howard, Philip K. *The Death of Common Sense: How Law Is Suffocating America.* New York: Random House, 2011.

Humboldt, Wilhelm von. *Werke in fünf Bänden.* Edited by Andreas Flitner and Klaus Giel. 5 vols. Darmstadt: Wissenschaftliche Buchgesellschaft, 1960–81.

Jacquette, Ozan, Bradley R. Curs, and Julie R. Posselt. "Tuition Rich, Mission Poor: Nonresident Enrollment Growth and the Socioeconomic and Racial Composition of Public Research Universities." *The Journal of Higher Education* (forthcoming).

Jaschik, Scott. "How to Cut Ph.D. Time to Degree." *Inside Higher Ed,* 17 December 2007. www.insidehighered.com/news/2007/12/17/phd.

Jaschik, Scott, and Doug Lederman. *The 2014 Inside Higher Ed Survey of College and University Chief Academic Officers: A Study by Gallup and Inside Higher Ed. Inside Higher Ed,* 23 January 2014. www.insidehighered.com/surveys.

———. *The 2015 Inside Higher Ed Survey of College and University Chief Academic Officers: A Study by Gallup and Inside Higher Ed. Inside Higher Ed,* 22 January 2015. www.insidehighered.com/surveys.

Jaspers, Karl. *Die Idee der Universität.* Berlin: Springer, 1946.

Jencks, Christopher, and David Riesman. *The Academic Revolution.* New York: Doubleday, 1968.

Johnson, Jean, and Jon Rochkind. *With Their Whole Lives Ahead of Them.* With Amber N. Ott and Samantha DuPont. New York: Public Agenda, 2009.

Johnson, Valen E. *Grade Inflation: A Crisis in College Education.* New York: Springer, 2003.

Johnstone, D. Bruce, and Pamela N. Marcucci. *Financing Higher Education Worldwide: Who Pays? Who Should Pay?* Baltimore: Johns Hopkins University Press, 2010.

Jones, Diane Auer. "The Federal Regulatory Compliance Fee." *Inside Higher Ed,* 12 January 2010. www.insidehighered.com/views/2010/01/12/jones.

June, Audrey Williams. "It All Comes Down to the Dean." *Chronicle of Higher Education,* 28 November 2014, A19–A21.

Kalaitzidakis, Pantelis, Thanasis Stengos, and Theofanis P. Mamuneas. "Rankings of Academic Journals and Institutions in Economics." *Journal of the European Economic Association* 1 (2003): 1346–66.

Kaplan, Thomas. "The Sad, Suffering Ivy League." *Vanity Fair,* 1 July 2009. www.vanityfair.com/news/2009/07/the-sad-suffering-ivy-league.

Karabel, Jerome. *The Chosen: The Hidden History of Admission and Exclusion at Harvard, Yale, and Princeton.* Boston: Houghton Mifflin, 2005.

Keirsey, David. *Please Understand Me II.* Del Mar, CA: Prometheus, 1998.

Keller, George. *Transforming a College: The Story of a Little-Known College's Strategic Climb to National Distinction.* 2nd ed. Baltimore: Johns Hopkins University Press, 2014.

Keup, Jennifer R., and Ellen Bara Stolzenberg. *The 2003 Your First College Year (YFCY) Survey: Exploring the Academic and Personal Experiences of First-Year Students.* Columbia, SC: National Resource Center for the First-Year Experience and Students in Transition, 2004.

Kimball, Bruce, and Benjamin A. Johnson. "The Inception of the Meaning and Significance of Endowment in American Higher Education, 1890–1930." *Teachers College Record* 114 (2012): 1–33.

Kiplinger. Best College Values, 2016. Washington, DC: Kiplinger, 2016. www .kiplinger.com/article/college/T014-C000-S002-kiplinger-s-best-college -values-2016.html.

Knight Commission on Intercollegiate Athletics. *Athletics and Academics Spending Database for NCAA Division I.* 2016. http://spendingdatabase .knightcommission.org/.

Knox, William E., Paul Lindsay, and Mary N. Kolb. *Does College Make a Difference? Long-Term Changes in Activities and Attitudes.* Westport, CT: Greenwood Press, 1993.

Kolodny, Annette. *Failing the Future: A Dean Looks at Higher Education in the Twenty-First Century.* Durham, NC: Duke University Press, 1998.

Kronman, Anthony T. *Education's End: Why Our Colleges and Universities Have Given Up on the Meaning of Life.* New Haven, CT: Yale University Press, 2007.

Kuh, George D., Ty M. Cruce, Rick Shoup, Jillian Kinzie, and Robert M. Gonyea. "Unmasking the Effects of Student Engagement on First-Year College Grades and Persistence." *Journal of Higher Education* 79 (2008): 540–63.

Kuh, George D., Jillian Kinzie, John H. Schuh, Elizabeth J. Whitt, and Associates. *Student Success in College: Creating Conditions That Matter.* San Francisco: Jossey-Bass, 2005.

Kuhn, Thomas S. *The Structure of Scientific Revolutions.* 2nd ed. Chicago: University of Chicago Press, 1970.

Langewiesche, Dieter. "*Humboldt* als Leitbild? Die *deutsche Universität* in den Berliner Rektoratsreden seit dem 19. Jahrhundert." *Jahrbuch für Universitätsgeschichte* 14 (2011): 15–37.

Lederman, Doug. "The Academic Pork Barrel, 2010." *Inside Higher Ed,* 29 April 2010. www.insidehighered.com/news/2010/04/29/academic-pork-barrel-2010.

Levine, David O. *The American College and the Culture of Aspiration, 1915–1940.* Ithaca, NY: Cornell University Press, 1987.

Lewis, Harry R. *Excellence without a Soul: How a Great University Forgot Education.* New York: PublicAffairs, 2006.

Light, Richard. *Making the Most of College: Students Speak Their Minds.* Cambridge: Harvard University Press, 2001.

Lombardi, John V. *How Universities Work.* Baltimore: Johns Hopkins University Press, 2013.

Loss, Christopher P. *Between Citizens and the State: The Politics of American Higher Education in the 20th Century.* Princeton, NJ: Princeton University Press, 2012.

Lovitts, Barbara E. *Leaving the Ivory Tower: The Causes and Consequences of Departure from Doctoral Study.* New York: Rowman, 2001.

Lucas, Christopher J. *American Higher Education: A History.* 2nd ed. New York: Macmillan, 2006.

Machiavelli, Niccolò. *The Prince.* Indianapolis: Hacket, 1995.

Mael, Fred, and Blake E. Ashforth. "Alumni and Their Alma Mater: A Partial Test of the Reformulated Model of Organizational Identification." *Journal of Organizational Behavior* 13 (1992): 103–23.

McCabe, Donald L., Linda Klebe Trevino, and Kenneth D. Butterfield. "Cheating in Academic Institutions: A Decade of Research." *Ethics and Behavior* 11 (2001): 219–32.

McPherson, Michael S., and Morton Owen Schapiro. *The Student Aid Game: Meeting Need and Rewarding Talent in American Higher Education.* Princeton, NJ: Princeton University Press, 1998.

Mitchell, Michael, Michael Leachman, and Kathleen Masterson. *Funding Down, Tuition Up: State Cuts to Higher Education Threaten Quality and Affordability at Public Colleges.* Washington, DC: Center on Budget and Policy Priorities, 2016.

Morey, Melanie M., and Dennis M. Holtschneider. "Leadership and the Age of the Laity: Emerging Patterns in Catholic Higher Education." In *Lay Leaders in Catholic Higher Education: An Emerging Paradigm for the Twenty-First Century,* edited by Anthony J. Cernera, 3–27. Fairfield, CT: Sacred Heart University Press, 2005.

Morey, Melanie M., and John J. Piderit. *Catholic Higher Education: A Culture in Crisis.* New York: Oxford University Press, 2006.

Mortenson, Thomas G. "Family Income and Unequal Educational Opportunity, 1970–2011." *Postsecondary Education Opportunity* 245 (November 2012): 1–20.

Münch, Richard. *Akademischer Kapitalismus: Über die politische Ökonomie der Hochschulreform.* Frankfurt: Suhrkamp, 2011.

Munk, Nina. "Rich Harvard, Poor Harvard." *Vanity Fair,* August 2009. www .vanityfair.com/news/2009/08/harvard200908.

National Center for Education Statistics. *Digest of Education Statistics: 2014.* Washington, DC: National Center for Education Statistics, 2016. https:// nces.ed.gov/programs/digest/d14/.

National Center for Education Statistics. *Postsecondary Attainment: Differences by Socioeconomic Status.* Washington, DC: National Center for Education Statistics, 2015. http://nces.ed.gov/programs/coe/indicator _tva.asp.

National Science Board. *Science and Engineering Indicators 2012.* Arlington, VA: National Science Foundation, 2012. http://wayback.archive-it .org/5902/20160210215920/http://www.nsf.gov/statistics/seind10/start .htm.

National Science Board. *Science and Engineering Indicators 2014.* Arlington, VA: National Science Foundation, 2014. www.nsf.gov/statistics/seind12/.

National Science Board. *Science and Engineering Indicators 2016.* Arlington, VA: National Science Foundation, 2016. www.nsf.gov/statistics/2016/ nsb20161/#/.

Neubauer, Aljoscha C., and Andreas Fink. "Intelligence and Neural Efficiency." *Neuroscience and Biobehavioral Reviews* 33 (2009): 1004–23.

Newman, John Henry. *The Idea of a University Defined and Illustrated in Nine Discourses Delivered to the Catholics of Dublin in Occasional Lectures and Essays Addressed to Members of the Catholic University.* Edited by Martin J. Svaglic. Notre Dame, IN: University of Notre Dame Press, 1982.

New York Times. "Top Colleges Doing the Most for Low-Income Students." 16 September 2015. www.nytimes.com/interactive/2015/09/17/upshot/top -colleges-doing-the-most-for-low-income-students.html.

Nixon, Howard L. *Athletic Trap: How College Sports Corrupted the Academy.* Baltimore: Johns Hopkins University Press, 2014.

Oakley, Francis. "The Humanities in Liberal Arts Colleges: Another Instance of Collegiate Exceptionalism?" *Daedalus* 128, no. 1 (1999): 35–51.

Oberdorfer, Don. *Princeton University: The First 250 Years.* Princeton, NJ: Trustees of Princeton University, 1995.

O'Brien, George Dennis. *All the Essential Half-Truths about Higher Education.* Chicago: University of Chicago Press, 1998.

Olson, Keith W. "The Astonishing Story: Veterans Make Good on the Nation's Promise." *Educational Record* (Fall 1994): 16–26.

Organization for Economic Co-operation and Development. "Education at a Glance 2014." *OECD Indicators.* Paris: OECD, 2014. www.oecd.org/edu/Education-at-a-Glance-2014.pdf.

Organization for Economic Co-operation and Development. "Education at a Glance 2015." *OECD Indicators.* Paris: OECD, 2015. www.oecd.org/edu/education-at-a-glance-19991487.htm.

Organization for Economic Co-operation and Development. "How Is the Global Talent Pool Changing?" *Education Indicators in Focus.* Paris: OECD, 2012. www.oecd.org/edu/50495363.pdf.

Panas, Jerold. *Mega Gifts: Who Gives Them, Who Gets Them.* Chicago: Bonus, 1984.

Pascarella, Ernest T., and Patrick T. Terenzini. *How College Affects Students.* Vol. 1, *Findings and Insights from Twenty Years of Research.* San Francisco: Jossey-Bass, 1991.

Pennington, Bill. "Rise of College Club Teams Creates a Whole New Level of Success." *New York Times,* 3 December 2008. www.nytimes.com/2008/12/02/sports/02club.html?_r=0.

Perry, Bliss. *And Gladly Teach: Reminiscences.* New York: Houghton, 1935.

Pew Research Center. *Is College Worth It? College Presidents, Public Assess Value, Quality and Mission of Higher Education.* Washington, DC: Pew Social and Demographic Trends, 2011.

Pryor, John H., Sylvia Hurtado, Victor B. Saenz, José Luis Santos, and William S. Korn. *The American Freshman: Forty Year Trends.* Los Angeles: Higher Education Research Institute, UCLA, 2007.

Putnam, Robert. *Our Kids: The American Dream in Crisis.* New York: Simon, 2015.

QS World University Rankings 2015/16. London: QS Quacquarelli Symonds, 2015. www.topuniversities.com/university-rankings/world-university-rankings/2015#sorting=rank+region=+country=+faculty=+stars=false+search=.

Quinterno, John. *The Great Cost Shift: How Higher Education Cuts Undermine the Future Middle Class.* New York: Dēmos, 2012.

———. *Making Performance Funding Work for All.* Chevy Chase, MD: The Working Poor Families Project, 2012.

Reardon, Sean F. "The Widening Academic Achievement Gap between the Rich and the Poor: New Evidence and Possible Explanations." In *Whither Opportunity? Rising Inequality, Schools, and Children's Life Chances,* edited by Greg J. Dunan and Richard J. Murnane, 91–115. New York: Sage, 2011.

Regents of the University of Michigan. *University of Michigan 2015 Financial Report.* Ann Arbor: University of Michigan, 2015.

Report of the Treasurer 2012–13. Princeton, NJ: Princeton University Office of Finance and Treasury, 2014.

Rhodes, Frank H. T. "The Art of the Presidency." *Presidency* 1 (Spring 1998): 12–18.

Rhodes, Frank H. T., and Inge T. Reichenbach. "Successful Fund Raising at a Large Private Research University." In *Successful Fund Raising for Higher Education: The Advancement of Learning,* edited by Frank H. T. Rhodes, 1–22. Phoenix: Oryx, 1997.

Roche, Mark W. *Dean's Report 2008: An Overview from 1997 to 2008.* Notre Dame: College of Arts and Letters, 2008. https://al.nd.edu/assets/16789/dean_report_2008.pdf.

———. *The Intellectual Appeal of Catholicism and the Idea of a Catholic University.* Notre Dame: University of Notre Dame Press, 2003.

———. "Notre Dame's Triadic Identity." Inaugural Address of Mark W. Roche, I. A. O'Shaughnessy Dean, College of Arts and Letters, University of Notre Dame, December 1997. https://mroche.nd.edu/assets/10959/inaugural address.pdf.

———. "Principles and Strategies for Reforming the Core Curriculum at a Catholic College or University." *Journal of Catholic Higher Education* 34 (2015): 59–76.

———. "Should Faculty Members Teach Virtues and Values? That Is the Wrong Question." *Liberal Education* 95, no. 3 (2009): 22–27.

———. *Was die deutschen Universitäten von den amerikanischen lernen können und was sie vermeiden sollten.* Hamburg: Meiner, 2014.

———. *Why Choose the Liberal Arts?* Notre Dame: University of Notre Dame Press, 2010.

Röhrs, Hermann. *The Classical German Concept of the University and Its Influence on Higher Education in the United States.* Frankfurt: Lang, 1995.

Rojstaczer, Stuart, and Christopher Healy. "Where A Is Ordinary: The Evolution of American College and University Grading, 1940–2009." *Teachers College Record* 114, no. 7 (2012): 1–23.

Rosenbaum, Joseph E. *Beyond College for All: Career Paths for the Forgotten Half.* New York: Sage, 2001.

Rosovsky, Henry. *The University: An Owner's Manual.* New York: Norton, 1990.

Ross, Kelly Mae. "National Universities Where Students Are Eager to Enroll." *U.S. News and World Report,* 25 January 2016. www.usnews.com/education/best-colleges/articles/2016-01-25/national-universities-where-students-are-eager-to-enroll.

Roth, Michael S. *Beyond the University: Why Liberal Education Matters.* New Haven, CT: Yale University Press, 2014.

Rüegg, Walter, ed. *A History of the University in Europe.* 4 vols. Cambridge: Cambridge University Press, 1992–2010.

Russo, Joseph A. *The Art and Science of Student Aid Administration in the 21st Century.* Washington, DC: National Association of Student Financial Aid Administrators, 2010.

Sacks, Peter. *Tearing Down the Gates: Confronting the Class Divide in American Education*. Berkeley: University of California Press, 2007.

Schelsky, Helmut. *Einsamkeit und Freiheit: Ideen und Gestalt der deutschen Universität und ihrer Reformen*. Hamburg: Rowohlt, 1963.

Schleiermacher, Friedrich. *Gelegentliche Gedanken über Universitäten in Deutschem Sinn*. Berlin: Realschulbuchhandlung, 1808.

Schuster, Jack H., and Martin J. Finkelstein. *The American Faculty: The Restructuring of Academic Work and Careers*. Baltimore: Johns Hopkins University Press, 2006.

Sonnert, Gerhard, and Gerald Holton. *What Happened to the Children Who Fled Nazi Persecution*. New York: Macmillan, 2008.

Sowell, Robert, Ting Zhang, and Kenneth Redd. *Ph.D. Completion and Attrition: Analysis of Baseline Demographic Data from the PhD Completion Project*. Washington, DC: Council of Graduate Schools, 2008.

Sperber, Murray. *Beer and Circus: How Big-Time College Sports Is Crippling Undergraduate Education*. New York: Holt, 2000.

Statistisches Bundesamt. *Bildung und Kultur. Studierende an Hochschulen. Wintersemester 2014/2015. Fachserie 11, Reihe 4.1*. Wiesbaden: Statistisches Bundesamt, 2015. www.destatis.de/DE/Publikationen/Thematisch/BildungForschungKultur/Hochschulen/StudierendeHochschulenEndg2110410157004.pdf?__blob=publicationFile.

Thelin, John R. *A History of American Higher Education*. Baltimore: Johns Hopkins University Press, 2004.

Tinto, Vincent. *Completing College: Rethinking Institutional Action*. Chicago: University of Chicago Press, 2012.

Toma, J. Douglas. *Football U.: Spectator Sports in the Life of the American University*. Ann Arbor: University of Michigan Press, 2003.

Toomajian, Charles R., Associate Dean and Registrar of Williams College. Letter to the author. 4 November 2011.

Trachtenberg, Stephen Joel, Gerald B. Kauvar, and E. Grady Brogue. *Presidencies Derailed: Why University Leaders Fail and How to Prevent It*. Baltimore: Johns Hopkins University Press, 2013.

Tucker, Allan, and Robert A. Bryan. *The Academic Dean: Dove, Dragon, and Diplomat*. 2nd ed. Phoenix: Oryx Press, 1999.

Turner, James, and Paul Bernard. "The German Model and the Graduate School: The University of Michigan and the Origin Myth of the American University." In Vol. 2 of *The American College in the Nineteenth Century*, edited by Roger Geiger, 221–41. Nashville: Vanderbilt University Press, 2000.

Turner, R. Steven. "University Reformers and Professorial Scholarship in Germany, 1760–1806." In *The University in Society*, edited by Lawrence Stone, 495–531. Princeton, NJ: Princeton University Press, 1974.

U.S. News and World Report Best Colleges. 2015 ed. Washington, DC: U.S. News and World Report, 2014.

U.S. News and World Report Best Colleges. 2016 ed. Washington, DC: U.S. News and World Report, 2015.

Vest, Charles M. *The American Research University from World War II to World Wide Web: Governments, the Private Sector, and the Emerging Meta-university.* Berkeley: University of California Press, 2007.

Veysey, Laurence R. *The Emergence of the American University.* Chicago: University of Chicago Press, 1965.

Walker, George E., Chris M. Golde, Laura Jones, Andrea Conklin Bueschel, and Pat Hutchings. *The Formation of Scholars: Rethinking Doctoral Education for the 21st Century.* San Francisco: Jossey-Bass, 2008.

Washburn, Jennifer. *University, Inc.: The Corporate Corruption of Higher Education.* New York: Basic, 2006.

Washington Monthly. College Guide Rankings 2015. Washington, DC: Washington Monthly, 2015. http://washingtonmonthly.com/college-guide/college-guide-rankings-2015-national/.

Wendler, Cathy, Brent Bridgeman, Fred Cline, Catherine Millett, JoAnn Rock, Nathan Bell, and Patricia McAllister. *The Path Forward: The Future of Graduate Education in the United States.* Princeton, NJ: Educational Testing Service, 2010.

Wildavsky, Ben. *The Great Brain Race: How Global Universities Are Reshaping the World.* Princeton, NJ: Princeton University Press, 2010.

Wilkinson, Rupert. *Aiding Students, Buying Students: Financial Aid in America.* Nashville: Vanderbilt University Press, 2005.

Williams, Ross, Anne Leahy, Gaétan de Rassenfosse, and Paul Jensen. *U21 Ranking of National Higher Education Systems.* Melbourne: University of Melbourne, 2016.

Wilson, Robin. "Penn State Eliminates Fines for Employees Who Skip Wellness Question." *Chronicle of Higher Education,* 27 September 2013, A6.

Wolniak, Gregory C., Tricia A. Seifert, and Charles F. Blaich. "A Liberal Arts Education Changes Lives: Why Everyone Can and Should Have This Experience." *LiberalArtsOnline* 4, no. 3 (2004). www.liberalarts.wabash.edu/lao-4-3-printer-friendly.

Woo, Jennie H., and Susan P Choy. *Merit Aid for Undergraduates: Trends from 1995–96 to 2007–08.* Washington, DC: Department of Education, 2011.

Worth, Michael J. *Leading the Campaign: Advancing Colleges and Universities.* New York: Rowman, 2010.

Young Invincibles. *2016 State Report Cards.* Washington, DC: Young Invincibles, 2016. http://younginvincibles.org/wp-content/uploads/2016/01/YI-State-Report-Cards-2016.pdf.

MARK W. ROCHE is the Rev. Edmund P. Joyce, C.S.C.,
Professor of German Language and Literature and concurrent
professor of philosophy at the University of Notre Dame.
From 1997 to 2008 Roche served as dean of Notre Dame's College
of Arts and Letters. His books include *Why Choose the Liberal Arts?*
(University of Notre Dame Press, 2010), which received the 2012
Frederic W. Ness Book Award from the Association of American
Colleges and Universities.